**C**ONTENTS

MW00453061

Acknowledgments vii

SECTION 1 ● The Wheel of Life: Life-Skills for College 1

1 Life-Skills for College: A Curriculum for Lifelong Learning 3

The Importance of Possessing a Repertoire of Skills 5
   The Changing Landscape of Colleges: What Is Changing and Who Is Attending College? 6
What a College Education Provides 8
Four Key Areas of Necessary Skill Development 9
   Interpersonal Communication/Human Relations Skills 10
   Problem-Solving/Decision-Making Skills 10
   Physical Fitness/Health Maintenance Skills 11
   Identity Development/Purpose-in-Life Skills 11
Life's Journey: An Accumulation of Skills 12
Needs as Perceived by Beginning College Students 12
   Pre-Orientation Needs 12
   Post-Orientation Needs 13
   My Top-Priority Need Prior to Orientation Was 13
   My Top-Priority Need Now Is 13
Developmental Theories Are Diverse in Nature— Each Offers an Advantageous Perspective from Which to Watch One's Future Unfold 14
Basic Life-Skills Assumptions 14
What Does All This Mean for You as a Student? 15
A Journey of Self-Exploration and Life-Skills Enhancement 15
Closing Remarks 16
Sources 18

Exercises

Exercise 1: Skill Building Profile 21
Exercise 2, Part A: Life-Skills Development Inventory (College Form) 23
Exercise 2, Part B: Life-Skills Wheel 27

2 Finding and Using One's Existing Motivation: Realignment and Enhancement 29

What Is Motivation? The Social Science View 30
   What Have Other Social Scientists Said About Motivation? 33
   External, Introjected, and Identified Regulation's Link to Persistence 34
What Is Motivation? The Perspective of Students 36
   What Does the Word Motivation Mean to You? 36
   Why Did You Decide to Go to This Particular College? 37
   How Is Motivation Related to Academic Success? 38
   Do You Think It Is the Responsibility of Professors to Motivate College Students? 39
   How Are Motivated Students Different from Students Who Lack Motivation? 39
   Six Factors That Align and Enhance Motivation 40
   Final Suggestions to Help Develop and Maintain One's Motivation 40
Closing Remarks 42
Sources 43

Exercises

Exercise 1: End Goals and Getting There 45
Exercise 2: Academic Motivational Orientation Assessment (AMOA) 49

SECTION 2 ● Problem-Solving/ Decision-Making Skills 53

3 Creating Time through Effective Time Management 55

Seeing the Big Picture in Relation to Time Management: Achieving Values-Congruence 56

Three Keys for Creating and Utilizing an Effective
    Time-Management Model   56
      Getting Organized   57
      To-Do List   58
      The Carry-Through   60
Emmett's Two Laws Governing Procrastination   63
Closing Remarks   64
Sources   65

Exercises

Exercise 1: Where Does My Time Go?   67
Exercise 2: Constructing a To-Do List   69
Exercise 3: Effective Planning for the Week   71
Exercise 4: Understanding Procrastination   73
Exercise 5: Plot Your Energy Level   75

4 Building a Repertoire of Good Habits for Academic Survival   77

Develop Good Classroom-Survival Tactics   78
Develop a Good System of Note-Taking   79
Adopt Good Study Methods   83
Learn about Academic Honesty   84
Learn the Grading System   86
Survival Skills for Students Belonging to a Minority
    Population on Campus   88
      Nontraditional Students   89
      First-Generation Students   90
Sources   91

Exercises

Exercise 1: Habits to Keep, Habits to Change   93
Exercise 2: Cornell Method of Note-Taking   95

5 Learning: The Connection to Memory and Memorization   97

The Autonomous Learner   98
The Connection between Learning and Memory   99
    The Creation of Memories   101
Six Factors That Optimize the Learning and Recall
    Process   102
One Last Recommendation   106
Sources   107

Exercises

Exercise 1: Unique Learning Approach   109
Exercise 2: Enhancing the Learning and Recall
    Process   111

6 Learning Style: One's Distinctive Manner of Learning   113

Whole-Brain Learning   114
    Brain Exercises   116
Multiple Intelligences   119
Perceptual Learning Modalities   121
Personality   122
    Introversion-Extroversion   123
    Intuition-Sensation   123
    Thinking-Feeling   124
    Perceiving-Judging   124
Your Own Personal Learning Style   125
Sources   126

Exercises

Exercise 1: How Fit Is Your Brain?   127
Exercise 2: Learning Style Skill Assessment*   129
Exercise 3: Discovering Your Personality Type   131
Exercise 4: Personal Learning Style   133

7 Winning Test Performance: Fine-Tuning Your Test-Taking Skills   135

Preparation before the Test   136
    General Preparation Tips   136
    Seek Information about the Test   137
    Cramming   137
Taking the Test   137
    Tips for Objective Tests   138
    Tips for Essay Tests   139
Evaluation of the Test   141
Performance Anxiety   143
    How to Recognize Performance Anxiety   143
Managing Test Anxiety   145
    Dealing with Thoughts   145
    Dealing with Physical Reactions to
      Anxiety   147
    Looking at Your Behavior   148
Sources   148

Exercises

Exercise 1: Test-Taking Quotient   149
Exercise 2: Objective Exam Analysis Worksheet   151
Exercise 3: Test Anxiety   153

8 Critical Thinking: Developing Critical Skills for the 21st Century   155

Thinking as a Developmental Process   156
    Models of Knowledge   156
    William Perry   157

Bloom's Taxonomy of Thinking and
Learning   157
Models of Critical Thinking/Problem Solving   159
Critical Thinking   159
Problem Solving   162
Arguments   164
Invalid Arguments   165
Closing Remarks   167
Sources   167

Exercises
Exercise 1: Stranded in the Desert   169
Exercise 2: Creating Breakthroughs   171
Exercise 3: Critical-Thinking Puzzle   177
Exercise Solutions   179

9   Acquiring Financial Skills: The Buck
Stops with You   181

Contemporary Meanings of Money   182
Human Development: The Money
Connection   182
Human Nature: The Money Connection   183
Managing Money to Achieve Academic Goals   185
Steps for Obtaining Financial Control   188
Quick Money Tips   188
Financial Aid and Student Employment   192
Debt Stress and Credit Problems   193
Closing Remarks   193
Sources   194

Exercises
Exercise 1: Money Management   197
Exercise 2: Investing with Personal Values   199

SECTION 3 • Interpersonal
Communication/Human Relations
Skills 201

10   Relationships: The Bridges That
Connect Self and Others   203

Relationships Fill Our Lives   204
Loneliness   204
Effects of Loneliness   205
Depression and Suicide   206
Unhealthy and Damaging Relationships   207
Sexual Relationships   208
Sexual Behaviors Gone Wrong   208
Acquaintance or Date Rape   208
The Key to Healthy Interactions: Communication
and Human Relations Skills   210

George Gazda's Approach to Effective
Communication   211
Nonverbal Communication   213
Assertiveness: A Special Skill   214
Closing Remarks   218
Sources   218

Exercises
Exercise 1: Receiving and Sending Messages   219

11   Connecting Common Threads
across a Diverse World   221

Multiculturalism   222
Demographic Changes   223
Living in a Pluralistic Society   224
Terminology   224
Developing Multicultural Competencies   225
Examine Your Attitudes   227
Sources of Prejudice   228
The Power of Prejudice   229
Developing a Multicultural View   230
Closing Remarks   231
Sources   231

Exercises
Exercise 1: Self-Examination of Ethnic
and Cultural Heritage   233
Exercise 2: Reflecting on Race Relations   235
Exercise 3: Why Do Stereotypes Endure?   237
Exercise 4: Spheres of Influence   239

SECTION 4 • Physical Fitness/
Health Maintenance Skills   241

12   Holistic Health: The Union of Mind,
Body, and Spirit   243

Holism and Holistic Health   244
Physical Benefits   245
Psychological Benefits   245
Spiritual Benefits   245
The Physical: Nutrition and Exercise   246
Nutrition   246
A General Guide to Healthy Eating   246
Learn How to Read Labels   248
Bulimia Nervosa and Anorexia Nervosa:
Nutritional Imbalances   249
Exercise   249
The Psychological: Stress and Sex   250
Stress   250
Sex   250

The Spiritual   254
    A Western Philosophical Approach   254
    An Eastern Philosophical Approach   254
Closing Remarks   255
Sources   255

Exercises
Exercise 1: Achieving Balance   257

13 Stress: Accentuate the Positive   259
What Is Stressful?   260
What Is Stress Exactly?   263
    Psychological Hardiness and Other Personality
    Differences   264
Learned Helplessness   266
Prolonged Stress and Impairment of
    Functioning   267
    Stage 1: Alarm (Fight/Flight)   267
    Stage 2: Resistance   267
    Stage 3: Exhaustion   267
Negative, Ineffective Ways to Handle Stress   268
Stress: What Can Be Done?   268
    Everyday Techniques for Reducing Stress   268
    Techniques for Periods of High Stress   270
Closing Remarks   273
Sources   274

Exercises
Exercise 1: Stress Assessment   275

SECTION 5 ● Identity Development/Purpose-in-Life Skills   281

14 Vocation: More than a Job, More than a Career   283
Self-Exploration   284
    Values   285
    Personality   285
    Interests   287
    Skills and Aptitudes   288

Career Exploration   289
    Computer-Assisted Career Exploration
      Programs   290
    Books   290
Occupational Exploration   290
    Resume   291
    Job Interview   292
    Employment Projections   293
Closing Remarks   294
Sources   296

Exercises
Exercise 1: Values Clarification   297
Exercise 2: Work Values   299
Exercise 3: Greatest Achievements   301
Exercise 4: Career Decisions   303

15 Campus and Community Connections: Development and Application of Life-Skills   307
Community Connections   308
    Service Learning   308
    Building Community through
      Volunteerism   309
Campus Resources   311
    Academic Affairs   311
    Student Affairs   312
    Libraries   313
    Cultural Opportunities   313
    Career Services   313
    People as Resources   313
Leadership   314
Moral Learning   315
Sources   316

Exercises
Exercise 1: Get to Know Your Campus
    Resources   317
Exercise 2: Interview Guide   319
Exercise 3: Who Are You at This Point in Your
    Life?   321
Exercise 4: Creating a Personal Mandala   327

Index   331

ACKNOWLEDGMENTS

The authors express appreciation to Shane Bowen for his artistic visuals. Earl J. Ginter and Ann Shanks Glauser shared equal responsibility in preparing this textbook.

SECTION 1

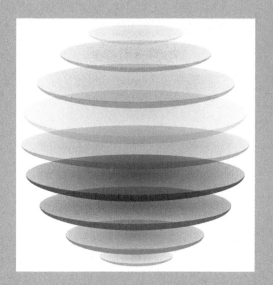

The Wheel of Life:
Life-Skills
for College

Life-Skills for College
A Curriculum for Lifelong Learning

College offers numerous challenges and opportunities to learn and develop lasting skills. The lasting skills referred to are those types of skills that enable a person to meet head-on the challenges encountered in college as well as those encountered for the rest of his or her life. Simply stated, there is much for you to discover about yourself and the world around you via the college experience.

According to the Oxford English Dictionary, the word *college* refers to "a society of scholars . . . formed for the purpose of study or instruction." The words *a society of scholars* imply that both students and professors are actively engaged in the learning process. Truly, a college is a dynamic city of learning for all its inhabitants.

In the United States of America, the first center for higher learning was Harvard, and it is widely recognized for its excellence since its inception in 1636. However, several famous centers for learning predate Harvard. For example, the University of Al-Azhas in Egypt was founded in 970, the University of Mexico was founded in 1551, the University of Bologna in Italy was founded in the 1000s, and Oxford University was founded around 1200.

All of these early centers of learning have long histories with layers of traditions and accomplishments. Oxford University, located in Oxford, England, exemplifies such a record of well-established customs and achievements. Oxford is the oldest English-speaking center of higher learning in the world. This particular center of learning endured over the centuries in spite of "civil wars, the Black Death, peasant uprisings, and royal orders to burn [some of its] scholars at the stake" (Cohen, 2002, p. A38). Even a cursory review of Oxford's history reveals a rich, continuous record of important occurrences. Oxford's name is associated with 47 Nobel Prize winners and many other well-known and talented individuals such as Oscar Wilde, John Ronald Reuel Tolkien, and Stephen Hawking. A number of students from the U.S. have also attended Oxford since 1902 as Rhodes Scholars. (See Table 1.1 for a partial listing of the Rhodes Scholars from just one of the universities in the U.S.)

Note Throughout the textbook, the authors use the word *college* to refer to both colleges and universities. The exception is when a specific institution of higher learning is mentioned.

While a college's unique history, traditions, and achievements certainly can contribute to why a student completes and submits an application packet, is it possible that other concerns play a larger role in the student's decision? If you were to ask other students why they are attending your college, you would hear them offer numerous reasons. Taking a closer look at their reasons would most likely reveal a few common themes. One of the most typical reasons given is that they are here to qualify for "a good job in the future."

Table 1.1

Partial List of Rhodes Scholars

1924: Hervey M. Cleckley A clinical professor and co-author of *The Three Faces of Eve*, which depicted a patient diagnosed with multiple personalities. Joanne Woodward won an Oscar for her portrayal of the patient in the 1957 movie based on the book.

1931: Milton P. Jarnigan, Jr. Headed the mathematical/computational arm of the U.S. Guided Missile Center during World War II.

1934: Eugene T. Booth Contributed to the Manhattan Project via utilization of uranium-235 to create the first viable atom bomb.

1939: Morris B. Abram Served as chairman of the U.N. Watch, located in Geneva, in SW Switzerland.

1973: Fred F. Manget Worked as legal counsel for the U.S. Central Intelligence Agency.

2003: Adam Cureton At age 22 he had earned three degrees, and subsequently used his Rhodes scholarship to pursue a doctorate in philosophy. Adam has a strong interest in social justice as it relates to others who are disabled. Legally blind, he has stated his goal is to "*Use all of my abilities to ensure that a perfect world need not be composed of perfect people.*"

Note. Worldwide the Rhodes scholarship is recognized as one of the most celebrated honors a student may be awarded. The scholarship is named for Cecil John Rhodes, a British colonial administrator assigned to South Africa, who accumulated a fortune through diamond mining. According to the specifications of his will, Oxford University set up a foundation in 1902 to provide financial assistance to exceptional students. Since its inception, only one U.S. president, Bill Clinton, has received a Rhodes scholarship to attend Oxford University.

SOURCE: The University of Georgia. (n. d.). UGA's Rhodes scholars 1903–1999. Retrieved November 3, 2009, from http://www.uga.edu/gm/archives/ArcRho.html

A college certainly helps one prepare for a career, but a college also offers many other opportunities. A college can help you to develop the skills you need for lifelong learning. To illustrate this point, you only need to look to the motto chosen by your college to express its goals or ideals. In most cases, the words selected for a college's official motto succinctly convey a principle or set of principles that reflect the broad nature of the skills the college wants to impart to its students. For example, the authors of this textbook work at a university whose motto states that its aim is "to teach, to serve, and to inquire into the nature of things." Our university builds upon this general definition of purpose by further asserting that the motto reflects the institution's concerted effort to play an "integral and unique role in the conservation and enhancement of the state's and nation's intellectual, cultural, and environmental heritage." Such remarks suggest that centers of higher learning are more than simply career training or job placement centers. It is your authors' experience that the more students embrace the greater purpose expressed by a college, the more enjoyable and ultimately rewarding the entire college experience becomes. After graduation, these types of students often rise to the upper levels of their careers (and they often seem to get more out of life in general).

Colleges are environments where students soon discover that, compared to earlier learning environments such as high school, they will not only be required to work harder, but more importantly, must be self-motivated to do well. Over time it is not unusual for some colleges to become increasingly competitive academically, since the academic potential of students attending has risen (in fact, it goes well beyond a matter of time—numerous factors contribute to such a change). Established colleges most often select the academically strongest students from the pool of applicants. For example, the average high school grade point average (GPA) of entering freshmen for a major state college in the southeast U.S. recently reached 3.85. This college's selection procedures have created a large pool of beginning students that is made up of academically strong high school students (with a few exceptions). It is typical for a sizable number of these beginning students to experience a drop in their performance. In some cases, the same effort that may have resulted in an A or A– in high school now results in a B– or C, and for a significant number of freshmen, that effort will result in a grade of D or lower.

The Importance of Possessing a Repertoire of Skills

It is our experience that this drop in grades frequently is the result of a lack of skills; thus, skill building in certain areas is needed to enable the student to achieve at her or his optimum level of performance. Rachel Sobel (1998) tells the story of Kingslea Chan, which illustrates the type of transition from high school to college that is typical of many entering freshmen. Chan had obtained a high score on the math portion of the SAT and decided he would apply to Rochester Institute of Technology. He was accepted and started college that fall. Even though he had passed advanced-placement calculus, Chan earned C's and D's on his first exams. According to Rachel Sobel, Chan's experience in a beginning math course is far from unusual and actually fits the profile of 41 percent of students entering a four-year college. These students lack one or more of the skills necessary to compete successfully during their first year. Chan was able to perform much closer to his optimal level of performance after he devoted attention to enhancing the skills he already possessed in note-taking, test-taking, and time management. After skill building in these three areas, Chan's grades changed to B's.

In addition to a lack of processing skills (i.e., effective note-taking), many students have a difficult time gauging the amount of time they should devote to meeting course requirements. This mismatch can represent several things. For example, some students may devote too much time because they rely on inefficient skills when studying course notes, while other students do not spend enough time studying because they do not accurately estimate how much study time is required to get a certain grade. Among those students carrying a full load, one finds considerable variability in the number of hours they set aside to work on class-related activities. When 60,000 students from 276 different colleges responded to a survey, their responses revealed that about 14 percent of the students devoted 26 hours or more to class preparation activities (e.g., studying, reading, and writing). Of the remaining students, 29 percent indicated they allotted between 16 and 25 hours, 49 percent reported 6 to 15 hours, and 9 percent reported that they devoted less than 6 hours a week to preparing for class (Mollison, 2000). When the colleges were compared to one another, it was discovered that the amount of time devoted to preparing for classes varied considerably from institution to institution among the 276 colleges.

The good news is that after the initial shock and experience of earning low grades, beginning students who obtain the needed skills often find the remainder of their college experience very rewarding. Rachel Sobel points to the example of Franklin Delano Roosevelt, who went on to become the 32nd president of the United States after earning a C– in his freshmen government class.

The Changing Landscape of Colleges: What Is Changing and Who Is Attending College?

Recent Trends among Institutions of Higher Learning. Colleges are not static landscapes that remain the same forever. In recent years, most colleges have undergone many changes. A number of different authors have emphasized that colleges are devoting much more attention to the following activities:

- **Curtailing Instances of Web Cheating**—Colleges are relying on computer programs capable of comparing an extraordinary number of existing documents to detect plagiarism, and increasing numbers of students have been reprimanded or expelled from college as a result.
- **Moving Away from Traditional Hiring Practices**—Many colleges have moved to hiring part-time staff rather than full-time tenure-track assistant professors. This change represents an attempt to keep costs down while meeting the needs of swelling student bodies.
- **Better Utilization of the Internet**—Colleges are exploring how Internet applications can be effectively used to create unique possibilities for instruction and learning. (The University of Phoenix relies extensively on Internet-based instruction and has become the largest post-secondary institution, with an enrollment that exceeds 450,000 students.)

Some professionals perceive these changes to reflect trends that are both troublesome and harmful. Even in the area of Internet applications, some individuals see recent developments as ultimately injecting greater distance between learners and teachers—the type of distance that will have a subtle but deleterious effect on students' ability to develop the interpersonal skills required to work effectively in a world that promises to become increasingly diverse and shrunken in terms of geographic distances due to emerging technologies. (Computer technology itself is contributing to a shrinking of physical distances.)

Recent Trends among Students Attending College. Researchers such as Hussar and Bailey (2009), Grant (2010), Pryor et al. (2007 & 2008), Sieben (2011), and Whelan (2011) provide evidence to conclude that several prevailing trends make present-day students very different from those students going to college several decades ago. In general, today's college students are older (increasingly over the age of 24), mostly female, and more ethnically diverse.

Of particular interest is information provided by the largest and longest-running survey of American college students (more than 13.4 million freshmen at 1,708 colleges spanning over four decades). The *Cooperative Institutional Research Program* (CIRP) *Freshmen Survey* has been administered by the Higher Education Research Institute at the University of California Los Angeles (UCLA). This large-scale data collection effort, combined with the data from the other studies mentioned earlier, has resulted in several conclusions:

- **Economic Landscape**—The current economic environment has influenced what students worry about and the decisions they make about attending college.
- **Affordability**—College affordability is a greater concern for students and largely accounts for the increasing number of students choosing to attend another college after receiving notification of acceptance by their "college of first choice."
- **Income Sources**—Students are seeking multiple income sources (i.e., family support, personal savings, and employment) to pay for college. Approximately 50 percent of students currently enrolled state they plan to get a job to help meet college expenses.
- **Psychotropic Medication**—Approximately 15 percent of students who begin college take medications for some type of psychological disorder.
- **Academic Reputation**—In spite of financial concerns, the most popular reason given by students for selecting a particular college is the academic reputation of the institution.
- **An Influx of Learning Disabilities**—The number of students reporting a learning disability continues to increase. These students anticipate that counseling, tutoring, and other supportive campus resources will be available to them once they start college.
- **Anxiety and Depression**—Directors from 424 campus counseling centers reported that approximately 40 percent of the clients seen suffer from some form of anxiety. For a number of years, depression was the most common condition reported by students seeking help at counseling centers, but it should be kept in mind that at 37 percent, the number of students reporting depression remains high. Finally, when today's students are compared to previous students, researchers have found a noticeable drop in the emotional health of incoming students, with many of these students starting college feeling overwhelmed.
- **Embracing Diversity**—The majority of students report they are tolerant of others who possess different beliefs. In addition to asserting that they are able to work cooperatively with diverse groups of people, they also report a greater interest in learning more about other countries and cultures.
- **Going Green**—A significant number of college students indicate they are supportive of green initiatives. The strength of students' environmental concerns is tied to a belief that the world's future hinges upon a healthy environment. (The authors of your textbook have recently observed that this growth of environmental concern is as strong, if not stronger, than students' economic concerns. Also, it appears that many students are starting to move from a stance of concern to some form of activism.)

- Participation in Politics—Increasingly, students are reporting greater political engagement. It is becoming obvious that students increasingly believe it is important to know what is taking place at national, state, and local levels of governance.
- Values Recognized—Among the most prevalent values reported by entering freshmen are the importance of being financially "well-off" and the great worth of helping others. Concerning this latter value, the percentage of students reporting they are likely to participate in some form of community service has increased significantly.
- A Guiding Philosophy—There has also been a noticeable tendency for students to indicate they believe it is very important to develop a meaningful philosophy of life as one outcome of attending college.
- Parental Consultation—Freshmen report they often rely on their parents when making decisions about college. Moreover, students report they see their parents' input as both important and useful.
- Egoism—There is evidence to indicate that both narcissism and a lack of empathy are on the rise in college students. Both of these traits seem to be exacerbated by periods of poor economic growth and high unemployment.
- Employable Skills—Employers have complained that many college graduates seeking work lack sufficient skills in two areas: *communication* and *decision making*. The message to all beginning students should be clear—these are critical skill areas that students must concentrate on sharpening throughout their college years.

According to the *Digest of Education Statistics*, it can be expected that an increasing number of high school graduates will pursue an advanced degree. Also, it appears that in the United States the population is becoming more educated (e.g., in 1980 only 17 percent had four years of college, compared to 1996 when the percentage jumped to 24 percent). Finally, while there is not total agreement, some professionals assert (e.g., Mallary, 2002) that the college experience and life in general have become more complicated for students since September 11, 2001.

The authors of this textbook believe it should be kept in mind that many institutions of higher learning, as illustrated by Oxford's long history, have successfully prepared students to meet the challenges created by profound societal changes. One thing that has remained essentially the same for centuries is the basic mission across all colleges—producing well-educated graduates through the provision of numerous opportunities to develop the balance of skills necessary to experience a genuinely meaningful and fulfilling life in the interdependent world of the 21st century.

What a College Education Provides

If a student knows where to look, he or she will discover that a college will help him or her to achieve the following:

1. Develop skills to become an autonomous learner. A college student is expected to read, listen, and process a considerable amount of information. While it is very important for the student to learn the information presented via lectures and other means, it is critical for all students to *learn how to learn*. The latter skill enables you to become an independent learner for the rest of your life. Learning how to learn means developing critical and creative thinking skills needed for making good decisions and solving problems, as well as learning how to effectively and efficiently select, process, and retain information.

Harvard is the oldest institution of higher learning in the United States.

2. **Develop skills for continuous personal growth.** A college offers wonderful opportunities to develop a greater awareness of your own qualities and to build upon your strengths; the diverse nature of a college's rich and varied student-faculty culture opens new doors for personal growth. In addition, you can further develop self-management skills in the areas of health, money management, relationships, time management, communication, and multiculturalism.

3. **Develop skills to seek and obtain a relevant career.** College is the time to engage in the vocational processes of self-exploration, career exploration, and occupational exploration. Choosing the right job path involves selecting work that is congruent with various factors such as interests, personality, values, aptitudes, and skills. A college can help you better understand these job-related factors.

4. **Develop skills to become a responsible member of the world.** To a large degree, the door to world membership is your local community. What will be your level of commitment to your community? Communities need leaders to survive and thrive. Will you be one? According to two researchers, Levine and Cureton, today's college students do not believe in quick fixes to the nation's social problems. They see the problems and are willing to put forth time and energy at the *local level* to try to resolve them.

Four Key Areas of Necessary Skill Development

Whether you are a freshman, a transfer student, a returning student, a nontraditional student, or a part-time student (or some other label that you believe more accurately describes you), there are basic life-skills that you need to develop to adequately meet the various objectives listed above. *Life-skills* are skills that can be learned and are necessary for effective living. Dave Brooks and George Gazda isolated four areas or dimensions of life-skills that cut across all potential college experiences as well as any experience a student will encounter post-graduation. The dimensions are **interpersonal communication/human relations**, **problem-solving/decision-making**, **physical fitness/health maintenance**, and **identity development/purpose-in-life** (each of the four dimensions is described in detail below.).

These four dimensions result from several developmental features of human existence that appear early in our life. These early developmental features—*affective, cognitive, ego, moral, physical-sexual, psychosocial, vocational*—have often been isolated to study their influence on human behavior, but to obtain a more complete understanding of complex human actions one must consider the more complex life-skills dimensions, which better mirror the actual complexity underlying human actions. Specifically, they mirror those actions taken by a person attempting to adapt to the challenges associated with four settings—*home and family, school, community at large*, and the world of *work*. (See Table 1.2 for a depiction of the relationships between the various developmental features that mix together to form the four life-skills dimensions and the four settings where life-skills are both learned and applied.)

Interpersonal Communication/Human Relations Skills

These are the skills necessary for effective communication, both verbal and nonverbal; along with others, they facilitate establishing meaningful relationships, small- and large-group and community membership and participation, healthy management of interpersonal intimacy, clear expression of ideas and opinions, and giving and receiving feedback in a multicultural world. Possessing strong skills in this area enables individuals to modify, correct, or strengthen their interactions in ways that lead to development of their social potential.

Problem-Solving/Decision-Making Skills

This category represents a set of skills necessary for information seeking; information assessment and analysis; problem identification, solution finding, implementation, and evaluation; goal setting; systematic planning and forecasting; time management; critical thinking; and conflict resolution.

Development theorist William Perry has added to our understanding of how difficult it is sometimes to arrive at an answer to a difficult problem or situation. It is more than simply deciding. According to Perry's theory, a student may operate at a level of *dualism*, where the student is thinking in terms of right and wrong or absolute categories. Operating from a dualistic perspective, a student believes a professor knows the right answer. *Multiplicity* represents a different approach. In this case, a student may not agree with another, but recognizes the other has a right to his or her own opinion: that is, all opinions are equally valid in the search for the answer. *Relativism* denotes the realization that information is relative and dependent on its context: that is, the realization that not all opinions are equally valid and opinions need to be tempered with reason. Relativism is reflected in situations where the student has made a commitment to values, beliefs, people, and ways of acting that establish identity, and his or her decisions are based on this commitment. Colleges are designed to provide an environment for students to achieve such a commitment in order to deal effectively with an increasingly complex world.

Table 1.2

A Model for the Development and Application of Life-Skills

Affective	Four	Home and Family
Cognitive	**Life-Skills**	Academic Sites (e.g., College)
Ego	**Dimensions**	
Moral		World of Work
Physical-Sexual	←——————→	Community and Beyond
Psychosocial		
Vocational		

The above represent raw developmental materials. These seven areas increase in complexity over time. They also mix together in unique ways to form each person's unique personality, which is expressed via the four life-skills dimensions.	SOURCE: Ginter, E., Gazda, G., Horne, A., Glauser, A., & Glauser, E. (2006, April). *School counselors working with teachers, students, and parents to build developmental strengths: A life-skills approach.* Presentation made at the 2006 American Counseling Association World Conference in Montreal, Quebec, Canada.	The above represent the four primary environments we are exposed to during our lifetimes. These are the main sites where people first display the developmentally based abilities they are born with. Through *learning*, these abilities are reshaped to meet the expectations held by *others* for each major developmental period (child, adolescent, and adult).

Physical Fitness/Health Maintenance Skills

These skills are necessary for coordination and motor development, nutritional maintenance, physical fitness, athletic participation, physiological aspects of sexuality, stress management, and leisure activity selection. Findings suggest that this category of skills is directly related to one's ability to handle stress effectively. Sometimes students with low skills in this developmental area may use drugs or alcohol or engage in other addictive behaviors to cope with stress rather than finding better or permanent solutions to what is causing stress in their lives.

Identity Development/Purpose-in-Life Skills

This set of skills is necessary for ongoing development of personal identity and emotional awareness, including self-monitoring, maintenance of self-esteem, manipulating and accommodating one's environment, clarifying values, sex-role development, developing a personal meaning of life, and establishing moral or value dimensions of sexuality.

Life's Journey: An Accumulation of Skills

The above four dimensions do not only apply to college students; they actually pertain to the three primary stages of human development (child, adolescent, and adult). In addition, each of the four categories of life-skills can be expected to manifest itself differently at various ages during one's lifetime. Consequently, developmental differences are largely due to what a person needs to accomplish at various times during his or her journey through life.

Knowing what to expect at different points in time enables us to better assess the developmental situation accurately. For example, when adults observe a young child in a sandbox with other children, they often misinterpret what is taking place. In this example, we have a beautiful illustration of how subtle developmental differences can be at various points in one's life. The child digging in the sandbox is most likely displaying a common form of solitary activity found in very young children, but relying upon our adult perspective, we will probably conclude that we are seeing a young child honing his or her interpersonal skills. In truth, we are observing an activity that is said to parallel the play of other children who just happen to be in the same sandbox (this type of behavior is called *parallel play*).

Needs as Perceived by Beginning College Students

The college years encompass many challenges and personal changes for students. (In fact, changes start to occur once the student receives notification of his or her acceptance to college. For example, a student's anticipation of what he or she will encounter at college can initially affect what occurs at college.) The authors of your textbook believe that it is possible to achieve a fuller understanding of *what happens to students during their college years*, but only by obtaining a deeper understanding of human development. The authors also recognize that college students typically do not think in developmental terms. For example, students who are confronted with obstacles often use a word such as *need* to discuss their developmentally based concerns (e.g., "I need more money to pay for school," "I need to study more," "I need to find out what courses to take next semester"). Nevertheless, regardless of the language used, the concerns of students become much more manageable if placed in the context of what we have learned about early adult development.

Mark Daddona studied what students report concerning their "needs," and his work provides a detailed snapshot of the developmental-based concerns for traditional-age college students. Daddona reported that students reveal they have one set of needs prior to entering college (a period referred to as pre-orientation) and another set after they arrive on campus (post-orientation). Daddona has also categorized these expressed needs as falling into one of the following three areas: academic, career, or personal/emotional. The **expressed needs** he uncovered are listed below from most important to least important as perceived by students.

Pre-Orientation Needs

- Planning my class schedule for the first semester (academic need)
- Finding a job after graduation (career need)
- Knowing how to get the grades I want (academic need)
- Learning about job opportunities after graduation (career need)

- Choosing a career direction that is right for me (career need)
- Having enough spending money while in college (personal/emotional need)
- Planning my class schedule after the first semester (academic need)
- Selecting courses that I feel I can be successful in (academic need)
- Knowing how to study for college-level courses (academic need)
- Getting accepted to a professional/graduate school (career need)
- Understanding expectations of professors (academic need)
- Finding my way around campus (personal/emotional need)

Post-Orientation Needs

- Knowing how to get the grades I want (academic need)
- Finding a job after graduation (career need)
- Learning about job opportunities after graduation (career need)
- Knowing how to study for college courses (academic need)
- Having enough spending money while in college (personal/emotional need)
- Choosing a career direction that is right (career need)
- *Knowing how to manage my time* (academic need)
- Understanding expectations of professors (academic need)
- Selecting courses that I can be successful in (academic need)
- *Where to go with trouble understanding course work* (academic need)
- *Matching career direction to interests and skills* (career need)
- *Knowing what to do if having course work trouble* (academic need)

The expressed needs in **bold italics** represent new pressing needs that were reported after the student participated in orientation. Also, notice that even though a large number of needs expressed during the post-orientation period are the same as those reported during pre-orientation, there has been considerable shifting in the priority of those needs.

Take the time to look carefully at what these students reported. Reflect on your own experience. What was the most pressing need for you during pre-orientation? What about now? In the space provided, list your own most pressing need for the period indicated.

My Top-Priority Need Prior to Orientation Was

_____

_____

_____

My Top-Priority Need Now Is

_____

_____

_____

Developmental Theories Are Diverse in Nature— Each Offers an Advantageous Perspective from Which to Watch One's Future Unfold

Other theorists and researchers have also concentrated on studying developmental issues that pertain to young adults attending college. Arthur Chickering is one such individual. According to Chickering, there are seven developmental areas (which he calls "vectors") to consider for a typical college student.

1. **Developing competence.** During a student's years at a college, if everything proceeds as it should, greater and greater competence is achieved in the areas of intellectual development, physical and manual skills, and social and interpersonal skills.
2. **Managing emotions.** This area pertains to the emotional side of development encountered during one's years at a college. Recognizing the appropriate expression of emotions, both positive and negative, is key to this area.
3. **Moving through autonomy toward interdependence.** Of course, a major task for a student is to achieve independence, but healthy independence really rests upon a foundation of recognizing the importance of others in one's life. One can expect the student to develop an awareness of his or her connectedness with others where the connectedness is not dependent on receiving assurance from others.
4. **Developing mature interpersonal relationships.** As a college student's identity begins to take shape, one outcome is an appreciation for differences, whether tied to values, appearance, interests, background, or experiences. A genuine openness to diversity can be expected to occur because of healthy development during the college years. Simply stated, the person respects and accepts differences.
5. **Establishing identity.** The person becomes comfortable with his or her body, appearance, gender, sexual orientation, and heritage. A positive self-concept is evident.
6. **Developing purpose.** During the college experience a student is confronted with the question "Where am I going in this life?" Finding a meaningful direction answers this question. In this case, we can expect to find the person developing vocational goals and making commitments to people, interests, and activities.
7. **Developing integrity.** Finally, as in William Perry's work cited earlier, a student can be expected to move away from a belief in a world of either/or to a perception that rules are not absolutes, but rather guides to help us make decisions. This is to say, a college student does not develop a set of beliefs that he or she takes to be universally valid: rather, the internal set of beliefs arrived at serve as a reliable way to consistently deal with life. Finally, the interests of others are balanced with one's own interests: that is, self-interest is balanced with social responsibility.

Upon closer inspection of Chickering's theory, one discovers that the seven developmental areas can be placed into one (or more) of the four life-skills dimensions. Finally, according to Brooks, Darden, Gazda, and Ginter, the life-skills approach, which serves as the foundation for this textbook, rests upon various general assumptions about human development.

Basic Life-Skills Assumptions

- Within the developmental matrix that constitutes human development, there are stages through which all people must pass to achieve effective living. Some of the stages are linked to certain age periods; others are not.

- These stages are defined by certain tasks that are representative of what needs to occur for each stage. These tasks are similar to the nuggets of gold found when panning in a mountain stream. At certain points in one's developmental journey, certain tasks shine brighter and should receive one's attention. Other tasks are returned to the "developmental stream" for the time being.
- Accomplishment of a particular task is directly related to mastery of certain life-skills. Life-skills represent a sort of developmental glue that binds stages to tasks and helps a person to grow further and to move on.
- During each person's lifetime, he or she is exposed to many *others* (e.g., parents, teachers, and friends) who are instrumental in helping the person learn necessary life-skills.
- At certain points in life, various life-skills are easier to master than at other points in life. In essence, this point can be summarized by the following statement: *a child must crawl before he or she can walk.*
- While one's ability to learn is somewhat dependent on innate factors, the actual maximization of life-skills is tied to external events or life experiences.
- Failure to develop certain life-skills may result in an inability to take part fully in life. One may develop a psychological disorder (i.e., neurotic behaviors or even a functional psychosis) because of such failure.
- Optimal human functioning is directly related to obtaining mastery of life-skills.
- Optimal functioning can be achieved in a learning environment (e.g., a college), since mastery of life-skills can be tied to instruction and direct learning of various life-skills.

What Does All This Mean for You as a Student?

According to Marcia Baxter-Magolda, survival in this century depends on a person's ability to adapt to rapid changes, increased complexity, ambiguous situations, and greater diversity. A high level of adaptability requires more than simple acquisition of college-based knowledge: the student must *author a new self* during the college years— the type of self that emerges from the interplay between your college experiences and the various characteristics referred to earlier (affective, cognitive, ego, moral, physical-sexual, psychosocial, and vocational).

This textbook is designed to help you develop the necessary life-skills to meet the challenges alluded to by Baxter-Magolda. The underlying theory and research is drawn not only from the work of the authors, Ginter and Glauser, but also from many others who have built upon the work of George Gazda. Gazda spent decades developing the comprehensive approach briefly outlined in this chapter. Each remaining chapter in this textbook offers information and activities to assist you in gaining personal insight that can be used to master relevant skills for the college environment and for your life after graduating.

A Journey of Self-Exploration and Life-Skills Enhancement

Look at the sequence of drawings (on the following page) that form an Egyptian hiero-glyphic sentence. What do you think they mean?

According to Joseph and Lenore Scott, this ancient sentence is a question: "Who are you?" A toddler who has finally mastered the pronunciation of his or her name through a great deal of practice and effort may simply give his or her name in response to this perennial question, but that is no longer a sufficient answer to satisfy you or others.

If the seemingly countless questions appearing throughout this textbook could be reduced to a single, encompassing question, it would be "Who are you at this point in your life?" At this stage in your life, this question is multilayered and is most likely to be answered only after careful consideration of its inherent existential nature. This course essentially provides you with a pathway to uncover a more complete answer to this very important and complicated question.

At the very end of the last chapter of this textbook, you will find an exercise that is intended to pull together all the things you have learned about yourself during this course. Karen Larson, who has explored the existential nature of people's lives, provides us with several different areas to consider when seeking an answer to the question *"Who are you at this point in your life?"* Specifically, she has you consider your level of engagement, degree of goal direction, sense of expectancy, understanding of capacity, sense of purpose, and perception of psychological resources (refer to Exercise 3 in Chapter 15, which is based on Larson's work).

Closing Remarks

Humans have a tendency to perceive and respond to events based on what is taking place in their immediate environment—whether we are aware of it or not, our surroundings often serve as a reference point to determine how we should respond next. For example, after reading this chapter, how would you respond if your professor asked, ***"What basic skills are needed to remain healthy, successful, and unaffected by the numerous challenges you will encounter in the future?"*** You are likely to answer the question by recalling some portion of this chapter.

But what if your professor framed the question by first creating an unexpected scenario? Imagine you are the sole survivor of a plane crash, and you find yourself stranded in an unfamiliar wilderness where the temperature drops below freezing each day. Assume that you will not be rescued until two weeks have elapsed, and you were able to salvage only a few items from the plane, since its contents were destroyed by a fire shortly after the crash (you retrieved a large blanket, three cans of soda, some thin rope made of several strands of cotton braided together, two chocolate candy bars, a magazine, a long piece of broken glass, and a small metal container).

How would you answer the professor's question in light of the scenario created?

Your response:

_____

_____

_____

Another question: *"Can you think of a way to create a critical survival tool from the soda can and chocolate candy obtained from the crash site?"*

Your response:

_____

_____

_____

See **Table 1.3** for five basic survival skills that fit the scenario described, and for an answer concerning the chocolate and an aluminum soda can.

Table 1.3

Five Necessary and *Sufficient Skills* to Prolong Survival

1. Starting a *fire*: Allows you to dry clothes, have light, keep warm, and sanitize water.

2. Knowing how to find **water** and **food**: Depending on conditions, a person's life is likely endangered after three days without water. In addition, knowing how to pull together the necessary environmental ingredients to create crude *fishing* equipment and those to create a *loop snare* to catch small animals will prove invaluable. Even though food is less of a factor, in many cases, a long period without food will lead to death.

3. Using various **shelter tactics**: Skills related to building a debris hut or creating a tarp from available materials can be a lifesaver. In this case, the term *shelter* also implies taking care of your clothing. If your clothing becomes torn, the ability to sew a *locking stitch*, unlike a simple running stitch, allows you to make a repair that will not unravel.

4. Possessing **basic first aid** skills: Basic first aid can prevent minor scrapes, burns, and cuts from developing into something worse.

5. Knowing about effective **signaling**: Find items that reflect sunlight, such as pieces of shiny metal or a mirror, and brightly colored items such as clothing that can be used to signal.

Note. Tory and Grant, hosts of the popular televised show *Mythbusters* (Episode 45: Shredded Plane, Fire without matches), confirmed this fire-starting technique by having Tory polish the bottom of a soda can until it generated sufficient heat to produce smoking embers using a leaf.

SOURCE: "The 5 Basic Survival Skills." (2011). *Survival Topics—Your Online Survival Kit.* Retrieved from http://www.survivaltopics.com/survival/the-5-basic-survival-skills

Answer to soda can and chocolate question: The bottom of the aluminum can is concave, but requires polishing before it can become a useful survival tool. A pure chocolate candy bar can be broken up and with a small piece of rag used as a polishing agent. Once streaks are removed and the concave area becomes highly reflective, you can use the can to heat combustible tinder (any dry substance that readily takes fire when heated). When the sun is at its brightest, tinder should be held approximately an inch away from the center of the can's concave circle until it ignites.

Go to the following site for a detailed, step-by-step presentation on how to convert an aluminum soda can into a fire-starting tool. *Source:* Muma, W. (2003, February). Fire from a can of coke and a chocolate bar. *Wildwood Survival.* Retrieved from http://www.wildwoodsurvival.com/survival/fire/cokeandchocolatebar/

The above activity was intended to emphasize the importance of being prepared for the future, especially the unexpected future. The speed at which changes are taking place in today's world has never been equaled in recorded history, and graduating from college with your head full of facts is much less important than graduating from college *after you have learned how to learn*. During your lifetime, you should expect that much of what constitutes today's foundation of knowledge will have to be modified as a result of new information, or simply discarded due to new discoveries. This is why the single most important goal to achieve before you graduate is to develop those life-skills that will enable you to become *a lifelong learner*.

Finally, our use of the "stranded in an unfamiliar wilderness" scenario may have struck some readers as a bit much for the purpose of making a point, but you only have to think back to March 11, 2011 when Japan was struck by a massive earthquake and tsunami to realize that anyone's life can be immediately transformed by an unforeseen event. If you had been one of the stranded victims in Japan who had to endure one of the nights when the temperature plummeted, the ability to start a fire with a soda can and a piece of chocolate might have been a lifesaver. As the authors of this textbook, we believe the best advice we can offer to a beginning student is to keep an open mind and acquire as many life-skills as possible during your college years.

Sources

Barr, S. (2000, May). Campus cheaters: Too many students are earning an F for honesty. *Reader's Digest*, 108–113.

Baxter-Magolda, M. B. (2001). *Making their own way*. Sterling, VA: Stylus.

Brooks, D. K., Jr. (1984). *A life-skills taxonomy: Defining elements of effective functioning through the use of the Delphi technique*. Unpublished doctoral dissertation, The University of Georgia, Athens.

Chickering, A., & McCormick, J. (1973). Personality development and the college experience. *Research in Higher Education, 1*, 43–70.

Cohen, D. (2002, January 25). Is "Modern Oxford" a sign of the times or an oxymoron? *The Chronicle of Higher Education*, pp. A38–A41.

Daddona, M. F. (2001). *The needs of UGA freshmen: Implications for academic assistance*. Presentation made to faculty and staff of the Division of Academic Assistance, The University of Georgia, Athens, GA.

Darden, C. A., Gazda, G. M., & Ginter, E. J. (1996a). Life-skills and mental health counseling. *Journal of Mental Health Counseling, 18*, 134–141.

Darden, C.A., Ginter, E. J., & Gazda, G. M. (1996b). Life-skills Development Scale (Adolescent Form): The theoretical and therapeutic relevance of life-skills. *Journal of Mental Health Counseling, 18*, 142–163.

Digest of Education Statistics. (1997). Retrieved from http://nces.ed.gov/pub/diget97/d977001.html

Evans, N. J., Forney, D. S., & Guido-DiBrito, F. (1998). *Student development in college theory, research, and practice*. San Francisco, CA: Jossey-Bass.

Farr, M. (2002, February 17). Hot jobs: College and university faculty members. *The Atlanta Journal-Constitution*, p. R3.

Gazda, G. M., & Brooks, D. K., Jr. (1980). A comprehensive approach to developmental interventions. *Journal for Specialists in Group Work, 5*, 120–126.

Gazda, G. M., Ginter, E. J., & Horne, A. M. (2001). *Group counseling and group psychotherapy*. Boston, MA: Allyn & Bacon.

Ginter, E. J., & Glauser, A. (1997, March). *A developmental life-skills model: Comprehensive approach for students*. Paper presented at the 22nd Annual University System of Georgia's Learning Support/ Developmental Studies Conference, Augusta, GA.

Glauser, A. S., Ginter, E. J., & Larson, K. (2002, March). *Composing a meaningful life in an ever-increasing diverse world*. Program presentation at the American Counseling Association's Annual Conference, New Orleans, LA.

Grant, D. (2010, November 11). Art students' mental health: A comprehensive picture. *The Chronicle of Higher Education*. Retrieved from http://chronicle.com

Gross, N. (2006). *University of Georgia: Off the record* (A. Burns, M. Dowdell, & K. Nash, Eds.). Pittsburgh, PA: College Prowler.

Higher Education Research Institute (HERI). (2011, January). *Your first college year survey, 2011*. Los Angeles, CA: HERI at the University of California, Los Angeles.

Hussar, W. J., & Bailey, T. M. (2009). *Projections of Education Statistics to 2018* (NCES 2009-062). National Center for Education Statistics, Institute of Education Sciences, U.S. Department of Education. Washington, DC.

Larson, K. R. (1999). *Female college students: Exploring how they manage affective and cognitive resources in response to heightened stress levels*. Unpublished doctoral dissertation, Kansas State University, Manhattan, KS.

Levine, A., & Cureton, J. S. (1998). *When hope and fear collide*. San Francisco, CA: Jossey-Bass.

Liu, A., Ruiz, S., DeAngelo, L., Pryor, J. H. (2009). *Findings from the 2008 Administration of the College Senior Survey (CSS): National Aggregates*. Los Angeles, CA: Higher Education Research Institute, UCLA.

Mallary, M. (2002, February 17). Security field the best bet in tech sector. *The Atlanta Journal-Constitution*, pp. R1, R5.

Mollison, A. (2000, November 13). College studying studied, and the marks aren't high. *The Atlanta Journal-Constitution*, p. A4.

Oxford University Press. (1971). *The compact edition of the Oxford English dictionary* (Vol. II, P–Z). New York, NY: Author.

Perry, W. (1970). *Forms of intellectual and ethical development during the college years: A scheme*. New York, NY: Holt, Rinehart & Winston.

Picklesimer, B. K., & Miller, T. K. (1998). *Life-Skills Development Inventory (College Form)*: An assessment measure. *Journal of College Student Development, 39*, 100–110.

Pryor, J. H., Hurtado, S., DeAngelo, L., Sharkness, J., Romero, L.C., Korn, W. S., & Tran, S. (2008). *The American freshman: National norms for fall 2008*. Los Angeles, CA: Higher Education Research Institute, UCLA.

Pryor, J. H., Hurtado, S., Saenz, V. B., Santos, J. L., & Korn, W. S. (2007). *The American freshman: Forty-year trends*. Los Angeles, CA: Higher Education Research Institute, UCLA.

Sieben, L. (2011, April 3). Counseling directors see more students with severe psychological problems. *The Chronicle of Higher Education*. Retrieved from http://chronicle.com

Scott, J., & Scott, L. (1968). *Egyptian hieroglyphs for everyone: An introduction to the writing of ancient Egypt*. New York, NY: Barnes & Noble.

Simmons, K. (2002, February 18). Pinched colleges using more part-timers. *The Atlanta Journal-Constitution*, p. Al.

Sobel, R. K. (1998, August 31). The problem with all those A's: Even high achievers often need remedial help. *U.S. News & World Report*, p. 78.

The University of Georgia Undergraduate Bulletin (1999–2000). (1999). Athens, GA: Office of Undergraduate Admissions.

Whelan, C. B. (2001, April 22). Helping first-year students to help themselves. *The Chronicle of Higher Education*, A56.

Chapter 1

Exercise 1: Skill Building Profile

This exercise is designed to gather information that will be used by your professor to structure the remainder of the class experience (e.g., the amount of class time devoted to a topic will be partly determined by the interest you and your fellow classmates indicate in the topic).

Phone (Cell) _____ **E-mail address** _____

Check all areas that you believe you will need information about and/or skill building in:

_____ Choice of a major/career

_____ Time-management tactics

_____ Assertiveness skills and how to best apply them

_____ Ways to enhance my motivation level

_____ How to cope with stress

_____ Find ways to boost my self-confidence

_____ How to cope with math anxiety

_____ Explore how I can develop better problem-solving and decision-making skills

_____ Discover how my values can be used to make decisions compatible with *who I am*

_____ Explore what is meaningful to me so I can establish clear goals

_____ Learn ways to become a better communicator

_____ Discover my style of learning

_____ How to relate better with others

_____ How to cope with test anxiety

_____ Health and physical fitness

_____ Multicultural skills

_____ Discover how to overcome my tendency to procrastinate

_____ Learn about critical-thinking skills

_____ Discover what resources are available on campus

_____ Learn more about financial aid

_____ Find employment while I am in college

_____ Simply learning more about myself (e.g., how *who I am* impacts on my life)

_____ Other area(s)? List and briefly explain:

1. _____ Explain _____

2. _____ Explain _____

3. _____ Explain _____

Have you decided on a major? What is it?_____

Why did you select this major over other majors offered at college?

_____

_____

_____

What type of courses do you expect (or know) you will find most difficult?

_____

_____

Why do you predict this (or how do you know)?

_____

_____

_____

The most important information/skill for me to leave this class with is

_____

_____

_____

When I experience a problem academically (e.g., a poor grade on an exam), I typically respond by

_____

_____

_____

_____

When I graduate from college, I want to look back and be able to say

_____

_____

_____

_____

_____

The **adjective** that best describes me at this point in my life is _____

Ten years from now, the **adjective** that will best describe me is _____

Chapter 1

Exercise 2, Part A: Life-Skills Development Inventory (College Form)

Respond to each statement by writing the appropriate number on the line.

3 = Completely agree
2 = Mostly agree
1 = Mostly disagree
0 = Completely disagree

Section I

_____ 1. If I have a different opinion from what is being said, I am afraid to express my views.

_____ 2. I can accept different values in people my age.

_____ 3. My feelings keep getting in the way when I relate to people.

_____ 4. I have no problem saying no to friends and people my age.

_____ 5. Laws are necessary but can be questioned if unjust.

_____ 6. I am able to adapt to get along with different groups of people.

_____ 7. I do not understand why people behave the way they do.

_____ 8. I do not understand my parents.

_____ 9. When I listen to others, I am able to understand their feelings.

_____ 10. I get very little emotional support from people my own age.

_____ 11. I am able to maintain meaningful relationships with members of the opposite sex.

_____ 12. When I am with people my own age, I feel like an outsider.

_____ 13. I maintain my independence within my friendships.

_____ 14. I choose my friends by the way they look.

_____ 15. I do not get along with most members of my family.

_____ 16. Other people can depend on me.

_____ 17. I have good relationships with my peers.

_____ 18. I am able to communicate my needs and wants to my peers.

_____ 19. I make friends easily.

_____ 20. I respect people who have different backgrounds, habits, values, or appearances.

_____ 21. I am involved in community service.

_____ 22. I am able to manage any conflicts that might arise between home and school.

SOURCE: Picklesimer, B. K., & Gazda, G. M. (1996). *Life-Skills Development Inventory—College Form* (1996 version). Athens, GA: Authors.

_____ 23. I am able to give and receive from people.

_____ 24. I frequently discover important things by interacting with peers.

_____ 25. Being in a group is satisfying to me.

_____ Total

(*Note:* Do not total any of the sections at this time. Answer all the items and read the instructions at the end. Then total each section.)

Section II

_____ 26. I am able to take directions and follow through on tasks.

_____ 27. I have set goals in life for myself.

_____ 28. I do not know which strengths to work on that will help me in the future.

_____ 29. There is no role model for me to look to in order to find out about the kind of work I might like to do.

_____ 30. I know how to find reliable information about jobs.

_____ 31. When solving problems, I am willing to explore multiple solutions.

_____ 32. I gather as much information as possible when making educational decisions.

_____ 33. I feel that I have to sacrifice my personal values when I make decisions.

_____ 34. Once I have made a decision, I do not usually change my mind.

_____ 35. I am able to use my experience in part-time work to help me decide my future occupation.

_____ 36. I know what steps to take to get the kind of job I want.

_____ 37. I do not have an effective way of making decisions.

_____ 38. I have made the right educational decisions so far.

_____ 39. I am able to handle my own money matters.

_____ 40. I have confidence in the decisions I make.

_____ 41. I can envision my future.

_____ 42. My emotions interfere with my ability to deal with the facts.

_____ 43. I know how to think clearly and solve problems in a crisis.

_____ 44. I am able to understand ideas and issues from different points of view.

_____ 45. I understand how emotions influence my decisions and actions.

_____ 46. I am able to use my problem-solving skills when encountering new situations.

_____ 47. I am able to resolve inner conflicts.

_____ 48. I think about the success or failure of my plans and goals.

_____ Total

Section III

_____ 49. I am unsure about what is normal in terms of sexual arousal and expression.

_____ 50. I do not like to participate in individual or team sports.

_____ 51. I have good health habits.

_____ 52. I exercise at least 20 minutes a day, three times per week.

_____ 53. I do not actively pursue my interests and hobbies.

_____ 54. I have satisfying leisure-time activities.

_____ 55. I understand the importance of choosing healthy foods.

_____ 56. I do things regularly that help me keep fit and healthy.

_____ 57. I practice preventative measures such as exercise, stress management, and maintaining a healthy diet.

_____ 58. I am aware of methods to control stress.

_____ 59. I have the willpower to eat healthy foods in moderation.

_____ 60. I understand the effects of alcohol on the body.

_____ 61. I understand how nicotine affects the body.

_____ 62. I consume caffeine on a daily basis.

_____ 63. I am aware of foods that are high in fat content.

_____ 64. I limit the daily intake of sugar in my diet.

_____ 65. I am overly concerned with my body weight.

_____ 66. I would like to have a perfect body.

_____ 67. I realize the psychological benefits of maintaining an exercise program.

_____ 68. I understand how to prevent the spread of sexually transmitted diseases.

_____ Total

Section IV

_____ 69. I have a positive attitude about work.

_____ 70. I get confused as to what is appropriate behavior for males and females.

_____ 71. When I interact with people, I am able to be myself.

_____ 72. I understand the role of sexual intimacy in love relationships.

_____ 73. I want to be more independent but cannot do it without hurting others.

_____ 74. I understand there are broad ranges of differences among individuals.

_____ 75. My personal values guide me when I do things.

_____ 76. Everything considered, the way I am developing is fine.

_____ 77. Though I consider other people's ideas, I am not controlled by them.

_____ 78. I have a good sense of humor.

_____ 79. I do not act responsibly in relationships.

_____ 80. I have a specific career goal.

_____ 81. I am bothered by the differences between what I believe and what society expects.

_____ 82. I am able to deal positively with any frustration and failures I face.

_____ 83. The way I express my anger either hurts me or somebody else.

_____ 84. Life is boring, and I really cannot get excited about it.

_____ 85. The way I handle my emotions often hurts me or someone else.

_____ 86. I am able to handle ambiguous situations.

_____ 87. I often think and act on my own.

_____ 88. There are certain people besides teachers from whom I learn.

_____ Total

Figuring Your Score

Return to each section and for *every item* **printed in bold** *reverse the score*. **Thus, 3 = 0, 2 = 1, 1 = 2,** and **0 = 3**. Then add up the column of numbers for each section and enter the totals in the spaces provided below.

SECTION I: Interpersonal Communications/Human Relations (IC/HR)
Total = _____ Divide by **25**. This number is your **IC/HR score** = _____

SECTION II: Problem-Solving/Decision-Making (PS/DM)
Total = _____ Divide by **23**. This number is your **PS/DM score** = _____

SECTION III: Physical Fitness/Health Maintenance (PF/HM)
Total = _____ Divide by **20**. This number is your **PF/HM score** = _____

SECTION IV: Identity Development/Purpose-in-Life (ID/PIL)
Total = _____ Divide by **20**. This number is your **ID/PIL score** = _____

Utilizing the Information Provided by Your Scores

It is not so much a matter of having all low or all high scores (even students with high scores can improve and strengthen the skills they possess), think more in terms of what each life-skills dimension means to you. If a particular overall score strikes you as low compared to the other scores, go back to the items listed for that life-skills area. Determine which items contributed the most to obtaining your low score. Of these items, identify those which you consider most important to achieving your future goals in life. During the remainder of this course, these are the areas you will want to focus on and build skills in.

Stop! Bring your textbook to class to complete the final part of this exercise, the Life-Skills Wheel. This will be done in class, after which your professor will discuss the results, indicating how they can be used to enhance your skill levels.

Chapter 1

Exercise 2, Part B: Life-Skills Wheel

Transfer your scores (from Part A) to the spaces provided.

IC/HR _____ PS/DM _____ PF/HM _____ ID/PIL _____

(If any of your scores **exceed the value of 3**, **there is an error** somewhere. Return to "Exercise 2, Part A" and recalculate your scores.)

This represents the last part of Exercise 2, and it will be completed in class. You are to transfer your mean scores to the wheel and darken in the area that corresponds to a mean score. Review the example provided on the next page before you start.

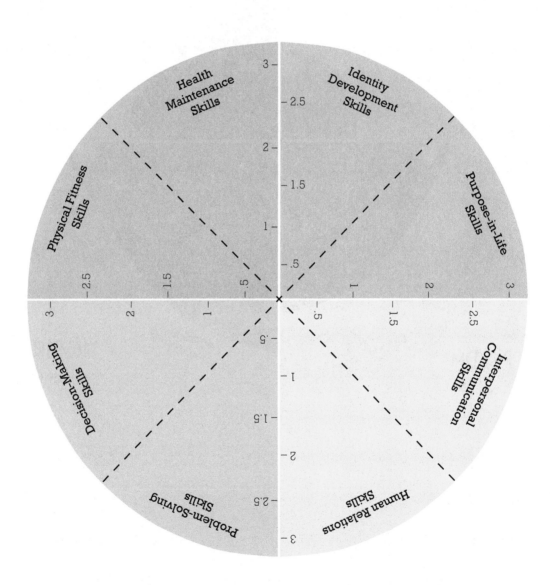

Example of a Completed Life-Skills Wheel

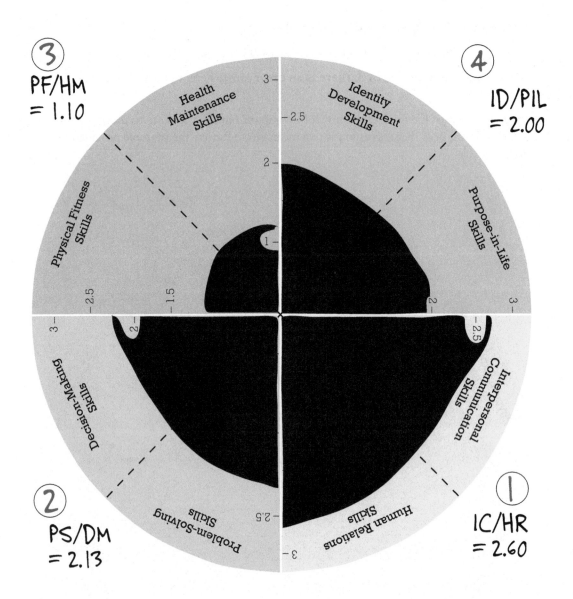

③ PF/HM = 1.10

④ ID/PIL = 2.00

② PS/DM = 2.13

① IC/HR = 2.60

Finding and Using One's Existing Motivation
Realignment and Enhancement

2

ver the years, we have worked with a large number of students seeking assistance on a wide variety of concerns. Many of these students provided initial explanations of their difficulties that indicated they were affected by a lack of motivation. Essentially, each student claimed that an absence of motivation caused his or her problem (e.g., poor test performance, not having enough money to go out on weekends, failing to schedule a meeting with a professor because of reluctance). Interestingly, when such a student is asked what he or she must do to change the situation, the student usually offers a relevant answer (e.g., study more, spend less time worrying about money and just go out and get a part-time job, talk to the professor to find out what she expects for the major project). It seems that these students know what actions they should take, but they choose not to carry through on the actions. (Curiously, it is not unusual for these students to devote about the same amount of time to setting up a meeting with one of us as they would have devoted to implementing the action itself.) The students' comments, considered in their totality, reflect a type of twisted logic that imprisons the students and prevents them from reaching the expressed goal.

Before we present some suggestions to counteract these kinds of problems, it is useful to consider the validity of the students' explanations for their lack of motivation. A typical explanation goes like this: "Since I earned low grades on all three tests, and because I know I want to do well, the problem must be that I lost my motivation to study." We have labeled this the *"empty tank explanation."* It is as if the person claims to possess a motivation tank somewhere in his or her body that is now empty. In a sense, the person has sought help to find a new source of motivational fuel to fill the tank and drive off to his or her destination.

The authors operate from the assumption that everyone is motivated to do something (e.g., one student who reported having "no motivation for anything" also revealed that he "always" played video games for "several hours each day"). The question we seek to help students answer can be stated as follows: *"What changes can be made to realign or enhance the motivation you currently possess?"*

The **realignment approach** is advocated when students display a lack of interest in an expressed goal, but do not realize the mismatch between the stated goal and their low level of motivational energy tied to that goal. For example, a student is pursuing a major because a parent wants her to, rather than because she is interested in the major and believes it will eventually satisfy her personal system of values. The **enhancement approach** is advocated when the goal is appropriate for students, but their existing level of motivation requires a boost. When we work with a student, we do not decide for the student which of the two approaches is the one to take: rather, the appropriate approach emerges after the student explores and gains insight into what lies behind the initial claim that he or she is suffering from a lack of motivation.

Before listing changes students can make to strengthen their existing motivation or bring it into line, it is necessary to review what has been uncovered about motivation in general. Having general knowledge about motivation will enable you to better select interventions that will provide the greatest amount of return for the effort you make. We believe useful knowledge can be obtained by considering the opinions of two different groups who are close to the issue of motivation: highly motivated students who have thought about motivation's effect in their lives and social scientists who have studied motivation. Each of these groups is a rich source of information to consider.

What Is Motivation? The Social Science View

Life is a continual series of choices for the individual in which a main determinant of choice is the person as he already is (including his goals for himself, his courage or fear, his feelings of responsibility, his ego-strength or "will power," etc.). We can no longer think of the person as "fully determined" where the phrase implies "determined only by forces external to the person." The person insofar as he is a real person, is his own main determinant. Every person is, in part, "his own project" and makes himself.

Abraham H. Maslow

Maslow is perhaps best remembered for his views on *self-actualization*. **Self-actualization** can be thought of as the last level in a motivational hierarchy where each level represents a set of needs the person is innately driven to fulfill (see Figure 2.1). According to Maslow, there are five essential levels of need that serve to motivate our actions, and satisfying them sequentially, starting at the lowest level, allows us to reach the summit. At the summit, we are driven to satisfy our unique potentiality—all those latent aspects of the self that we are capable of calling into being.

At the base of Maslow's pyramid of hierarchical needs are basic physiological needs. Scaling the pyramid beyond the first level, one finds next safety and security, then recognition, then self-esteem, and finally, at the capstone, self-actualization (see Figure 2.1). Once we satisfy one level of need, we are free to focus on the next level.

While at first glance it may seem relatively easy to satisfy these needs on our journey up the pyramid's slope, the difficulty of the tasks involved increases significantly at each new level. For example, there are markets where I can buy food, but there are no markets where I can purchase $20 worth of self-esteem over the counter. Of course, there are places on the earth today, including the United States, where people are mostly concerned about satisfying just basic physiological needs each day of their life.

Concisely, Maslow's theory proposes that a person cannot simultaneously be a self-actualized artist forging a new medium for artistic expression and a person foraging from a dumpster because he or she is hungry and homeless. In other words, a severely malnourished person who is forced to seek warmth during a winter blizzard by climbing into a large cardboard box and shutting its lid is probably not a person whose immediate actions are driven by needs related to self-actualization. Even when one is not confronted with a situation of severe deprivation, it is not that easy to satisfy all of the needs listed by Maslow. Maslow himself recognized the many implications of his the-

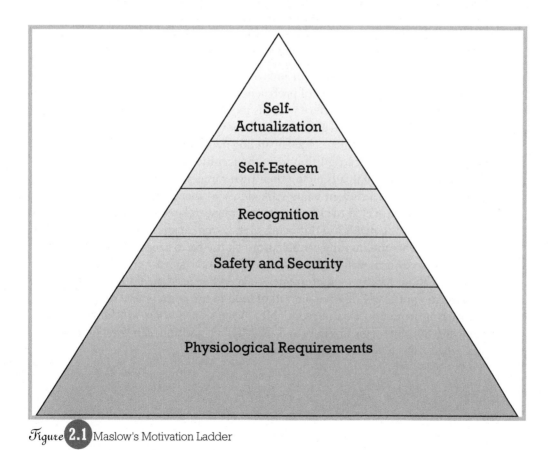

Figure **2.1** Maslow's Motivation Ladder

ory and its underlying complexity (e.g., an attack on one's self-esteem can simultaneously feel like an attack on one's sense of security). In fact, the difficulty of moving up Maslow's pyramid of needs is evident in the low percentage of individuals who consistently reside at the highest level. At one point Maslow indicated it was a very small percentage of the population. Whatever the actual percentage is, it should be assumed to be relatively small, since Maslow believed people such as Abraham Lincoln, Eleanor Roosevelt, and Albert Einstein were good examples of those operating at the highest level of potentiality. Finally, because Maslow's idea of self-actualization is often misunderstood, we use Maslow's own words to describe this final motivational dimension of life:

> Self-actualization does not mean a transcendence of all human problems. Conflict, anxiety, frustration, sadness, hurt, and guilt can all be found in healthy human beings. In general, the movement, with increasing maturity, is from neurotic, posed problems to real, unavoidable, existential problems, inherent in the nature of [the person] (even at his [or her] best) living in a particular kind of world. Even though [the person] is not neurotic [the person] may be troubled by real, desirable and necessary guilt rather than neurotic guilt (which isn't desirable or necessary), by an intrinsic conscience. Even though [the person] has transcended the problems of Becoming, there remains the problem of Being. To be untroubled when one should be troubled can be a sign of sickness. Sometimes, smug people have to be scared "into their wits."

Maslow's work can help us understand what is meant by the word *motivation*, and especially what the phrase "I lack motivation" tells us about a particular student. The student's claim that motivation is unreliable (it cannot be found when it is needed) takes on new meaning when one considers that most individuals are not operating at Maslow's highest level of motivation, and that most people are struggling to meet primary and social needs. Thus, the student's difficulties are more accurately understood and solved if seen as linked to causes such as the following:

- The student's opinion, favorable or unfavorable, about his ability in a certain area: if he is ashamed of his low level of proficiency in math, the resulting negative opinion of the self will likely interfere with his motivation to study for a math test.
- A perceived failure to receive acknowledgment and rewards for her hard work: a student's level of commitment to a demanding major can be expected to drop if her efforts do not result in recognition from the faculty, especially if the faculty members are too caught up in advancing their own careers.
- A fear for his safety: a student being stalked by a former lover who threatens bodily harm cannot be expected to concentrate on course-related activities.
- The student's basic needs are not being met: a student that is confronted with financial problems and literally cannot afford all the basic necessities of life will find it difficult to perform well in courses when she tries to subsist on a meager diet and is worried about having enough money to keep her residence. Or what about the student who purposely deprives herself of food to the point where she is diagnosed as suffering from anorexia nervosa? Her skeletonized body will block her from achieving healthy forms of safety and security, recognition, self-esteem, and obviously the final state of self-actualization.

What Have Other Social Scientists Said About Motivation?

Cokley, Bernard, Cunningham, and Motoike (2001) reviewed the motivation literature and provided an overview of what they found. Based on their findings, it can be concluded that people experience three different types of motivational conditions or states, referred to as *intrinsic*, *extrinsic*, and *amotivation*. Each is tied to a certain level of **autonomy**; the highest level of autonomy is found with intrinsic motivation.

Intrinsic Motivation. This type of motivation comes into play when we stop to figure out why we are compelled to perform a certain activity and realize it is because the activity itself creates pleasure or satisfaction. Regardless of the specific type of pleasurable pursuit that drives us to act, intrinsic motivation is believed by the experts to reflect a form of **self-determined behavior** (i.e., "I select to do the activity").

Breaking this down further, Cokley et al. report that a person typically acts in a certain way for one of three reasons, or a combination of these three:

- *to know,*
- *to accomplish things, or*
- *to experience stimulation.*

Extrinsic Motivation. In this situation, the person is basically acting in a way that would cause an outside observer to conclude that the person's actions reflect some form of **instrumental behavior** ("I am doing this for a reason that originates outside me"). Thus, the person's actions are serving as a means to some end beyond any pleasure the activity itself may provide the person. Three types of extrinsic motivation are said to exist: *external regulation*, *introjected regulation*, and *identified regulation*. Considering how each is defined points out the difference between extrinsic motivation and intrinsic motivation.

- **External regulation** occurs when there is a definite outside consequence that drives an activity (e.g., "Next year I can get my own apartment if I earn a B average my first year").
- **Introjected regulation** occurs when the external reason for acting in a certain manner has taken up residence in the person, and typically takes the form of an inner voice or monologue that persuades or pressures the person to act in a certain way (e.g., "When I go out the night before a test, I feel guilty, so I stay in and study to reduce the amount of self-scolding that goes on in my head").
- **Identified regulation** occurs when the person acts in a certain fashion because he or she has adopted a ready-made set of rules or established guidelines from someone else. The person has allowed himself or herself to identify with another person's or group's standards (e.g., "My parents socialize only with other professionals and I see no reason to do differently"). In this case, the person is essentially governed by unexamined rules.

Identified regulation results in the person feeling connected to a certain pattern of behavior, and thus, the person essentially follows the same approach to life as another person. (Unlike introjected regulation, identified regulation lacks the quality of taking orders from an internalized drill sergeant.) While this third type seemingly differs from the other two forms of extrinsic motivation, it does have an instrumental quality because it is basically the result of an unexamined acceptance of something that originated outside the person. (A fourth type, integrated regulation, is introduced in Exercise 2 at the end of this chapter.)

Amotivation. This represents the lowest level of autonomy. It is difficult to tie the person's behavior to either an intrinsic or an extrinsic explanation because the person sees his or her actions as beyond his or her control ("I am doing poorly in my psychology class and there is nothing I can do because the professor comes up with tests I can't prepare for"). We rarely see this type of student in our offices, not because they are rare, but rather because they view seeking help as a waste of time and effort. For them a lack of control is the same as destiny—it cannot be changed. (We will return to the issue of perceived control later in this chapter.)

External, Introjected, and Identified Regulation's Link to Persistence

Social science theories of motivation help explain much about human behavior—why we do certain things in one situation and why we sometimes see ourselves as stuck in another situation. Moving from one environment to another can affect our motivational status because a new environment challenges our motivational resilience in ways it has not been tested before. Certainly, attending college is one of those times. Colleges are unique learning environments that can challenge a student in many ways. For example, most professors, unlike high school teachers, were not formally trained to be teachers. They were hired because of their particular degrees, their research skills, or other skills and abilities. It may seem strange, but some professors do not even see themselves as teachers; rather, they identify themselves as researchers. (For them, teaching is something that occurs between research activities.)

At some large research institutions (e.g., the University of Georgia, the University of British Columbia, and Louisiana State University & Agricultural & Mechanical College), a large segment of the professors devote much of their time and energy to professional duties in addition to any teaching they are responsible for during an academic term. Because of the many responsibilities that professors assume, they tend to expect students to take a very active role in the learning process—that is, to be self-motivated.

In such large, sometimes impersonal learning environments, does it even matter what type of motivation serves to push a student to study, as long as the student studies? Specifically, does it matter if the student studies because of extrinsic motivation ("My parents will be upset if I don't do well since they are paying") or because of intrinsic motivation ("I want to study because learning about psychology—why people do what they do—is fascinating")? It turns out that it does matter. Researchers have found that the type of motivation governing our behavior can make a significant difference over time. According to Cokley et al. (2001), different types of motivation affect a person's ability to persist, or endure obstacles. **Persistence** can be defined as the degree to which a person refuses to give up on a goal even when confronted with interference.

It seems reasonable to assume that different types of motivation would be associated with different levels of persistence. Furthermore, it seems logical to assume that higher levels of persistence are likely to contribute more to a student's completion of a course than lower levels of persistence. When Cokley et al. tested such assumptions, they found that "students who persist and finish the course had higher levels of intrinsic motivation toward academic activities than students who drop out of the class."

The researchers also found that one type of extrinsic motivation contributed to a student's level of persistence. It was found that identified regulation (which is further along the continuum of autonomy than other forms of extrinsic motivation) positively affected the "staying power" of students. External and introjected regulation did not contribute one way or the other, but it does appear that the more a student embraced an amotivational explanation for life events, the less likely the student was to stick it out in a course. Table 2.1 depicts what was found for various types of motivation in relation to persistence.

Table 2.1 Different Types of Motivation: Their Impact on Staying in a Course	
Type of Motivation	Impact on Persistence
Driven to know (intrinsic): "I need to learn"	Positive Influence (+)
Driven to be stimulated (intrinsic): "Learning is exciting"	Positive Influence (+)
Driven to accomplish (intrinsic): "Finishing is good"	Positive Influence (+)
Pushed by regulations one identifies with (extrinsic): "A good student is expected to work hard so I study hard"	Positive Influence (+)
Pushed by rules or demands (extrinsic): "I study because it is expected by my parents"	None (0)
Pushed by what happens (extrinsic): "If I don't study I will have to go out into the real world"	None (0)
Not driven or pushed but controlled (amotivation): "Life is like being a puppet—I move to the pull of my strings"	Negative Influence (−)

Other sources of evidence for the claim that intrinsic motivation contributes to a person's ability to persist and achieve a difficult goal are found in published interviews, biographies, and autobiographies. Stories of how highly motivated people have persisted to win against great odds are plentiful. Randi Altschul's story is an example (Ryan, 2000). Randi's career started at age 25 when she created a board game based on a popular television series. Her initial attempts to obtain permission to market the game were rejected. However, she refused to give up and became even more tenacious. Realizing that the real power to grant the permission she sought resided with the executive producer of the television series, she decided to target him for approval. Finally, her dogged pursuit paid off and she was granted a meeting with this pivotal person, who said yes to her idea. This was the start of a successful career that has led to 2,000 copyrights and several important consulting jobs with major companies, which grant her the freedom she requires to think and create in her own style. During an interview, Randi made a comment concerning her overall perspective that was very revealing in light of the above research findings. She stated, "You don't get anything unless you make it happen. My middle name is Persistence. I don't wait for anyone else and don't take 'no' for an answer."

Being driven by intrinsic motivation has not only contributed to Randi Altschul's high level of persistence, it has also fueled her trust in the creative process, and as a result she has developed many intriguing prototypes for possible production. She has conceived of an interactive breakfast cereal that depicts various cartoon shapes that revert to a regular cereal shape once milk is poured into the bowl; she has created various novelty toys; and at the time of the interview, she had just created a disposable "phone-card-phone" (a combination of two frequently used items) that could be kept in a wallet or purse and used in emergencies. Not only is her career achievement an excellent example of how persistence and motivation interact, it is also an excellent example of how intrinsic motivation can lead to the same tangible types of rewards (in her case, wealth) that so many extrinsically motivated people hope to acquire.

What Is Motivation? The Perspective of Students

While it is obvious from what has already been discussed that motivation is one of the most important factors in your future success at college and in your career, the views of social scientists and theorists are just one side of the story. What can students say to add to our understanding about motivation? We contacted students identified as being highly motivated and asked them five questions about motivation. Their comments and the themes uncovered provided us with a clearer image of what constitutes motivation and what ingredients contribute to its presence.

What Does the Word *Motivation* Mean to You?

Highly motivated students respond to this question in various ways. Here are some responses we have received.

"Motivation is the incentive to achieve."

"It is a drive or push that we feel."

"Motivation is a 'kick-starter' that gets us going."

Such responses suggest that motivation essentially involves effort and goals and that motivation may be summarized as *the willingness and ability to put forth effort.*

Activity

Answer the following questions. Circle either **Yes** or **No**.

1. I am a self-starter. I do not need to be pushed to start studying.   Yes   No

2. If I receive a failing grade, it is because I did not do what was needed to earn a good grade.   Yes   No

3. Even in a class with a poor instructor, I can learn the material and do well.   Yes   No

4. The grades I earn are due to my own effort.   Yes   No

5. I usually feel I have control of situations.   Yes   No

6. Some people are just plain lucky.   Yes   No

7. It is useless for me to try hard in school because a person will do well or poorly regardless of his or her effort.   Yes   No

8. If something bad is going to happen, it will just happen.   Yes   No

9. When people are angry with me, it is usually for nothing I did or said.   Yes   No

10. Some students are just born good students and so they earn high grades.   Yes   No

While we cannot expect ten questions to capture who you really are, your responses may reveal the typical manner in which you perceive your world as to how much it affects you and how much you affect it.

If you answered Yes to questions 1–5 and No to questions 6–10, you may typically believe that your effort can make a difference, which probably means you believe you can affect outcomes. In this case, you should be able to put forth the effort required to succeed because you believe your actions can make a difference. If your answers did not match this pattern (showed a mixed or reverse pattern), you should not be overly concerned, but we do suggest that you stop and consider that you may have more power to direct your academic future than you believe.

It is important to point out that you may perceive yourself as capable of affecting outcomes in your favor in the academic world, but less so in your interpersonal world. For example, you may have answered questions 5, 6, 8, and 9 in a manner that indicates you see yourself as having little influence on aspects of your life outside the classroom. Regardless of what area or areas of your life are affected, if you have doubt about your ability to influence your future positively, you might want to speak to the instructor of this course or even a college counselor to explore whether these beliefs are negatively influencing your life.

A final point to make before moving to the next question relates to a comment made by a highly motivated student. She stated that motivation "is something that starts outside of ourselves when we are young, and as we get older motivation begins to come from within us." Highly motivated students are driven by something from within, and because of this, they are willing to put forth effort. Motivated students understand that good grades are related to effort. While some students find it easier than other students to earn high grades, we have never encountered a college student earning A's and B's who did not put forth effort. To succeed in a college setting, a student must see the connection between grades and one's own effort.

Why Did You Decide to Go to This Particular College?

In responding to this question, highly motivated students provided the following types of answers:

"I thought I would feel comfortable and happy at this college."

"It was the best deal in terms of cost and quality of education. It was a good fit."

"I live in the area and felt at home."

"I just feel connected to this college."

It is very evident from such comments that motivated students typically report a *strong sense of belonging* at the college they have selected to attend. A large part of succeeding at a college and maintaining a high level of motivation is based on perceiving the college as a sort of home away from home. Interestingly, it has been found that students who do not take the time to decorate their dorm rooms after starting college frequently feel more alienated, and this sense of alienation has been linked to dropping out during their first year. While reasons for dropping out can be many-faceted, we trust that what highly motivated students have taught us about belonging is probably true of all students (e.g., freshmen, transfer students, nontraditional students, and international students). And, yes, in some cases, establishing a sense of belonging can be as simple as devoting a little time and effort to decorating your room or apartment with favorite possessions, making the place yours, and creating a sort of personal sanctuary or territory. Of course, a sense of connectedness can be fostered in other ways, such as taking time to meet other students and learn about campus and community resources. Also, some beginning students just out of high school can benefit from starting during the summer term, before most other freshmen enter the college. Allowing yourself to become familiar with the college you have selected before the crowds show up in the fall can help foster a sense of belonging that fuels your motivation.

How Is Motivation Related to Academic Success?

This question posed to motivated students reveals important aspects of what constitutes motivation. These were some of the responses:

"One's motivation level is tied to earning certain grades—grades that lead to what you want."

"Being interested in a future career helps to motivate a student to achieve."

"Motivation is the drive to succeed, not being passive."

"Motivation means taking ownership."

These comments introduce the notion of goals. Goals are a sort of psychological adhesive that holds a series of motivated behaviors together. Of course, these motivated behaviors, once strung together, lead to some type of meaningful achievement. Simply stated, *college students must possess goals to possess motivation*.

As a result of working with many students over the years, both as professors and as counselors, we have found that a crude but significant indicator of motivational level or motivational strength can be found by asking a student to discuss his or her academic goal and why that goal is important. Some typical responses that possibly indicate a weak motivation level follow:

"My parents wanted me to go. They always wanted me to go here. They are graduates of this college."

"All my friends went to college, so I followed. I also want to be a medical doctor because they make a lot of money. There's some kind of medical program here, right?"

"I want to make money to enjoy life, and a friend told me you can make a lot of money by going to college."

Here are two examples of responses that indicate a strong motivation level.

"I spent a lot of time exploring different majors, and I decided to major in business because it matches my values. I like to work with people and I like a lot of variety, and this college has a very good business school that matches my values and interests."

"I have always been interested in learning. I like to learn and this college is known for excellence in several fields of study. It has a major in accounting that will enable me to get into a good graduate program."

These latter two goals are specific in nature, and they are built upon knowledge about what is available. When the motivated student tells us what he or she wants, the student's remarks present us with a clear indication of what is desired and leaves little doubt concerning what the student plans to accomplish or experience. It is also obvious that the stated goals are realistic. The goals expressed by a motivated student are the result of careful thought and using various resources to obtain good advice and accurate information. This brings us to the issue of *locus of control*. **Locus of control** refers to whether a person sees himself or herself as having control over his or her life or as being controlled by some outside influence. Students who allow themselves to be controlled by others (e.g., "My parents told me what to major in") are less likely to succeed than students who decide important questions for themselves.

Students who tend to succeed have a good reason for going to a particular college. They can explain why they are going there, and they frequently know what they will major in. They have a clear goal in mind. Having a definite reason for going to college is often a better predictor of academic success than a high SAT score. Goals are such an important contributor to academic success that we have concluded this chapter with two exercises, one of which is a goal exercise. The goal exercise has proven to be very helpful for many students—our advice is to think carefully about your goals.

Do You Think It Is the Responsibility of Professors to Motivate College Students?

While it may be up to a professor to devote attention to what he or she presents in class, it is not the professor's job to foster or maintain a high level of motivation in students. When asked, motivated students will typically agree that students, not professors, are responsible for maintaining student motivation. Their comments are directly related to the belief that successful students *possess skills for personal problem-solving and decision-making*, so they can overcome setbacks rather than just giving in. Motivated students know how to approach a problem, and if they do not know, they find out.

Many of the college students referred to us for academic assistance have a difficult time solving problems or making decisions. Such students frequently possess distorted information about what to do. For example, they might say, "You can't question a professor about a grade earned on a test" or "I am feeling a lot of stress right now, but I can't go to the counseling center for help—they only deal with people who are seriously disturbed." The truth is that you have a right to approach a professor concerning a grade, and college counseling centers are for all students with a wide range of concerns. In fact, there are many free services available on campus to assist students with finding answers to problems. Furthermore, just taking some type of action can help you improve, enhance your problem-solving skills, and positively affect your motivation level.

If you encounter a problem, or have a difficult decision to make, and you lack the skills or knowledge to find a solution, take action. Find someone who can help you find a solution. If you are having difficulty with the course, seek out and speak with the professor. If you do poorly on a test, decide how you should change your manner of studying for the next test. Visit a college tutor when you do not understand material covered in class. The point is to take appropriate action.

How Are Motivated Students Different from Students Who Lack Motivation?

Motivated students speak about many things in connection with this question, but a comment made by one student caught the authors' attention. She indicated that *motivated students enjoy more of what is going on, take part in the college, and seek out others*. We believe that motivated students are the students who maintain and develop relationships that provide support. They establish and maintain a circle of interpersonal support.

To summarize, successful students not only possess firm goals, they put forth effort and know how to approach problem situations. They also report knowing others whom they can count on. This support can come from a number of people (parents, a stepparent, friends, an uncle, a professor). The availability of support from others can have a tremendous impact on a student's academic performance. This support creates an emotional buffer that helps a student get through all the initial changes that are part of starting college and those that come during the years leading up to graduation.

When most students start at a college (even seasoned transfer students), they should expect to experience a period of loneliness. This is normal, but it also makes students vulnerable at that time. As a new student, it is very important for you to maintain contact with family members, make an effort to develop new friendships, and establish a good relationship with your academic advisor and others who can provide additional support during the transition period. Motivated students enjoy taking part in campus activities, meeting people, and finding many reasons for staying in college. Motivated students establish links with many people—links that serve to fill interpersonal needs. Having support enables a motivated student to maintain confidence in his or her own ability even if the student is going through a rough period. Evidence suggests that personal problems can negatively influence one's level of motivation. It is very common for students to experience periods of depression or loneliness while at a college. (One of the leading causes of death on campuses across our country is suicide due to persistent, severe depression.)

If you are lonely, join a campus organization. This may also help with feelings of minor depression. You can even use relaxation techniques to reduce negative feelings and enhance thoughts of succeeding. In many cases, the initial feelings of loneliness and even depression experienced by a new student weaken and vanish over time. But if such loneliness or depression persists, or you are simply concerned about such feelings, you should seek help on your campus. Consider meeting with one of the college's counselors. Develop a plan of action. Do not let personal problems control you or your future by disturbing your level of motivation.

Six Factors That Align and Enhance Motivation

The theories and research of social scientists and the comments made by highly motivated students reveal that various elements and characteristics contribute to being highly motivated. It is also apparent that these elements are intertwined. To summarize, highly motivated students share these six characteristics:

- Are willing to put forth effort to achieve their goals
- Possess a strong sense of belonging on campus
- Possess firm goals that are
    - explicit (clear and not built on whimsy),
    - linked to careful planning,
    - established by obtaining useful information from various resources
- Possess skills for personal problem-solving and decision-making
- Report having support from others
- Experience a range of motivations, but are mostly driven by intrinsic forms of motivation

Final Suggestions to Help Develop and Maintain One's Motivation

Develop a Motivating Perspective toward the World. David E. Schmitt, who wrote *The Winning Edge*, writes about a motivating attitude. Based on our experiences and the views of Schmitt, we have concluded that it is important to feed and strengthen (1) an optimistic perspective, (2) a passion for our identified goals, (3) a critical, truth-seeking approach to learning, (4) an ability to approach situations with curiosity, (5) a desire to achieve, (6) a belief in ourselves, (7) our creative potential, and (8) our sense of control. While some of these elements will be discussed in greater detail in other chapters, we will expand on a few here.

When you experience anxiety or fear about a college course, you should not allow such feelings to affect your motivation. For example, let us say you are required to enroll in an introductory speech class and you have always found it difficult to speak in front of others. You could dwell on the negative aspects of the situation, or you could take control of the situation by approaching it from a positive, optimistic perspective. For example, you could write out the first speech. You could go to the classroom when no one is there and sit in your chair and imagine being called upon by the professor, then go to the front of the classroom and give the speech. Reciting a speech while picturing one's classmates being present and seeing oneself earning a good grade can significantly reduce one's fear in many cases.

When a student uses this technique, frequently the student is able to do what is required—to take control of a situation rather than letting it control him or her. An optimistic perspective enables a person to focus on what he or she can do rather than what he or she cannot do.

Possessing the various elements of a motivating perspective enables one to recover sooner from the stress and confusion that is sometimes encountered during one's academic journey toward graduation. For example, sometimes a person becomes confused as to why he or she is attending a college. Goals are no longer clear, and the student finds it difficult to concentrate on class work because the student is unsure about what the future holds. There is a sense of lacking direction. If you ever find yourself in a situation where you doubt your original reasons for going to a college, you should stop and ask, "Why did I want to attend college in the first place?" Such self-examination may lead you to realize that the motivation that has carried you this far is weak and your motivational energy is missing. The solution is to establish new goals or modify old ones by moving through the steps listed below, keeping in mind that intrinsic motivation is associated with high rates of persistence.

- Examine your priorities (values).
- Examine alternatives.
- Obtain needed information and assistance.
- Find something that will generate passion.
- Finally, reestablish goal(s).

The following examples illustrate the connection between values and motivation:

A student may value and be motivated by a desire to help others.

A student may value and be motivated by an interest in working as a member of a team.

Other values that may motivate someone are competition, power and authority, working alone, acquiring knowledge, or financial security.

The college career of one of the authors provides a case in point: I (Ginter) started college wanting to gain knowledge, but also to guarantee myself financial security after graduating. As a beginning freshman, I decided to major in philosophy. But over time, maintaining my motivation became difficult because I became very concerned about whether I would ever obtain a job teaching philosophy, since such jobs are relatively rare. This meant I did not see myself as having a financially secure future (something I valued). I gathered information and sought assistance. The result of these efforts was that I examined appropriate alternatives and decided to switch to a major in psychol-

Motivation gets us to our top goal.

ogy, a major that at the time promised a future career. I had a passion for both philosophy and psychology. Thus, by carefully considering my values and the alternatives, I was able to reestablish a clear goal, and this boosted my motivation level to do well in college.

Everyone has strengths. Students admitted to a college are not selected with the aim of having those students fail. Colleges want students to succeed. This is where having carefully thought-out goals pays off. Keep in mind that your college goals should be tied to your strengths. If you are interested in working with people, you might want to consider going into majors related to social work, nursing, or psychology. If you are the type of person who likes to be in a position of leading others or convincing others, you might want to consider going into law or business. If you enjoy investigating problems and you enjoy science-related activities, you may want to consider biology, math, or computer programming as a career.

The right major can be a powerful contributor to success. Some students even change colleges once they figure out what to major in because the new college offers the major desired. As indicated earlier, students without a clear direction often do not see themselves as part of the college they attend. They have a difficult time seeing anything positive about the college. These students are more likely to lose whatever motivation they started college with, perform poorly, and even drop out.

When a successful, motivated student begins to feel alienated, the student works to establish a connection in some manner. The main point here is that if you major in an area that fits your personality, you will be more likely to remain optimistic and curious, develop critical thinking skills, and foster your creative potential: that is, more likely to stay motivated in college.

Use Motivational Boosters to Maintain Your Motivational Level. In addition to possessing a motivating attitude, there are many simple techniques that you can employ to maintain a high level of motivation. Time-management techniques can be helpful. Keeping a list of what needs to be done in each of your college classes, breaking the tasks down into manageable units of time, and marking off what has been accomplished can reduce stress and help maintain your motivation.

Another motivational aid is to plan for a vacation, but only work on the details of the vacation after reaching a goal: for example, after having completed and turned in a major assignment on time. Such a reward system will help you stay motivated.

Closing Remarks

Motivation is often a focus of interests in such areas as education and sports. Since individuals differ in terms of motivation, researchers have found it helpful to use various motivational categories (termed *motivational styles*) to uncover weaknesses and strengths. The primary purpose of such research is to develop various methods or even series of stratagems to improve performance and learning. In a sense, this chapter can place you in the role of such a researcher—knowledge you acquired about what constitutes effective motivation, insights you gained about your own motivational style, and your new understanding about applying various techniques that best match your situation will certainly improve your own performance and learning.

Sources

Cokley, K. O., Bernard, N., Cunningham, D., & Motoike, J. (2001). A psychological investigation of the academic motivation scale using a United States sample. *Measurement and Evaluation in Counseling and Development, 34*, 109–119.

Glauser, A., Ginter, E. J., & Larson, K. (2002). *Composing a meaningful life in an ever-increasing diverse world.* Presentation made at the 2002 World Conference of the American Counseling Association, New Orleans, LA.

Maslow, A. H. (1968). Abraham H. Maslow. In W. S. Sahakian (Ed.), *History of psychology: A source book in systematic psychology* (pp. 411–416). Itasca, IL: F. E. Peacock.

Reeves, J. (Producer). (1997). *Getting motivated.* [Videotape]. Athens, GA: GPTV. Earl J. Ginter (Writer of script).

Reeves, J. (Producer). (1997). *Maintaining motivation.* [Videotape] Athens, GA: GPTV. Earl J. Ginter (Writer of script).

Rotter, J. B. (1966). Generalized expectancies for internal versus external control of reinforcement. *Psychological Monographs, 80* (1, Whole No. 609).

Ryan, M. (2000, October 8). My middle name is persistence. *Parade Magazine*, pp. 24–25.

Schmitt, D. E. (1992). *The winning edge: Maximizing success in college.* New York, NY: HarperCollins.

VandenBos, G. R. (Ed.). (2007). *APA dictionary of psychology.* Washington, DC: American Psychological Association.

Chapter 2

Exercise 1: End Goals and Getting There

1. During the next ten minutes, list all those things you want to do in the future (after graduation). These can be thought of as **end goals**. At this stage in the exercise, the number of items listed is more important than how well-thought-out each one may be. Just list things as you think about them without being too critical of what has popped into your head.

   #1 to find a minimum wage Job
   #2 to aford a small apartment
   #3 Pay for my rent
   #4 support my family
   #5 to be finaully stable

2. Select two of the **end goals** listed that you find personally meaningful. Rewrite these end goals in a manner that is clear and specific. Provide details.

   End Goal 1

   to find a minimum wage Job and to afford a small apartment

   Since im inschool twice a week I have been trying to find a minimum wage Job for the longest but I cant seem to get it far so for the forture im trying my best

   End Goal 2

   So for the future I would like to afford a small apartment not somewhere far but something I can afford so that I can be able to pay bills and be stable

3. Devote five minutes to listing **intermediate goals** and **stepping-stone goals**. These are smaller goals that lead to completing your **two end goals**.

Stepping-stone goals are the smallest goals. They might be accomplished in a day or a week. Their contributions lead to the next category of goals (intermediate goals). Think of *intermediate goals* as goals that might take several weeks or longer to accomplish.

List **End Goal 1** here: _____

Stepping-Stone Goals

Intermediate Goals

List **End Goal 2** here: _____

Stepping-Stone Goals

Intermediate Goals

4. This exercise has allowed you to establish an outline of a motivationally driven plan to accomplish two long-term goals. In 50–100 words, indicate what you have learned about the necessary steps to achieve your two end goals.

Exercise 2: *Academic Motivational Orientation Assessment (AMOA)*

Using the rating scale below, indicate to what extent the following statements correspond to your decision to attend college. Place the appropriate number in the space before each statement.

1	2	3	4	5	6	7
Had no influence on my decision	Influenced me a little		Had a moderate influence on my decision	Influenced me a lot		Is the exact reason for my decision

Why Do You Go to College?

1. __6__ My family has always stressed the importance of me getting a college education.

2. __3__ I really enjoy engaging in the academic tasks of college.

3. __6__ Earning a college education will make my family very proud of me.

4. __5__ I'm earning a college education mainly to ensure a good standard of living.

5. __6__ The things I will learn while in college will make me a more competent person in many areas of my life.

6. __1__ Without a college education, I risk an uncertain financial future.

7. __2__ I will feel very guilty if I do not earn a college degree.

8. __4__ I do not really have a clear reason for being in college at this time.

9. __6__ Because I need a college education if I want to secure an important career in the future.

10. __7__ A college education will provide the opportunity to hone many life-skills I will need in the future.

11. __3__ My primary reason for getting a college education is to maximize my earning potential.

12. __0__ Being college educated symbolizes who I am as a person.

13. __5__ For the inherent pleasure I experience doing academic work.

14. __7__ Because I believe that my career options would be seriously limited without a college education.

15. __7__ A college education will allow me to utilize, throughout my life, the knowledge I gain.

16. __6__ A college education is an integral part of my own personal value system.

17. __4__ I enjoy the academic work involved in college.

18. __7__ A college education is necessary to ensure that I obtain a well-paying job.

19. __7__ The things I learn in college will enable me to face important life challenges.

SOURCE: Pisarik, C. (2009). *Academic Motivational Orientation Assessment (AMOA)*. Athens, GA: Author. Reprinted by permission.

20. __3__ The academic tasks involved in college are pleasurable.

21. __5__ My intentions for pursuing a college education are not yet clear.

22. __4__ A college education will make me competitive within the job market.

23. __7__ I feel I owe it to my family to get a college education.

24. __6__ A college education will make me a more capable individual.

25. __1__ I enjoy meeting the academic challenges in college.

26. __7__ A college education will define me as a person.

27. __1__ There was nothing better to do.

28. __6__ It will be difficult to support myself without a college degree.

29. __6__ The knowledge I gain in college will be important in many ways.

30. __4__ In many ways, I am following the flow.

31. __7__ I do not want to disappoint my family.

32. __6__ I have come to realize how central a college education is to my own identity.

33. __5__ It is very satisfying to accomplish difficult academic tasks.

34. __7__ I want to secure a meaningful career in the future.

35. __7__ I grew up believing that I should get a college education.

36. __1__ I am in college passing time until I know what I want to do.

Instructions

Sum the values you assigned for each group of items listed below to determine your overall score for each category of motivation.

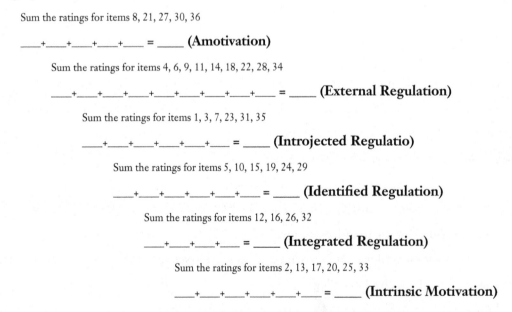

Sum the ratings for items 8, 21, 27, 30, 36

___+___+___+___+___ = ____ (Amotivation)

Sum the ratings for items 4, 6, 9, 11, 14, 18, 22, 28, 34

___+___+___+___+___+___+___+___+___ = ____ (External Regulation)

Sum the ratings for items 1, 3, 7, 23, 31, 35

___+___+___+___+___+___ = ____ (Introjected Regulatio)

Sum the ratings for items 5, 10, 15, 19, 24, 29

___+___+___+___+___+___ = ____ (Identified Regulation)

Sum the ratings for items 12, 16, 26, 32

___+___+___+___ = ____ (Integrated Regulation)

Sum the ratings for items 2, 13, 17, 20, 25, 33

___+___+___+___+___+___ = ____ (Intrinsic Motivation)

Interpretation of Results

The higher the score, the more likely you are to rely upon this form of motivation. The lower the score, the less likely you are to rely upon this form of motivation.

Review

Read over the explanation for each type of motivation.

- **Amotivation** represents the lowest level of autonomy. It is difficult to tie the person's behavior to either an intrinsic or an extrinsic explanation because the person sees his or her actions as beyond his or her control (e.g., "*I am doing poorly in my psychology class and there is nothing I can do because the professor comes up with tests I can't prepare for.*").
- **External regulation** occurs when there is a definite outside consequence that drives an activity (e.g., "*I can get my own apartment if I earn a B average fall semester.*").
- **Introjected regulation** occurs when the external reason for acting in a certain manner has "taken up residence" in the person, and this typically takes the form of an inner voice or monologue that essentially serves to persuade or pressure the person to act in a certain way (e.g., "*When I go out the night before a test I feel guilty, so I stay in and study to reduce the amount of self-scolding that goes on in my head.*").
- **Identified regulation** occurs when the person acts in a certain fashion because the person has adopted a ready-made set of rules or established guidelines from someone else. The person has allowed himself or herself to identify with another person's or group's standards (e.g., "*My parents socialize only with other professionals and I see no reason to socialize differently.*"). In this case, the person is essentially governed by unexamined rules.
- **Integrated regulation** refers to when a person has evaluated those regulations which were assimilated into the *self*. In addition, an effort is made by the person to maintain congruence between behaviors and goals <u>and</u> needs and values. However, any particular activity carried out by the person is done to obtain a desired outcome, not because of the inherent enjoyment one may find in carrying out the activity itself (e.g., "*I decided to attend college because I value having a college degree, not because I enjoy learning a lot of stuff.*").
- **Intrinsic motivation** comes into play when a person performs a certain activity because the activity itself creates pleasure or satisfaction. Regardless of the specific type of pleasurable pursuit that drives a person to act, intrinsic motivation is believed by the experts to reflect a form of **self-determined behavior** (i.e., "*Since I like to read about history, I decided to enroll in this class.*").

Questions

1. Of the various types of motivation listed above, which one most accurately reflects your reason for attending college? Explain why this is true.

2. Which of the above types of motivation least accurately reflects your reason for attending college? Explain why this is true.

SECTION 2

Problem-Solving/ Decision-Making Skills

Creating Time through Effective Time Management

3

Frequently, a student's reason for not succeeding at a college is attributed to such things as not being able to devote sufficient time to studying, overloading himself or herself with too many tasks, putting things off until the last minute, or having difficulty utilizing time that has been set aside to complete academic tasks. In the last instance, the problem may be poor concentration, an often-cited complaint that may result from anxiety, sleep deprivation, stress, personal problems, or any number of interfering factors. All these reasons for not doing well are related to time management—or, more accurately, time mismanagement. The major areas of discussion in this chapter are time management strategies tied to one's personal values, getting organized via a schedule, utilizing a to-do list, and effectively carrying out what you have planned.

Seeing the Big Picture in Relation to Time Management: Achieving Values-Congruence

To accomplish major tasks (the "big picture") in one's personal, academic, social, and professional life requires consideration of one's values. When goals are in line with our values, they have values-congruence. Achieving a values-congruent perspective will help you maximize your academic performance and your overall potential. Another outcome is likely to be greater general happiness.

Steps necessary to achieve values-congruence are the following:

1. Identify the most significant values in your life (e.g., financial security, working with others, utilizing creative ability, supervising others, influencing others, working with computers).
2. Identify how your academic preparation and choice of a major are tied to your values.
3. Identify all the steps, activities, and academic opportunities involved in accomplishing lifelong educational and career objectives.

Now, identify, apply, evaluate, and modify your time-management plan for academic and career success. Simply stated, you should develop your own personal model of time management to accomplish what is of true value to you. The basic ingredients of this model are fourfold.

- **T**ie your plans to specific objectives (e.g., "I think I will take a survey course to decide what area of a particular career I want to enter.").
- **I**nvest the necessary time to establish how you will implement, evaluate, and effectively modify, if necessary, your personal model (e.g., "I will take the survey course in the spring, visit a career counselor after completing the course, and discuss the major I am interested in to determine if this is the correct career path for me.").
- **M**anage your time in a way to reach your goals, but do this in a flexible manner without losing your focus on key objectives—objectives that are based on your personal values (e.g., values such as wanting to have a career in an area where you will be allowed to creatively express your ideas and work with others so you can apply your people skills).
- **E**nd each day (or some other specifically designated period, such as a week) by achieving at least one positive step to meet your objectives. The positive step can be a major step or a minor step; the most important thing is to be moving in a direction that results from values-congruence.

Three Keys for Creating and Utilizing an Effective Time-Management Model

Keys for putting this model in effect involve the following areas: getting organized, the to-do list, and the carry-through.

Getting Organized

The following are points to consider when scheduling or structuring your time.

- Be reasonable. Construct a schedule you will actually live by. Do not try to change everything in your life to "finally get organized, once and for all." Keep this silly-sounding but useful rhyme in mind: "Inch by inch, it's a cinch. Yard by yard, it's too hard."

- Time management is really self-management. There are 24 hours in a day, 168 hours in a week, and 2,520 hours in a semester (i.e., 15 weeks). Use it or lose it.

- Maintain flexibility when scheduling. Allow for mishaps. Schedules that are too tight with no buffers for the unexpected can create stress when you get off track because of an interruption.

- Establish time limits for tasks being scheduled. Move on to the next task when the established time limit is up. (If you are not allowing enough time for tasks, learn from the experience and in the future allow yourself more time.)

- At the end of your efforts (usually at the end of the day), reward yourself for accomplishing a step toward reaching a big goal. Visit downtown and walk around, purchase that item you have wanted, eat at your favorite restaurant. Just take a break and enjoy your accomplishment.

- When getting organized and setting your schedule, think in terms of prioritizing the tasks you are listing. Periodically ask yourself, "Is this the best use of my time now?"

- Use a planner or appointment book with a daily, weekly, and monthly calendar. We advise purchasing the type of planner sold at the college bookstore because these note important academic calendar dates, such as when the residence halls open, new student orientation is scheduled, classes begin, the midpoint of the academic session falls, classes end, the reading day is assigned, final exams are given, commencement ceremonies are scheduled, holidays fall, and special exams are given.

- Always allow time for breaks. Breaks of at least 10 minutes after studying for an hour will rejuvenate you and help to maintain a higher level of efficiency of learning.

- When working on a task, concentrate on the task. Do not allow yourself to be distracted. (We will discuss handling distractions in much more detail later.)

- When setting up your schedule, be sure to break tasks into manageable units. Spending one or two hours per evening studying a topic is much more efficient than trying to cram in 10 straight hours of studying. Avoid marathon study sessions.

- Schedule time to relax. This is an extended period (e.g., an hour) when you set aside time for yourself. Allow time for creative incubation to occur; sometimes serious students are studying so hard they forget to take time to think creatively.

- Complete a task. Finish each task before moving on (unless you misjudged the time required). Finishing a task creates a sense of accomplishment and psychological closure. Researchers have found that unfinished tasks tend to linger in our minds, contributing to a sense of frustration and possibly stress.

- Know what resources are available and use them as part of your time-management efforts. For example, if you are taking a difficult course, schedule time to take advantage of any free tutoring offered through your college's academic assistance services.

- Organize your schedule to allow yourself to review difficult curricular material soon after being exposed to it (e.g., stop and look over the notes taken in the psychology class where the professor lectures in a rapid manner; aim to achieve an overview and fill in gaps left in the notes while the lecture is still fresh in your mind). Even in cases where there is a delay (you have classes scheduled back to back and have to wait to review the material), aim to review the material within 24 hours of first being exposed to it, even if for no longer than 10-15 minutes. Failure to review in this manner might result in a significant portion of the information (understanding) being lost. Keep in mind that the sooner the review takes place, the better the result.

- Know when to stop. Some individuals work past the time scheduled or needed. The result, if this becomes an established pattern, is decreasing return for the effort and possibly even stress because the work never seems to end. Find ways to stop yourself if you have to (use a kitchen timer to remind yourself to stop).

- Before going to sleep at night, use five minutes to visualize your future and see yourself as moving toward the goals you are striving to reach. Such visualizations can serve as motivation boosters.

- Some individuals find it helpful to make an oral (or written) contract with another person (e.g., significant other, study partner) concerning an important task. Knowing this other person is "watching" can foster and maintain motivation. Sometimes even writing a contract with ourselves can provide added initiative to meet a goal.

- Write reminders and post them if need be. Jotting down your most important time-management goals on a note and sticking the note on your computer, bathroom mirror, or textbook can help you stay on task. Plan in terms of specific and realistic academic goals.

- Periodically review your goals (from small intermediate goals to large end goals you are working toward), reassess the steps you are taking, and make appropriate changes when necessary.

- Schedule the things you like to study last. The importance of this is illustrated by the typical behavior of math-anxious students. Math-anxious students frequently study for the math course they are enrolled in at the end of their study time. By this time they are getting tired, so they become easily frustrated and thus do not devote the needed time to a subject they are having a difficult time understanding.

- Plan to carry your schedule with you. In questioning students over the years, we have found that some good organizers forget important tasks simply because they have forgotten to carry their schedules with them.

To-Do List

This is not to be confused with a schedule that is set up in a planner. A to-do list can stand alone or it can be incorporated into the pages of a planner. Many individuals have found a to-do list to be an indispensable time-management technique. In its simplest form, a to-do list is a list of things that must be accomplished that have been prioritized. Some people mistake a simple list of things to do for a to-do list; the two are not the same. A genuine to-do list keeps a person on track. A random, un-prioritized listing of tasks can keep us off track.

If you simply list items to do (e.g., go to library to read a reserved book, study two hours for next week's history test, buy a new pair of shoes at the mall, drop off camping tent at friend's house), you may wind up spending too much time on items that could have been put off (you go to the mall and decide to also see a movie, or you spend three hours at the friend's house because of a spontaneous invitation to stay for some barbecue being cooked) and not devoting enough or any time to important tasks and then rationalizing your mismanagement of time ("I can study the night before the test."). Thus, to have a genuine to-do list, you should list and prioritize the items. Mark the most important task with a star, an asterisk, the letter A, or any symbol that denotes importance.

Another tip is to have a variety of things to accomplish that are not all top priorities (some items should be things you will get to if you can, but if you do not, it is not really a problem). Follow the 20/80 rule. If you construct a to-do list with ten items, aim to have two (maybe three) items that are designated top-priority items. Think of it this way: we never read everything in a magazine, only certain sections (20 percent) and leave much of it unread (80 percent); office workers refer to a few filing drawers in an office (20 percent) and not the others (80 percent) except on rare occasions; and we walk mostly on a small amount of floor space where we live each day (20 percent) but do not walk on the rest (80 percent). While there is not always a clear 20/80 breakdown, the point is that when we list things to accomplish, the top priority items should be fewer in number.

Adding the use of a to-do list to your repertoire of time-management skills can increase your efficient use of time dramatically. The effectiveness of a to-do list is reflected in the world of business, where whole-day workshops on time management are often sponsored by major companies to get employees to be efficient users of time, which, of course, adds to a company's earnings. It is unlikely that large corporations would invest in such workshops if there were not a monetary return. For people in the business world, time-management techniques can become almost second nature. To-do lists are constructed for important tasks automatically. Review the two examples of to-do lists in Figure 3.1. Which example represents a poorly constructed to-do list? Why is it an example of a poor to-do list?

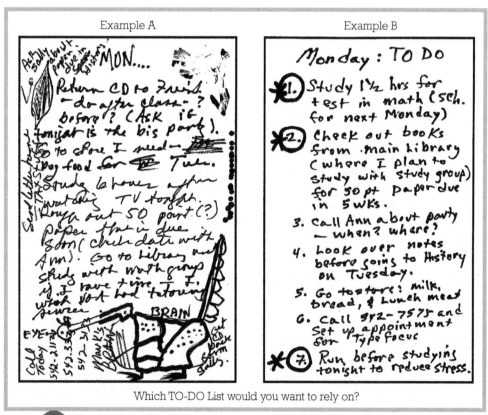

| Example A | Example B |

Which TO-DO List would you want to rely on?

Figure **3.1** Two Examples of To-Do Lists

The Carry-Through

A vital part of being an effective time manager is to be able to carry through on what you have planned. Your scheduling skills and to-do lists may be impeccable, but the perfect schedule and perfect to-do list will do nothing for you if you cannot achieve what you have planned. Here are some points to consider.

- Think of the place you study as a ***study territory*** to be defended. The notion that all that is needed to establish a place to study is a neat desk with sharpened pencils is antiquated. In many ways, a place to study is more of a frame of mind that fits your needs and unique personality. However, regardless of the place, it should be one you can claim as your property. If you mark this place as yours, others are less likely to intrude on your study time. Interestingly, this sort of response to another's territory cuts across many life forms.

  Dogs protect their territory (e.g., a student's apartment) from strangers and other dogs. The protector in this case is likely to win in a battle with an even stronger dog, because fighting in one's territory provides a competitive edge. This is even true in some wars between countries, where stronger countries have attempted to invade and take over weaker countries only to lose the war to the weaker country defending its home territory.

  Having areas that we claim as ours is more common than most people realize. For example, early in the academic term, part of settling into a classroom is finding a chair. Students frequently mentally mark a chair as theirs. Think of those times when you entered a classroom where you have sat in the same chair for several weeks, only to find another student seated in "your" chair. You felt irritated because you had come to view that particular chair as your territory.

  Interestingly, we even have portable territories that we carry around with us. It is as if we all move about with invisible bubbles that shield us from others. One's invisible bubble extends out to differing distances depending on the environment and who is approaching. At night, on a street without lights, it may extend so far that seeing a stranger walk toward us might cause us to cross the street. In addition, even though during the day the bubble's boundary is much smaller (extending only a few feet from our bodies), think of those times when another student whom you did not know crossed this invisible boundary by standing too close. During such "invasions," we maneuver to reestablish the boundary. We step back or look away (similar to what occurs on crowded elevators where everyone looks at the door). Intrusions coming within a few inches of our faces or bodies are rare because most people understand innately that territories (stationary and portable ones) are not to be violated.

  The point is to have a place to study that is yours. For example, if a person knocks on your dorm/apartment door to visit at a time when you must study for an important test, you should stand at the door (the boundary) and tell the person you are studying and will see or call him or her later. Use assertiveness skills if necessary (see Chapter 10). Learn to say no to requests that involve invasion of your scheduled time. Mark the territory with a sign on the door such as "Do not disturb" or "Back in three hours." The reader of the latter sign does not need to know you are behind the door and really mean that you will be back from studying in three hours.

- Cut down or eliminate possible distractions. If you live in a noisy dorm or apartment, schedule time to go to one of the college's libraries or campus areas for studying. If you keep getting phone calls, turn off your phone. Anticipate possible distractions, and take steps to block the interference before it occurs.

Emmett's Two Laws Governing Procrastination

First Law: The dread of doing a task uses up more time and energy than doing the task itself.

Second Law: Obsession with perfection is the downfall of procrastinators.

In her second law, Emmett uses the words *obsession with perfection* to refer to various fears that block us from starting on a project, task, or assignment. A number of fears that Emmett believes can cause procrastination are listed below:

Fear of . . .

Low proficiency

Unknown

Judgment (What will others think or say?)

Making mistakes

Success

Having to live up to a high standard

Change

Too much responsibility

Feelings (e.g., not doing something because you fear the reaction of another person)

Finishing (e.g., "Once I finish this project, I have to start that other project—the project I am dreading.")

Being rejected

Making the wrong decision

Emmett believes the best way to manage procrastination is to identify your fear and then face your fear. "Once you identify your fear and face it, once you magnify that fear and decide you'll survive it and perhaps even learn from it, you can start moving and do whatever it is you've been putting off—and start taking control of your life" (Emmett, 2000, p. 94).

Procrastination is not an unusual event. Everyone procrastinates from time to time (e.g., scheduling a doctor's appointment may be consistently put off), but procrastination can become a vicious cycle. This vicious cycle can become a mental and behavioral prison. Individuals caught in such a cycle reveal its strength when they say things such as "There's no point in getting started—I can't get anything done," or "I feel overwhelmed and stressed out and don't know where to start." Such self-defeating thoughts and behaviors tend to intensify the problem and frequently contribute to lower self-esteem. For example, a student puts off doing math homework because he does not like math. Because less time is being devoted to math, the student starts to do poorly in math. This drop in performance leads to longer delays and increased avoidance of the topic, which results in another drop in grade average. The student now repeatedly states self-defeating messages about math whenever confronted with the topic. Sometimes these statements are made to others, but most of the time they are simply repeated silently, as if a message were playing repeatedly inside this person's head. According to David Burns, a *mindset* has been established.

According to Burns, some mindsets interfere with motivation, and once established grow in strength over time. A syndrome is created, in which a group of signs are found together. The procrastination mindset is characterized by a feeling of hopelessness, a sense of being helpless, magnification of events leading to feeling overwhelmed, a tendency to jump to conclusions, negative self-labeling ("I am a loser"), undervaluing rewards due to perceiving outcomes as not worth the effort, self-coercion in the form of *should* and *ought* (e.g., "I should study math; otherwise I am a rotten person"), low tolerance of frustration, and a general sense of guilt and self-blame.

According to Burns, procrastination can be effectively dealt with. He suggests taking actions such as these.

1. **Use a schedule.** Prioritize tasks and do so using a weekly/monthly/annual planner.
2. **Keep a record of dysfunctional thoughts.** Record the self-defeating language you are feeding yourself and use cognitive restructuring techniques to break this pattern. This involves changing the negative scripts in your head and creating and using self-affirming scripts ("I am a capable person, so I can find ways to learn math!")
3. **Endorse one's self.** If you find yourself operating from a perspective of "what I do doesn't count," you should argue with yourself. Turn the old perspective around. ("I have always thought others were more deserving, but there is no reason to not place myself in the deserving group of people. The people I have been placing on a pedestal also have strengths and weaknesses. I am just as deserving as they are!")
4. **Avoid the oughts and shoulds that are governing your behavior.** Albert Ellis has referred to the destructive impact of absolutes on our quality of life ("I must always be the A student. Less than an A means I am a failure") by saying we are performing **"*must*rbation."**
5. **Use disarming techniques.** If something or someone is contributing to a negative mindset, disarm it or the person by taking its or the person's power away. In cases involving others, you can call upon assertiveness skills to change the situation (see Chapter 10).
6. **Think about little steps.** Seeing too far into the future sometimes leads to procrastination. If you have to write a 25-page paper for an early American history class, you might see the finished product in your mind and become overwhelmed, wondering, "How can I ever write that 25-page paper?" When this takes place, stop and think about the task a step at a time. Break up what you see as the product into manageable smaller stages.
7. **Visualize success.** Envision yourself completing the task. See yourself as succeeding when you start to experience self-doubt.
8. **Test your can'ts.** When you say you cannot do something, stop and do a specific assessment of what is involved in completing something. Often, when we carefully assess what is required, we start to understand exactly what steps are needed to succeed, and the feeling of "I can't" loses its power.

Everyone is allotted 168 hours a week.

Closing Remarks

This chapter covers many tips and concepts that deserve careful consideration. Above all, you should leave this chapter knowing you possess valuable tools for gaining control over your time. Keep in mind the information and skills discussed are to be used when needed. Using time-management tactics should not gobble up a lot of your time. If you are spending hours each week getting organized, that in itself is a time-management problem. Start using those things suggested in this chapter that seem to fit your time-management needs best, and add other tactics when appropriate. Over time the time-management technique you employ will become positive habits that require little effort.

Sources

Burns, D. D. (1980). *Feeling good: The new mood therapy.* New York, NY: Morrow.

Emmett, R. (2000). *The procrastinator's handbook: Mastering the art of doing it now.* New York, NY: Walker.

Lakein, A. (1973). *How to get control of your time and your life.* New York, NY: New American Library.

Schmitt, D. E. (1992). *The winning edge: Maximizing success in college.* New York, NY: HarperCollins.

Taylor, H. L. (1981). *Making time work for you.* New York, NY: Dell.

Tuckman, B. W. (1991). The development and concurrent validity of the Procrastination Scale. *Educational and Psychological Measurements, 51*(2), 473–480.

Chapter 3

Exercise 1: Where Does My Time Go?

Estimate the amount of time you typically devote to each activity listed below in a full week. After entering your estimates, record the exact amount of time spent on each activity during one week. Then answer the questions posed at the end.

	Estimated Hours/Minutes	Actual Amount of Time
Attending classes	_____	_____
Working at job	_____	_____
Sleeping (include naps)	_____	_____
Showering/bathing	_____	_____
Traveling to and from work	_____	_____
Eating (include snacks)	_____	_____
Studying for test(s)	_____	_____
Completing homework	_____	_____
Socializing (include time just talking to friends)	_____	_____
Organizational activities (band practice, fraternities/sororities, clubs, special groups, etc.)	_____	_____
Time devoted to physical fitness	_____	_____
Shopping (clothing, groceries, other)	_____	_____
Religious/spiritual activities	_____	_____
Time with family	_____	_____
Other (list)		
a. _____	_____	_____
b. _____	_____	_____
c. _____	_____	_____
d. _____	_____	_____
Totals	_____	_____

1. How accurate was your estimated total compared to the actual total?

2. Look over the list. Which three activities are of greatest importance to you? Does the actual amount of time you are devoting to each seem to be enough?

3. How might you change the manner in which you manage time to boost your time-management skills to a higher level? Provide five ways to do this.

    a.

    b.

    c.

    d.

    e.

Chapter 3

Exercise 3: Effective Planning for the Week

Week of _____

	Monday	Tuesday	Wednesday	Thursday	Friday	Saturday	Sunday
6:00							
7:00							
8:00							
9:00							
10:00							
11:00							
12:00							
1:00							
2:00							
3:00							
4:00							
5:00							
6:00							
7:00							
8:00							
9:00							
10:00							
11:00							
12:00							
1:00							
2:00							
3:00							

To complete your planning, continue to the next page.

Priorities for the Week

List Tasks Here   **Write Due Date Here**

1. _____   _____

2. _____   _____

3. _____   _____

4. _____   _____

5. _____   _____

6. _____   _____

7. _____   _____

8. _____   _____

Evaluation

1. Discuss the strengths of your time-management approach based on the plan you completed.

2. Discuss ways you may plan each week differently in the future to increase your effective use of the 168 hours in a week.

Chapter 3

Exercise 5: Plot Your Energy Level

Review the example below. Then plot your typical pattern of mental energy for a day.

Example: Changes in Mental Energy Level during a Typical Day

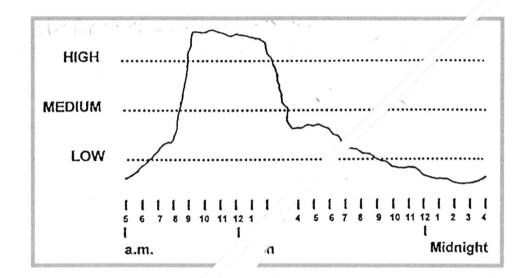

Questions

How might you use the information and insight you obtained from plotting your energy level? Specifically, how could you schedule some activities differently to take full advantage of your periods of peak mental energy?

Building a Repertoire of Good Habits for Academic Survival

4

s indicated in Chapter 1, a life-skills approach to academic success rests upon learning. Effective learning requires a repertoire of good habits. Everyone has familiar, routine ways of doing things. Some of these habits are good and help to guide our lives in positive directions, while others are not so good and tend to interfere with achieving what we want. Although "bad" habits often form unconsciously, a committed, conscious effort is required to change them.

How committed are you to being a successful student in college? Most students come to college believing that they have the requisite skills and motivation to succeed in college. Not all students understand that achieving academic excellence requires that you consistently engage in the process of developing and strengthening good learning habits while eliminating poor habits that interfere with your academic performance. Coming to class prepared, taking good lecture notes, paying attention in class, developing a stronger vocabulary, and reviewing notes are often good habits that can help you to survive academically in college. Skipping class, turning in assignments late, slouching in your chair in the back of the class, and not completing the assigned readings before coming to class are bad habits that interfere with academic performance.

Take an inventory of your academic habits, and differentiate between habits that can contribute to your academic success and ones that create barriers to success. Habits have a profound influence on the way we approach academia and future learning situations beyond college. Making a conscious decision to replace ineffective learning habits with more effective ones can have a powerful effect on your potential and capacity to process and retain vital information. Begin to change your behavior by initiating small changes to avoid overwhelming yourself. Throughout this chapter you will find helpful tips that can become good habits for developing effective learning approaches.

Develop Good Classroom-Survival Tactics

Remember when you were in elementary school and received a grade on your report card for classroom behavior? Even though you may not be given a conduct grade now, professors do have expectations related to your behavior in their classes. Certain behaviors tend to differentiate the more successful academic students from other students.

- **Attend class regularly and arrive on time.** Students who attend class on a regular basis do better than other students. Attend class every day, *including the first day*. Professors generally give out the class syllabus and begin to lecture on the first day of class. A professor who is requesting a lot of assignments or presenting a fairly complex syllabus may choose to spend the entire period going over the syllabus and addressing other expectations related to the course. We have had many students in our classes over the years who seem confused about an assignment, paper, or project two weeks into the semester. Often, it's because they were not in class the first day. On the first day, we thoroughly review the syllabus and advise students on not only how to survive our classes, but how to excel.
- **Know your class syllabus.** Your class syllabus is a "contract" between the students in the class and the professor teaching the class. Take notice of assignments, readings, tests, the grading procedure, and when and how to get in touch with your professor. As you read through the syllabus, take the time to transfer all deadlines to a master calendar. Know what is expected of you and when it is expected. What if you lose your syllabus? Replace it as soon as possible. See if your professor has a copy online or ask directly for a replacement. You could always borrow one from a classmate to copy. Do not try to navigate the class without a syllabus.
- **Get a good seat.** (No, not in the back as far away from the professor as possible.) Sit up front, focus your attention on your professor, and remember to make eye contact. Your professor will notice you and will also notice if you appear interested. Sitting close to the professor will help you (or force you) to concentrate better. During class, avoid unnecessary communication with students seated around you. Also avoid reading a newspaper, eating, using your phone, checking your computer for e-mail or other messages, and other activities that show your disinterest.

- **Prepare for class.** Read assignments and work problems, be familiar with terminology, and come to class with good questions. Bring all needed supplies such as a calculator, paper, pencils, pens, a blue book, or other books.

- **Get to know your professors.** What are your professors' office hours? E-mail addresses? Your professors are part of an educational system that can be difficult to maneuver in. When searching for answers to questions related to your college experience and career, remember to use your professors as resources. Professors are also often more willing to write a letter of recommendation for a student who has taken the time and interest to get to know them.

- **Get to know some of your classmates.** Identify a responsible student in each class whom you can contact to get notes if needed. You might also want to identify students in class who may want to form a study group. When forming a study group, be sure to set up guidelines that spell out expectations for group members (e.g., commitment, regularly scheduled meeting times, and collaborative teaching within the group).

- **Know each professor's policy about absences.** Does your professor want you to call, text, or e-mail? Is it okay to go by the professor's office to obtain handouts that you may have missed? You are responsible for all assignments and notes.

- **Participate in class.** Ask questions and share comments, appropriately. When you have a question to ask or a comment to make, think about it first and then ask yourself, "Will my question reveal the fact that I have not completed the assigned readings?" If so, do not take up class time with your question. Also consider the timing of your comments or questions, avoid monopolizing class discussions, and respect different points of view.

Develop a Good System of Note-Taking

Whether you find yourself in an auditorium with 300 fellow students or a small class of only 25 students, you will be expected to take good notes. Some college professors pull the majority of their material for their tests from their lecture notes. Without good notes, you may be lost when the test comes around. You already know not to write down everything the professor says, but how do you differentiate between what is important and what is not, or what's going to be on the test and what's not? Taking good notes involves more than merely showing up for class and recording all that your professor recites. Note-taking is comprised of many skills: the ability to concentrate, the ability to listen well, and the ability to analyze and then synthesize information into patterns of meaning to help you remember information from the lecture. Take the responsibility to develop better note-taking skills. Allow the following activities to become rituals throughout your college experience:

- **Learn to adapt your note-taking to the course.** Biology notes will include many diagrams and terminology, whereas math notes may have a lot of examples of problems, but fewer words. Be sure to read the assigned readings *before class*. The organization of the readings in your textbook (headings and subheadings) can help you to organize your notes in class as you write. Whether you are taking notes on your computer or using a notebook, focus on recording the main points of the lecture and remember to skip lines to highlight important ideas. If you are using a notebook, buy a separate one for each class and buy notebooks that are large enough so you have plenty of space to write. Crammed, disorganized notes can be indicative of a crammed, disorganized mind.

- **Become a good listener, an active listener.** Being a good note-taker is dependent on being a skilled listener. Think about how well you listen in class to lectures, videos, and questions and comments from fellow students, and then answer the following questions: What listening skills do you have? How engaged are you in the process of listening? Do you pay as much attention to what is being said in class as you do listening to your favorite radio program or television show? What is your attitude? Are you motivated to listen with an intent to learn? When you are actively listening, you are analyzing and organizing information, listening for key words, formulating questions, and relating new information to old information. Listening actively in class helps maintain an alert mental state. Some students are easily distracted. If you are one of them, try sitting near the front of the class away from chatty friends. Other behaviors that are likely to affect your ability to pay attention and listen effectively in class are apathy toward the topic being discussed, prejudgment, lack of concentration, excessive concentration, focusing on the irrelevant, faking attention, and allowing physical and personal barriers to interfere. These factors are described in more detail in Table 4.1.

Table 4.1

Factors That Inhibit Listening

Apathy toward the topic—As a listener, you have the potential to tune out a message at any time. And like many people, you probably tune out those messages that you do not care about.

Prejudgment—Forming judgments about an idea before listening to the entire message will likely inhibit the effectiveness of your ability to listen. It is difficult to listen with an open mind when your mind is already made up.

Lack of concentration—Listening is an active process that requires energy and concentration, which means failure to concentrate will likely inhibit effective listening.

Excessive concentration—Trying to take in every word and/or detail of a message is frustrating and impossible and may inhibit effective listening.

Focusing on the irrelevant—Focusing on things such as personal appearance or the speaker's mannerisms may inhibit effective listening.

Faking attention—Faking attention, that is, acting like you are listening even though you are not, sends false feedback to the other person(s) and will inhibit effective learning.

Allowing physical and personal barriers to interfere—The physical surroundings can often be a barrier to effective listening. Such things as room temperature, outside noise, etc., can be distracting. If you have a headache or are hungry, it can be difficult to process information.

From Conner, D., & Huguley, W. *The Auburn experience.*

- **Use a note-taking system that works for you.** There are many different ways to approach note-taking. You can adopt a well-known system of note-taking (e.g., the Cornell method or mind mapping) or create one that reinforces your personal learning style.

    In the 1950s, while at Cornell University, Walter Pauk developed the Cornell method of note-taking. Pauk's goal was to create a structured and efficient method of note-taking (Figure 4.1 provides an example). Key points of the method are listed next:

    - Number each page and include the date, your professor's name, the name of the course, and the title of the lecture.

- Draw a vertical line about 2½ inches from the left edge of your paper and then record notes in your own words, legibly, to the right of the line. Record as many facts as you can, writing in paragraph form and outlining as you write.
- Use the left side of the page for key terminology, annotations, questions, and relevant examples.
- Leave a two-inch margin at the bottom of the page for a summary of the day's notes.
- As soon as you can after class, make corrections, add clarifications, and summarize the day's lecture in your own words. An example of note-taking using the Cornell method is shown in Figure 4.1.

Cornell Method of Note-Taking	
Questions, examples, definitions, clarifications	Class: UNIV 1103　　　Page: 1　　　　Date: 11/22/12 Professor: Glauser　　　Topic: Test Anxiety (TA)
What is anxiety?	A pervasive sense of apprehension, a bad feeling that something bad is about to happen and feeling unable to cope w/it
Test anxiety?	A type of performance anxiety exp. before, during, and maybe after tests
What are some of the symptoms associated with test anxiety? Albert Ellis (cognitive psychologist said to stay away from absolutes) *ex (catastrophic thinking): I will never be able to pass this test, the class, graduate, or get a job.	Physical symptoms: accelerated hb, sweating, musc tension, nausea, and insomnia Cognitive symptoms: irrational thoughts (self-defeating and catastrophic) Behavioral: compulsive and impulsive behave, procrastination
How to Manage TA? What is cognitive restructuring? *ex.: "I don't know the answer to this question, but I will know other answers to other questions on this test." *ex in class of guided imagery: taking a math test	Deal with thoughts, behavior, and physical manifestations of anxiety. You can reduce neg self-talk through REBT (Rational Emotive Behavior Therapy) which cognitive psy Albert Ellis has written ext @. Also use techniques of cognitive restructuring* by replacing self-def thoughts w/rational, pos ones. Other ways to manage thoughts are to avoid catastrophic thinking, separate self-worth from performance, and use creative visualizations and guided imagery.
How to deal with physical manifestations?	Engage in abdominal breathing, exercise, and progressive muscle relaxation
Behaviorally?	Learn effective test taking, study, and time management strategies
Summary	TA is a pervasive problem that many people experience. It has physical, cognitive, and behavioral components. To deal with thoughts, you can engage in cognitive restructuring, separate self-worth from performance, and use creative visualizations and guided imagery. To deal with TA physically, exercise, do abdominal breathing, or progressive musc relax. Behaviorally, learn test taking, study, and tm techniques.

Figure **4.1** Note-Taking Using the Cornell Method

Another system of note-taking that is less linear and might be more appealing to visually oriented learners is mind-mapping (see Figure 4.2). Tony Buzan developed mind-mapping as an effective, creative, visual approach to recording and retaining information. Essential information from the lecture is reduced to key points that are then linked together through a central image relevant to the topic of the lecture. Buzan suggests that when you create a mind map, you do the following:

- Begin with a central image that represents the sum and substance of the lecture topic.
- Build a structure for your diagram by connecting through drawings related ideas and information. Words that represent key points should be written (in capital letters) on lines that connect to other words.

From Conner, D., & Huguley, W. *The Auburn experience.*

- Use as many symbols and colors as you can to capture and then differentiate ideas and information gleaned from the lecture. Colors and symbols used will serve as memory aids.
- When you are through with your note-taking, you will have created a one-page visual diagram that summarizes key points of the lecture.

A mind map allows for creative additions as you develop more connections between information presented in class and information derived from readings. When creating a mind map, you are creating a personal image that represents your knowledge of a specific topic. You can also create your own system of note-taking.

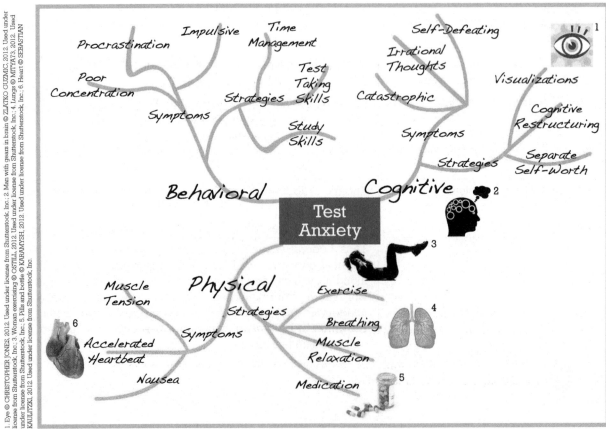

Table 4.2

Tips for Note-Taking

Do not write down everything. Be selective and pace yourself. Listen to the lecturer's sentences and paragraphs, not to each and every word. Try to summarize the main ideas presented in your own words, being careful to differentiate between relevant and irrelevant information.

Learn to identify cues about what is important. Information written on the blackboard, specific dates and other information from overheads, summaries, and any series of points the professor recites should be recorded in your notes. Finally, some professors indicate something is important by changing the tone of their voice to call attention to certain lecture points.

Use abbreviations whenever possible. You can use standard abbreviations or develop your own. Just remember to be consistent, making abbreviations a habit.

Pay close attention to how you organize your notes. Your professor will probably give you some good verbal cues to help with the organization of your notes (e.g., "Today we will talk about test anxiety; what it is, how to recognize it, and how to effectively deal with it.").

Write down any examples given. Also think of similar examples and record them in your notes.

After class, review your notes as soon as possible. Do they make sense based on what you remember from class? If not, speak with your professor or ask questions the next time your class meets to clarify your notes.

Students typically retain about 70 percent of what is communicated in the first ten minutes of a typical 50-minute lecture, but retain only about 20 percent of the last ten minutes of the lecture (McKeachie, 1994). So, whether you use the Cornell method, mind-mapping, or a note-taking system of your own, keep in mind the good habits listed in Table 4.2.

Adopt Good Study Methods

Whether you are just starting out in college, an upperclassman, or a transfer student, good study habits are important survival tactics to help you get through college successfully. Every year, more than 2.5 million college students transfer to different colleges throughout the United States for a variety of reasons. Students transfer due to financial reasons, to find a better major or program of study, or maybe to be closer to (or farther from) home. Some students find the college they have transferred into to be more academically challenging than their previous college and might experience a drop in grades; if you find yourself in this situation, schedule frequent and regular meetings with your academic advisor or with a knowledgeable person from your academic support center. Remember to schedule tutoring early and enroll in an orientation course that can help you to make a smoother transition to your new college. All students can benefit from taking advantage of all the academic support services at their college.

We have found the following tactics to be helpful and applicable to all students:

- Get to know your textbooks. Preview the reading material before you actually begin to read. Create a meaningful system for organizing all of the information you are about to read.
- Make studying a habit. Make study periods routine, breaking at regular intervals of time. Get in the habit of reviewing your notes regularly. Use any time you have between classes or before your first class to go over your notes.

- **Learn how to actively study.** Think about what you are reading. Relate new information to what you have learned previously. Have intent to read and learn study strategies that engage you and work for you.
- **Learn the right way to mark your text.** Use annotations. Annotations are explanatory notes that you write directly in your text, notes, or handouts. Annotating is an effective learning strategy that can help you make a more personal connection to your reading, deepen your understanding of the material, and improve on your retrieval of the material from long term memory. When you annotate, summarize important information in your own words before writing notes in the margins (if space is provided). Before you annotate, read the entire paragraph and then summarize key points. Highlight only the important information. Be sure to underline important concepts and key statements found within the reading. You can circle unfamiliar words and then write the definition ("def") of the words in the margin close by. Come up with your own marking system for identifying examples ("ex" or "x"). Write down personal questions and comments, but remember to keep your annotations concise and clear.
- **Create a study environment that is conducive to learning.** Identify where and under what conditions you concentrate best. Do you study best in a particular library or in your room? If you study in your room, does the order or lack of order in the room affect your studying? Reflect on your ideal learning environment. How closely does your current learning environment match the ideal? What can you do to make some positive changes that are more conducive to studying and learning?
- **Learn to organize your time.** Students in college are always wanting to know how to manage their time more efficiently and effectively. Try to study at those times during the day when you are the most alert.
- **Develop a better vocabulary.** College is a great time to build your vocabulary. When else in your life are you going to be expected to read from so many books representing so many disciplines? Words help us to clarify our thinking and express our understanding of things. Make it a point to record new words that you come across that you want to introduce into your vocabulary. Get to know these words—not just the pronunciation, spelling, and definition, but also the various ways the word can be used to express an idea or thought. I (Glauser) remember the first time I heard the word *epistemology*. I became fascinated with this word, and as I explored its meaning, I became acquainted with all sorts of other captivating words like *phenomenology*, *existentialism*, and *solipsism*.
- **Learn to concentrate better.** How good is your memory? Do you remember all you have read so far in this book? Are you good at remembering names, birthdays, definitions, street names, appointments, or the functions of the pituitary gland? Learning is associated with the ability to concentrate and store information in long-term memory. When you concentrate, you are focusing all your attention on the task before you. To improve concentration and retention of information, try some of the tips listed in Table 4.3.

Learn about Academic Honesty

Are you familiar with your college's policies and procedures regarding academic honesty? Do you know which office on campus is responsible for promoting and enforcing the policies of the academic honesty system? How does your college define academic honesty?

Table 4.3

Tips for Improving Concentration and Memory

If your mind starts to wander, switch to another reading assignment for a different class.

Remind yourself to look for patterns of meaning in the information you are studying.

Discover the source of any distractions. Are your distractions based on internal barriers (anxiety, procrastination, lack of confidence) or external barriers (noise, people, and other environmental influences)? Whatever is causing your inattentiveness, take appropriate action to deal effectively with the distraction.

Be selective about what you choose to learn. You do not have enough time to learn things verbatim. Focus on learning meanings rather than learning word-for-word content (the exception is technical definitions).

Organize information into meaningful associations. These associations might be logical (based on the subject) or absurd (based on a mnemonic, i.e., memory cue). For example, commonly used mnemonics are ROY G. BIV to remember the colors of the rainbow in order (red, orange, yellow, green, blue, indigo, and violet) and HOMES to remember the names of the Great Lakes (Huron, Ontario, Michigan, Erie, and Superior). Memory cues allow one to condense a great amount of information into a memorable sentence, phrase, or acronym. When creating a mnemonic, it's fine to be silly, nonsensical, or outlandish. The crazier the sentence or other cue, the less likely you are to forget it and the information it carries.

Repeat information that you are studying continually and consistently.

Arrange information within a familiar context.

What is your college's definition of academic dishonesty?

Academic Dishonesty = _____

_____

_____

Academic honesty policies are intended to regulate the performance of academic behavior. Consequences related to lying, cheating, stealing, tampering, receiving unauthorized assistance, and using unauthorized sources of information are generally spelled out in your school's academic honesty policy. At most colleges, you sign an honor code as part of the application process for admission. As a student, you are responsible for knowing and understanding the university honor code and the academic policy at your school. You are engaging in academic dishonesty any time you intentionally represent someone else's work as your own (plagiarism). You are also engaging in plagiarism and other forms of cheating if you

- Directly quote someone else's written or spoken words without using quotation marks
- Paraphrase someone else's work (including their statistics) without making a reference to it
- Take an exam for someone else or have someone else take an exam for you
- Copy from someone else's test, allow someone to copy your work, or bring in a cheat sheet (whether written on your arm, on a shirt cuff, inside a baseball cap, on a sheet of paper, or electronically)
- Turn in someone else's paper as your own, obtain a paper off the Internet, or pay someone else to do the work for you
- Receive any kind of unauthorized assistance (including a calculator or any other electronic device, notes, or information from a fellow student about what a test covers prior to taking a test)

- Give any unauthorized assistance
- Make up information, including statistics
- Deceive your professor about an absence
- Turn in the same paper for two different classes
- Change an answer on a graded test and then resubmit it to your professor to change the grade

Whether the act of cheating is intentional or unintentional, the punishment is the same, and students are responsible for reading and understanding their school's academic honesty policies. Students often wonder why academic dishonesty is so widespread on campus. Research suggests that more students are cheating because they see their peers engaging in plagiarism, unauthorized collaboration on assignments, cheating on tests, and other forms of academic dishonesty and getting away with it (Barr, 2000). Aristotle and other philosophers wrote that moral character is formed by habitual action, and the longer a student is in an environment where cheating is allowed to exist, the greater the chance that the student will develop the habit of cheating (Cole & Kiss, 2000).

To create an academic environment that promotes greater academic integrity, some professors have begun to give writing assignments with more specific topics, give more pop quizzes, and use antiplagiarism computer programs that compare students' papers with all available literature within a particular database to assess students' work. Many colleges are working to create honor codes that are clearer, and disciplinary actions against students for violations are being strengthened and used more frequently. Punishment for violators can be suspension or expulsion, a grade of F on the assignment or in the course, or even a grade of XF for the course recorded on the student's academic record. The grade XF indicates to others that the failure was due to academic dishonesty. At a minimum, an incidence of academic dishonesty can stay on a student's record at some colleges for up to two years.

Learn the Grading System

Do you know the grading system at your college? Get in the habit of learning everything you can about grades, dismissal policies, withdrawals, probation, and honors. Your undergraduate bulletin has a wealth of information about these very topics and is often an official college resource for all academic information, including information about majors, courses, and other academic concerns such as current withdrawal policies and how withdrawals might affect student financial aid, scholarships, housing, full-time status, or health insurance. Your academic survival may be dependent on knowing about the following:

- **How to calculate your grade point average (GPA).** At most colleges, letter grades are converted into numerical equivalents. An **A** = 4 points; **A–** = 3.70 points: **B+** = 3.30 points; **B** = 3 points; **B–** = 2.70 points; **C+** = 2.30 points; **C** = 2 points; **C–** = 1.70 points, **D** = 1 point; and **F** and **WF** = 0 points. To calculate your GPA, you need to know the number of hours each course you have taken represents and the grade you received. Multiply credit hours by grade point equivalent. For example, if you got a B in a 3-hour class, you would receive 9 points. To arrive at your GPA, add up all of your grade points and then divide your total by the total number of credit hours to get your GPA. For example, in the example below, the student would have a 3.00 GPA (45 divided by 3 = 3).

Course	Grade	Point Equivalent		Credit Hours		Grade Points
MATH 1113	A	4	×	3	=	12
ENG 1101	B	3	×	3	=	9
MUSI 2020	B+	3.30	×	3	=	9.9
PSYC 1101	C	2	×	3	=	6
HIST 2112	B–	2.70	×	3	=	8.1
Totals				15		45

- **When to withdraw from a class.** What is the withdrawal procedure at your college? How many times can you withdraw from courses? Do you know whether a professor is permitted to withdraw you from class if you have an excessive number of absences? Do you know the difference between a W and a WF? At what point in the semester can you no longer withdraw from a class and receive a W?
- **Appealing a questionable grade.** Always keep all tests, quizzes, and papers. If you want to appeal a grade, first meet with your professor. If you need to take your appeal further, follow the appeals procedure outlined by your school.
- **Academic probation.** Academic probation is a warning. Most colleges place students on academic probation if their cumulative average falls below 2.00. If you are placed on academic probation, talk with your advisor, and gather information about your school's policies governing probation. For how many academic terms can you remain on academic probation before being dismissed? Probation can be an opportunity for you to assess your academic survival tactics and make some positive, strategic changes.
- **Academic dismissal.** If you are dismissed, can you apply for readmission, and when? Who has the power to grant a student at your college readmission? Will other colleges or universities admit a student who has been dismissed from your college? When?
- **How to identify factors that interfere with your grades.** Assess your study strategies, test-taking skills, relationships, personal and social life, time-management skills, and anything else that might be preventing you from achieving better grades. Review your reasons for being in college.

Activity

Getting to Know Your College's Grading System

Go to your college's online undergraduate bulletin to answer the following questions:

1. What are the steps involved in appealing a grade? (If no procedures are listed, search other sources and summarize what you discover.)

2. If you audit a class, will you receive a grade? _____

3. After how many absences can your professor withdraw you from class? _____

4. Will you automatically receive a WF if you withdraw from a class after the midpoint of a semester?

_____

5. How long does a student have to complete the course work to remove an Incomplete (I)? _____

6. What would qualify you to graduate with honors?

7. How long can a student remain on probation without being dismissed from your college? _____

8. What is the difference between a first dismissal and a second dismissal?

• •

Survival Skills for Students Belonging to a Minority Population on Campus

Successfully completing a post-secondary education is a fairly complex process that involves the ability to identify the attitudes, skills, and habits needed to achieve academically, developing those attitudes, skills, and habits, and then using them to reach goals. Throughout this chapter, you have been encouraged to develop good academic survival skills. Developing these skills will lead to more effective learning, but for students who are part of a minority population on campus, there are some additional factors that may or may not influence your academic performance in college.

Padilla (1998) reported that successful completion of college is dependent on integrating socially and academically into the campus culture. While students need support, talent, motivation, and commitment to reach their educational goals, they also must feel that their knowledge and experiences are valued. These conditions are not always readily available for minority students on campus. Padilla's report on the success of Latinos and other minority students in higher education identified several barriers that can interfere with academic success:

> *Discontinuity barriers* are created by dramatic changes in life patterns, from rural to urban, urban to rural, south to north, or moving from living with a family to living on one's own.

Resource barriers include problems such as a lack of money or problems with financial aid.

Non-supportive barriers result from a feeling of not being nurtured. This can arise from having few or no minority role models, a lack of family support and understanding, or perceived low expectations of minority students held by faculty, staff, and peers.

Isolation barriers result from a lack of presence on campus. This might include a sense of racial and cultural isolation, few or no topics related to minorities in curriculum materials, lack of minority mentors including faculty, and few or no visible minority support programs.

Nontraditional Students

On many campuses, nontraditional and first-generation students are a part of the minority population. Today's college population includes a significant proportion of older students. According to the National Center for Educational Statistics (NCES) report (2011), between 2008 and 2019, enrollment for students who are 18–24 is expected to increase by 12 percent; for students who are 25–34, the projected increase is 28 percent; and, for students who are 35 and older, the projected increase is 22 percent. "Adult learner," "nontraditional student," and "returning student" are terms used interchangeably to broadly define students who do not enter post-secondary institutions the same year that they graduate from high school, may be beyond the "traditional age" of 18–22, may work full time, and are either beginning or returning to college full-time or part-time (Benshoff, 1991; Brookfield, 1999). Adult learners are often motivated to begin or return to higher education due to circumstances that have dramatically reduced their quality of life (e.g., a job change, the death of a spouse, divorce). Others may be returning to college to receive additional education needed to advance in their careers. Regardless of their reason for attending college, many adult learners find themselves juggling a number of commitments and responsibilities (e.g., family, work, and school).

Adults generally come to college achievement-oriented and with the expectation that a college education will have a significant positive impact on their lives. For some adult students, these high expectations are moderated by concerns related to finances and family, which reduce their self-confidence and elevate existing stress levels. Researchers have identified an experience shared by many adult learners of feeling like an "imposter." Adult learners may view themselves as pretending to be students and feel they do not have the talent or the right to be studying at their particular college or university (Brookfield, 1999). For some students, these feelings of inadequacy are exacerbated by a perceived lack of social acceptance and support for being a student. If you are an older student attending a college populated by predominantly younger students, you may have experienced similar feelings.

Some adult learners encounter barriers to their academic goals from non-campus sources. Family, friends, and coworkers are sometimes unable to understand and appreciate what an adult learner is attempting to accomplish. Research has shown that support for academic endeavors is crucial for adult learners to achieve academic success, yet as an adult learner, you may find that you do not have the kind of support experienced during other life transitions (e.g., first job, marriage, birth of children). One good way to achieve this support and feel a sense of legitimacy on campus is to seek out and join a peer learning community. If you are an adult learner, check with your university, college, or community to see if a support group exists for nontraditional, adult, or returning students. Due to the increase in the number of older students on campus, more colleges and universities are developing programs that recognize the unique needs of adult learners and plan programs where older students can come together and share relevant life experiences.

What are some of the unique needs of adult learners? First, if a person is beginning or returning to an academic setting after an extended absence, they may find that they need some academic assistance to renew or develop effective study strategies. Second, while adult learners need more flexible scheduling, some colleges and universities do not offer late-afternoon or evening classes needed to fulfill specific degree requirements. This lack of control over scheduling requires that the adult learner develop creative problem-solving skills to deal with this and various other external barriers. Distance learning may be a good alternative for some students. The number of online course offerings is growing at colleges throughout the country. Third, as adult learners juggle multiple responsibilities and commitments, some experience feelings of guilt related to not being as available to their families as they once were. Time- and stress-management skills, academic assistance, and a supportive peer community are all essential to avoid feeling overwhelmed by all the demands that adult learners experience.

If you are an adult learner, you may find that you need to actively recruit more support and assistance from family, friends, and coworkers. Learn to be more assertive by letting those around you know what assistance you require (do not expect others to read your mind about what you need), and offer suggestions for how they can help you to meet your academic goals. Share your experiences. Maybe your motivation and enthusiasm will be contagious, motivating others to begin or return to college or a university. If you have a family, try involving them in decisions about how many classes to take and scheduling of classes, so they feel a part of your life and better understand your academic obligations and challenges. Remember also to check out websites that cater to adult learners. The Association for Non-Traditional Students in Higher Education (www.antshe.org) is an international organization that offers support and information about careers, grants, and scholarships. There are other websites that offer support in the form of blogs and videos (check out *Take America to College:* http://www.takeamericatocollege.com/about/). Valuable information is available via the Internet from those who have successfully traveled the same academic route you have selected.

Academic success requires good study habits.

First-Generation Students

First-generation students, those who are the first in their families to attend college, often experience a sense of alienation from family and friends at home. Family members and relatives often send mixed messages based on a combination of pride and envy. Expectations from others to succeed are generally high, but empathy for the stresses of attending a college or a university may not be very strong. After all, what is so hard about going to college? For some who have not had the experience, attending college may sound like a vacation away from the real world. Some people at home may think that you have a glorious opportunity that they did not have, and when you communicate academic difficulties, they may respond that you only need to work harder and study more. Sometimes first-generation students find it impossible to explain just how difficult it is to adjust to all the demands of academic life.

Despite the difficulty encountered in sharing the challenges and frustrations, it is important for a first-generation student to self disclose such information. Share your experiences, reveal a sense of all the time and effort expended, and report your failures as well as your achievements, your hopes, and your doubts. As you have new experiences and form new friendships, it sometimes takes a little more effort to stay connected to family and friends. Be sure to share this period in your life via phone calls, texting, letters, e-mail, and visits, because even though new friends are a source of support, research has shown that family support of our life goals can be the most powerful influence in helping first-generation students (and all students) overcome obstacles.

Sources

Barr, S. (2000, May). Let's put the heat on campus cheats. *Reader's Digest*, 108–113.

Benshoff, J. M. (1991). Nontraditional college students: A developmental look at the needs of women and men returning to school. *Journal of Young Adulthood and Middle Age, 3,* 47–61.

Brookfield, S. D. (1999, January/February). What is college really like for adult learners? *About Campus,* 10–15.

Buzan, T. (1976). *Use both sides of your brain.* New York, NY: E. P. Dutton.

Cole, S., & Kiss, K. (2000, May/June). What can we do about student cheating? *About Campus,* 5–12.

Hussar, W. J., & Bailey, T. M. (2011). *Projections of educational statistics to 2019* (38th ed.). Washington, DC: U.S. Department of Education, National Center for Educational Statistics. Retrieved from http://nces.ed.gov/pubs2011/2011017.pdf

Kendall Hunt Publishing. (1999). *First-year experience sourcebook.* Dubuque, IA: Author.

McKeachie, W. J. (1994). *Teaching tips: A guidebook for the beginning college teacher* (9th ed.). Lexington, MA: D. C. Heath.

Padilla, R. V. (1998). *Chicana/o college students: Focus on success.* A report prepared for the Hispanic Association of Colleges and Universities.

Paul, W. (1974). *How to study in college.* Boston, MA: Houghton Mifflin.

Learning
The Connection to Memory and Memorization

"Learning is not a matter of filling a void with information. It is a process of internal organization of a complex of thought patterns, perceptions, assumptions, attitudes, feelings, and skills, and of successfully testing this reorganization in relation to problems of living."

LELAND BRADFORD, *Models of Influence*

Learning is the transformational process by which we acquire knowledge. Learning is an ongoing process that has the potential to create changes in existing knowledge, attitudes, skills, habits, and long-term behavior (e.g., learning techniques to overcome a snake phobia that has prevented one from going camping with friends). Learning is even powerful enough to change a person's appearance (e.g., learning and practicing yoga can significantly improve one's health and physique). There are numerous theories to explain how learning takes place.

Gross (1991) has reviewed and discussed the implications of a classification system developed by Reese and Overton that differentiates learning theories. Gross wrote that these two social scientists classified learning theories according to whether a theory's basic position reflected a mechanistic model or an organic model of the world. According to Gross, in **mechanistic learning theories** you find a metaphorical reliance on explanations that depict learning very much as one would describe the structure and function of machinery. Complex events can be reduced to predictable and measurable interactions, and results are quantitatively measurable and comparable (e.g., your SAT scores can be compared to other students' scores). A basic assumption of this model is that if you score low on a test, you must "not know" the material or you are somehow less capable of learning (a terrible conclusion considering that tests, including standardized tests, are not perfect measures and in some individual cases provide a grossly incorrect assessment of what a person has learned or is capable of learning). Finally, a mechanistic learning theory purports that if the learning environment can be controlled, the behavior of the learner can be conditioned or modified to some extent.

In contrast to the above theories are the **organic learning theories**. Instead of the metaphor of the machine, in this instance we have the metaphor of an "interconnected, developing organism" (Gross, 1991, p. 32). Operating from this organic perspective, the learner is viewed as a naturally active, creative individual who is continually searching for and assimilating new patterns of meanings. Theories developed by humanistic psychologists such as Abraham Maslow and Carl Rogers to explain the significance of the relationship between psychological needs of the learner and the learning process are classified as organic learning theories. Rogers (1969) formulated a set of principles related to how people learn that includes the following:

- People have a natural potentiality for learning based on a natural curiosity about the world.
- Significant learning occurs when the learner perceives the material to be learned as relevant to personal goals.
- People perceive and assimilate information best when external threats are at a minimum and they feel that there exists a supportive environment that encourages learning.
- Serious learning is acquired through doing, or active approaches.
- Learning is best facilitated when the learner participates responsibly in the learning process, choosing personal learning resources and strategies for learning.

Rogers (1969) believed that "the most socially useful learning in the modern world is the learning of the process of learning, a continuing openness to experience and incorporation into oneself of the process of change" (p. 163).

The Autonomous Learner

The first goal of a college education, which we noted in Chapter 1, is to help students develop skills to become **autonomous learners**. As a student, you certainly need to learn the information presented to you, but more importantly, you need to know how to learn so you can become an independent learner for the rest of your life. Consider the following questions as you read through this chapter.

1. Are you an involved, active learner?
2. Do you take responsibility for your learning?

3. Do you create a supportive environment for learning?
4. Do you take advantage of your natural sense of curiosity and search for relevancy in whatever information you are trying to learn?
5. Do you select appropriate strategies and resources for learning and retaining information?

When you are through reading this chapter, you will have a chance to answer these five questions (see Exercise 1). While other chapters of this textbook offer information to help you develop specific life-skills related to learning (e.g., learning styles and study skills), this chapter's aim is to help you understand the underlying elements of learning itself, which will better enable you to select the particular learning techniques, strategies, and approaches that fit your unique requirements for learning. Simply stated, the goal is to move you further along the dimension of autonomous learning. There is room for improvement for us all when it comes to being autonomous learners.

The Connection between Learning and Memory

Change is an essential and unavoidable experience in life. Even though at some level we believe this to be true, we still tend to cling to what we have and know, hoping those things will remain the same and last forever. According to Buddhist cosmology, nothing is permanent and much of human suffering is the result of the inaccurate belief that things that are important to us are permanent. Clinging to this notion of permanency, and rejecting the fundamental truth that all things in the universe change, is what brings misery. For example, a fairy-tale perspective on marriage can create problems when the natural changes in a marriage are mistakenly seen as a decrease in love. (Long-term intimate relationships are much more than a state of intense infatuation or some other initial emotional state experienced in the early stages of mutual attraction.) Similarly, some students resist change by refusing to learn new skills and strategies or to explore personal attitudes and beliefs that may be adversely affecting their learning (e.g., new college students may cling to study methods they used in high school as if their learning environment had not changed). These students find it difficult to make a personal commitment to becoming a different type of learner, and as a result, their current learning approach remains static and unproductive.

Some students tackle learning from an active and participatory stance, while others adopt a more passive approach to learning. The latter students may perceive learning as little more than attending class, taking notes, reading texts, writing papers, and taking tests. While these activities might get a few students to deeper levels of understanding, they are not synonymous with critical thinking, creative thinking, and other more responsible levels of learning that have repeatedly been shown to optimize learning. All students bring numerous ideas about learning with them to college. What ideas about learning did you bring to college?

Ideas about Learning

Answer the following questions.

What does learning mean to you personally?

_____

_____

_____

What do you think is your potential for learning?

_____

_____

_____

Have you experienced certain fears that have created barriers to learning?

_____

_____

_____

Are there interpersonal factors that prevent you from learning effectively in a group setting?

_____

_____

_____

By giving even a little thought to these questions, it's easy to see that emotional, motivational, attitudinal, and perceptual factors influence one's ability to learn.

© LIGHTSPRING, 2012. Used under license from Shutterstock, Inc.

The connection between learning and memories.

Learning and memory are intricately linked to one another. Can you imagine what it would be like to wake up every morning and not be able to remember what you had learned the day before? With no experiences upon which to build, how would you learn? How would this affect your personality? Danielle Lapp (1998) reminds us that memory brings continuity and meaning to our thoughts and actions by putting them into perspective. When we are comparing, contrasting, evaluating, choosing, daydreaming, and engaging in other forms of thinking, we are relying on our brains' ability to perceive, store, and retrieve information. We are relying on our memories. While the line that divides learning and memory may seem real, that line is no more real than the drawn borders on world maps. In the real world, you will not find lines drawn on soil to divide countries. In truth, we live in one world where actions in one part of the world eventually affect other parts of the world. Similarly, you cannot have memory without learning or learning without memory; these two aspects of our being coexist and represent a single system.

The Creation of Memories

A continuous interaction is going on between you and your environment. This interaction involves a complex sequence of electrochemical signals that are passed back and forth along a network of neurons in the brain and actually cause changes in the physical structure of your brain. In this section, we will explore different types of memory and what each contributes to the overall learning process.

Memory can be conceptualized in terms of three categories: sensory, short-term, and long-term (O'Brien, 2002). Information gathered by our senses flows into a sensory repository known as **sensory memory**. Although the amount of information that can be held at this point in the process seems "unlimited," information usually remains there for a mere fraction of a second before being replaced by new stimuli flowing into us—stimuli that are but a part of the existing ocean of sensory information that is available at any given time. What is a fraction of a second like? Dominic O'Brien (2002) indicates that an image, or "icon," on the visual cortex creates the illusion of live action because each icon begins to dissipate before the next image appears. The effect is similar to the projection of still images on a strip of film by a movie projector. The movie projector is projecting onto a screen 24 frames, or images, per second. Because of this rapid speed, the images blend in the brain and seem to offer a single, continuous flow of images that creates the impression of natural movement in linear time. Not all of the senses process information in the same way as the visual cortex. Auditory information might linger for several seconds because of the time required for it to fade away.

Before the information is even passed on to short-term memory, your brain has to connect with long-term memory to compare the incoming information with other information already stored in order to approximate what the new information is about. Long term memory provides a suitable reference, and this reference is eventually relied upon to complete the processing of the new information (thus long-term memory is also known as reference memory).

Your brain selects only a very small percentage of sensory information to pass on to **short-term memory** (STM). STM does not have a huge capacity like sensory memory and instead acts more like a screening center, either ejecting information from the process or holding and routing it to long-term memory. STM can screen roughly seven items of information during a period that lasts longer than a fraction of a second but less than a minute. During the brief period when screening occurs, if the information being screened is not sustained through some kind of activity (e.g., repetition, focused attention, emotional reaction) the information will dissipate and fade away.

Understanding the way STM works can help in developing effective learning strategies. Specifically, to learn information one must break the information down into manageable units. The general term for breaking information into smaller units is called chunking. **Chunking** is a characteristic of learning that George Miller discovered. The discovery is sometimes referred to as the "magical number seven, plus or minus two" (after the title of Miller's 1956 article, "The Magical Number Seven, Plus or Minus Two: Some Limits on Our Capacity for Processing Information"). The number of chunks of information that people can process runs from five to nine; most people can handle seven. Miller believed that short-term memory could hold much more information if the information was organized into meaningful chunks that represented a reorganizing of what was originally presented to the person. You can memorize information (e.g., names, terms, historical dates, listings) more efficiently than you may have believed possible just by reducing the information into seven or fewer meaningful associations, or chunks.

If the information at the short-term memory stage is acted on in some way (e.g., by repeating these manageable units of information), then the information is passed on to **long-term memory**, where it remains forever in some form. We can later retrieve the information when it is needed if the information has been stored well. This final step in the logging of information as memory leads to what is possibly the most important question related to learning: Why do we forget something? While serious physical deterioration of brain tissue and other physiological occurrences can certainly interfere with stored information, there are numerous psychological reasons to explain forgetting, as well as difficulty in learning new information. For example, racist beliefs can effectively block the processing of new information that disagrees with the already learned view that the other group is lazy, stupid, or dirty; high levels of math anxiety can block the recall of math information and learning of new math concepts; and maintaining a level of consistency between learned beliefs about good health and the unhealthy practice of smoking can cause smokers to block thoughts about their personal chances of getting lung cancer or forget to set up a doctor's appointment for breathing difficulties.

For the remainder of this chapter, we will focus on six factors that contribute to the effectiveness of many different types of learning strategies. Considering how you might incorporate these factors into your overall approach to learning will better enable you to combat common problems encountered when studying and recalling information later. Our aim is to help you alter your current approach to learning to avoid the types of problems that are common in the college environment. A common form of forgetting might be described as experiencing the somewhat paradoxical situation that we all have encountered of being aware that we do not remember something that we know we know. For example, during a history test you might be able to see in your mind the first letter of a general's name but not be able to recall the full name. Once you turn in the history test and leave the room, the full name of the general pops into your head. We refer to this type of recall problem as "hitting a memory iceberg," where just enough of the information pokes above the surface into our consciousness to convince us the information is stored in memory. Of course there are times when hitting a memory iceberg is analogous to the Titanic going down, on those rare occasions when the mind goes completely blank and a large segment of information has been lost.

Six Factors That Optimize the Learning and Recall Process

The word *memory* comes from the Latin *memoria*, which is derived from *memor*, meaning "mindful." Mindfulness, or awareness, is the foundation of memory. When we take the time to truly attend to what is before us, we notice what is unique to the situation, and we tend to remember what is special, what affects us in some way. Applying this perspective of mindfulness to various learning strategies can help you overcome learning and memory difficulties. The following tips (summarized in Figure 5.1) have helped many students with both memorization and retrieval of information.

- **Reorganize information to better consume it mentally.** As pointed out earlier, George Miller (1956) believed a primary component of effective learning is to organize and consolidate large amounts of information in a way that makes sense to you. Look for patterns, differences, similarities, and shared characteristics. Use the information to create maps, charts, outlines, or other mnemonic devices. The point is to reduce the information to bite-sized pieces of information that enable you to mentally consume it. For example, counselors working as family therapists sometimes use genograms to help themselves and family members understand the family's patterns of interaction. A genogram is a visual map of family connections and descriptors that enables counselors and family members to better see the patterns of family interaction that are poorly understood by the family. This device changes the information from a chaotic bundle of seemingly unconnected data that family members are choking on to something that is a manageable size for their consideration.

- **Shatter the time you devote to studying into bits.** Distribute the total amount of time you spend studying into shorter periods of time (try 30, 50, or 60 minutes of studying depending on your personal attention span) and follow each block of studying with a short break (five to ten minutes). Discover and adopt those lengths of time (study and break) that produce the best learning results. Keep in mind that this is likely to vary depending on subject area.

  Decades ago, the German philosopher Hermann Ebbinghaus conducted a series of experimental studies on memory and learning. He uncovered a curious finding that has implications for us today. Through experiments in which people were asked to learn a series of nonsense syllables (e.g., ETG-ASG-JJS-MFD-KRL-QRTYHD-MNB), he investigated the effects of the length of the series of syllables and the order in which they were presented. His research demonstrated that the learner tends to remember what comes first, then what comes last, and then what comes in the middle. In fact, the material learned earliest seems to even interfere with learning the remaining material.

  Have you ever taken the time to make out a list of items to buy or things to do, but then left the list at home? Chances are good that you were better at remembering the items at the beginning and end of the list, but not the items that fell in the middle of the list. Ebbinghaus's research suggests that an effective way to study is to distribute your time studying. The short breaks between learning periods lessen the effect of memories interfering with the retention of new material.

- **Sweep your mind clean of mental clutter.** Many accidents occur when a person allows his or her focus to wander. Frequently we go through life doing one thing while our thoughts are elsewhere. For example, when we are studying, we might obsess about an argument we had with someone close. The next day, having worked things out with the person, we are now enjoying the person's company, but we find that we are obsessing about not having studied enough the day before. It appears a person can be in two different places at once.

  Adopting another cultural perspective for the moment we could say that before studying one should practice *feng shui* on his or her mind. This Chinese concept involves balancing and harmonizing the flow of natural energies in our surroundings to create a beneficial effect in our life. An essential component of this approach to life is to get rid of clutter, both *external clutter* (e.g., the desk where you study may have a large number of things that are scattered about in a disorganized manner) and *internal clutter* (e.g., when you sit down to study, you find your mind is filled with various worries). The term *clutter* comes from the Middle English word *clotter*, which means "coagulate." What kind of thoughts or surroundings do you allow to clot the flow of energy you are trying to devote to studying?

  Identify some action that will sweep away the clutter in your mind and use it before you start a study session. This will differ from person to person. It might be exercising for one person; for another person it might be calling a friend to discuss old times. One of the authors of this textbook finds that sitting on the garden bench at home for 15 minutes while focusing on nature results in much less mental clutter.

- **Do not allow stress to drink up your energy.** During the initial stage of stress, a person can become very alert and focused. To a large extent, stress is a warning that we need to take action in relation to a threat, and in this context the hyper-alert state experienced makes sense. But if we do not effectively handle the source of the stress, after a period of time the stress begins to affect us negatively. Even single stressful events, if of great enough magnitude, can profoundly affect "the ways in which memory is encoded, stored, and retrieved" (Chu, 1998, p. 55). The end result is that the way we process new information is affected. There is little doubt, based on research findings, that stress can adversely affect learning.

  In responding to stress, individuals have two responses: **a remediation response** and a **prevention response**. First, when stress occurs we should take appropriate action to reduce its level. A remediation response in this case might be to directly confront the source of the stress. Second, we should incorporate behaviors in our life that lessen the chance of that stress occurring, and when it does occur, lessen its effect on us. A prevention response could be getting regular exercise, which has been shown to create a buffer against the stress.

  Some of our students tell us that they can talk on their cell phones while driving, watch television while studying, and change into their sweats in the car when driving down a street on the way to the gym because that is the kind of world we live in—a world that crowds in on us and demands that we multitask. In truth, multitasking can easily increase one's level of stress, whether the person is aware of this or not. If you want to process information more efficiently, you will need to control, or appropriately respond to, stress-producing situations or events. Handling stress will reduce the likelihood of feeling pulled in several directions at once. For example, suppose you want to study in your dorm room, but your intrusive and talkative roommate is there and the roommate refuses to turn the TV down. Instead of being pulled in three different directions (trying to study, arguing repeatedly with the roommate, and watching the TV because the volume pulls you in) leave and go to the library to study.

  Stress typically involves a situation where you have several things taking place in your life at the same time. For example, a student might be studying for two finals, meeting a 5 p.m. deadline for sending out her resume, packing clothes and belongings because the lease is up, and dealing with the news of a death in the family—all in a single day. In a nutshell, stress is having too many things to juggle at once. Once stress reaches a certain level, it can easily drink up all the energy you need for learning and memorizing course material.

- **Put your brain to sleep.** The amount of sleep needed will vary from person to person, but we each know when we are not getting enough. Recently the brain has been studied in a more direct fashion than ever before. Researchers are constantly creating more accurate and detailed maps of this unique organ. One area of study has focused on the brain's electrical activities, which have different frequencies. These investigations produced the means to identify different types of brain waves. For example, beta refers to a rhythm associated with being awake and alert; alpha is associated with resting; and theta (dreaming) and delta (deep level of sleep) are associated with the rhythms of a brain after the person drifts off to sleep. Just in this one area of study, some of the preliminary findings have proven intriguing. For example, theta and alpha rhythms coming together during a time when we are conscious appears to contribute to an increase in the ability to process information (memorization is optimized), but to achieve the combined effect, one needs to learn how to achieve a certain type of relaxed state.

Regardless of what the ultimate brain map reveals, one particular finding has immediate application for all of us: sleep has a positive effect on memory. Evidence indicates that sleeping affects the storing of information that we encountered during the day. Specifically, sleep appears to play an important and essential role in the consolidation of memory. One theory is that during sleep there are fewer external stimuli, so it is a good time for your brain to turn its attention to reviewing and organizing information.

Whatever the final relationship turns out to be between sleep and memory, we do know that people process information better if they are rested. For example, Pliskin and Just (1999) note that studies support the conclusion that sleepy drivers are more accident-prone than drunk drivers.

- **Be an imaginative processor of information.** Be creative and use your imagination when you are deciding on your plan to study. Be playful with information. Remember when you were a child and how there were times when learning just seemed easy? You may have been playing at some game or learning activity pertaining to science (e.g., building a volcano, using red food dye, vinegar, and baking soda to create eruptions). At other times during childhood, learning seemed more difficult. Maybe you were told that play was not allowed and you had to be serious about learning. Recapturing that playful state of mind can lead to active learning where a lot of new information is assimilated easily. Learning is more than spending time with something. If learning is perceived to be a chore, it will become a chore. Having a playful attitude and approach can help you avoid the role of a passive learner; spending a lot of time with a book or your lecture notes is no guarantee that you are actively involved in learning.

To maximize memory capacity, you should make an effort to engage both sides, or hemispheres, of the brain. The **left side** is associated with descriptive phrases such as "clock sense," "fact-oriented," "drawn to order," "writing to communicate," "responsive to lists," "language- and verbally oriented," and "drawn to details," and the **right side** is associated with descriptive phrases such as "drawn to overall patterns," "understanding the nonverbal," "reacts to colors and images," "draws to communicate," "misjudges time," "emotionally expressive," and "intuitively oriented." Most students already possess fairly strong left-brain abilities. It is left-brain abilities that have gotten you into college (such abilities help you find the single correct answer to an item on the SAT). Thus, to call upon more of your abilities to help you to learn information, you should engage more of your creative, imaginative side—that is, abilities typically associated with the right hemisphere of the brain. Combining our logical side with our creative side to create a more balanced approach to information processing can result in stronger, more widely distributed memories.

Finally, since **imaging** is a good way to incorporate more right-brain abilities, start repackaging information in terms of a mental image or images. We recommend you first try this out by using a course in your major area of study; you are already knowledgeable about the subject and comfortable with it, which should facilitate applying your imagination. For example, associate a technical term from your field of study with an image that will enable you to recall the term's definition (the word *association* is used to refer to the mental link created between two disparate items). Create an image that goes beyond having interesting colors and visual details; aim to create an image that incorporates other senses in addition to sight. Create an image that has elements of smell, sound, taste, and a certain quality of touch (e.g., can you associate the image created for the technical term with a quality like smooth, soft, greasy, rough, slick, or wet?). Another approach is to add a feeling to the image (happy, sad, angry). Feelings are associated with right-brain functions.

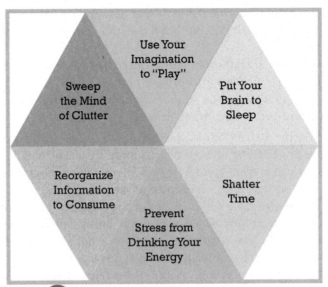

Figure 5.1 Optimizing Learning

Usually, the more surreal the image used to package the information you are trying to learn, the easier it is to process the information and to retrieve the information later. Some students take printed material found in a textbook or class notes and then transform key concepts into meaningful images. This imaginative approach has proven to be very helpful. Creating strange and dramatic images that combine several pieces of key information has allowed these students to memorize more easily and to later recall the information better than they would have if they had simply focused on material the way they had done in the past. Material once perceived as little more than a series of mundane words to memorize (terms and definitions) now has meaning after the material was changed into memorable images.

One Last Recommendation

When you are developing the skills of an autonomous learner, *keep your mind open to possibilities* as you try on different learning strategies to determine if they are a good fit. Let experience serve as a guide; the ultimate gauge in judging a strategy is whether it brings about the change in performance you are seeking. A final piece of advice is not to dismiss the learning approaches we advocate (or strategies you discover through another resource) just because they have been around for years, decades, or even centuries. "New and improved" is an advertising ploy used by sellers to get us to buy a product; it does not necessarily mean "better."

Some older learning strategies have withstood the test of time. One such strategy is using **loci**—mental hooks that are unforgettable (e.g., places in a student's dorm room) and can be used to hang new information on for later retrieval. This device was used by the Greeks to memorize the key points in long speeches that were filled with details. This memory strategy allowed orators in Greece over 2,000 years ago to speak for an hour or more without referring to anything like the note cards we cling to for comfort when giving a brief speech in a course such as *Introduction to Public Speaking*. Specifically, an orator would identify key words of his speech and mentally associate each key word with a different item found at his residence. During the speech, the orator simply recalled each item, which served to trigger the recall of each key word.

An appreciation of the history of learning strategies prevents us from reinventing the same techniques over and over. Ancient Greek and Roman history is long and rich, providing us with much useful information concerning memory training (they perceived memory training as a form of artistic endeavor). In the Middle Ages, scholars adapted classical memory techniques to teach religion and ethics and developed new ways to process information. In the 20th and 21st centuries, scientific advances have allowed us to achieve a much deeper understanding of the physiological processes behind learning—how certain neurological activities result in experiences being transformed and stored in the very fabric of the brain to cause memories.

When we pause to consider the shift in focus brought about by science in recent times, an interesting question arises. Is it knowing about physiological processes and neurological activities or knowing about certain learning skills that proves most helpful to the student? Obviously, knowing what learning skills to use to meet the requirements of a particular situation is of most help to students.

Finally, there may be some who ask, "Why should I learn a bunch of mental tricks when technology provides electronic tools such as language dictionaries and electronic organizers that can be used to kick-start my memories or access information?" These electronic devices should be thought of as aids (modern versions of printed language dictionaries and appointment books) that are not fail-proof. We cannot reject the role of autonomous learner if we want to achieve our full potential in life (it is analogous to the decision between taking the wheel of a car and driving it or releasing the wheel of the car in the hope that it will drive us where we want to go). One of the authors used electronic organizers for several years until three malfunctioned within the span of five months, each one losing its stored information. New technologies may remove one set of problems, but they introduce others.

A good example of calling upon the wisdom of the past and modifying what we know about learning strategies to meet our own unique learning requirements is provided by Dominic O'Brien (2002). O'Brien was the winner of the sixth World Memory Championships in 1999. During the competition, he memorized the order of 18 decks of shuffled cards (a total of 956 cards) in one hour and reproduced the sequence without any errors. He also memorized a 74-digit number, spoken to him at the rate of a digit per second, and was able to perfectly recall the sequence. O'Brien accomplished these feats through the use of mnemonic devices. The basic concept of the mnemonic device has been around and used for centuries. In fact, the term *mnemonic* is related to the name Mnemosyne, the Greek goddess of memory.

Sources

Bradford, L. P. (1962). Models of influence: The teaching-learning transaction. In W. G. Bennis, K. D. Benne, & R. Chin (Eds.), *The planning of change* (pp. 493–502). New York, NY: Holt, Rinehart and Winston.

Chu, J. A. (1998). *Rebuilding shattered lives: The responsible treatment of complex post-traumatic and dissociative disorders*. New York, NY: John Wiley.

Ebbinghaus, H. (1913). *Memory: A contribution to experimental psychology*. New York, NY: Teachers College Press.

Gross, R. E. (1991). *Peak learning*. Los Angeles, CA: Tarcher.

Lapp, D. C. (1998). *Maximizing your memory power* (2nd ed.). New York, NY: Barron's.

Levoy, G. (1997). *Callings*. New York, NY: Three Rivers Press.

Miller, G. A. (1956). The magical number seven, plus or minus two: Some limits on our capacity for processing information. *Psychological Review, 63*, 81–97.

O'Brien, D. O. (2002). *Learn to remember*. San Francisco, CA: Chronicle Books.

Pliskin, M., & Just, S. L. (1999). *The complete idiot's guide to interpreting your dreams*. New York, NY: Macmillan.

Rogers, C. R. (1969). *Freedom to learn*. Columbus, OH: Charles E. Merrill.

Chapter 5
Exercise 1: Unique Learning Approach

1. **Are you an involved, active learner?**   No   Yes   Sometimes

   What are some specific steps that you can take to become a more active learner?

2. **Do you take responsibility for your learning?**   No   Yes   Sometimes

   What specifically can you do to become a more responsible learner?

3. **Do you create a supportive environment for learning?**   No   Yes   Sometimes

   What could you do to set up a more supportive environment?

4. **Do you take advantage of your natural sense of curiosity and search for relevancy in whatever information you are trying to learn?**   No   Yes   Sometimes

   Describe your goals for being in college and how you use your goals to motivate yourself to learn.

5. **Do you select appropriate strategies and resources for learning and retaining information?**   No   Yes   Sometimes

   List learning strategies that you plan to implement to make you a better learner.

   List some resources, including people, that can help you to achieve your academic goals.

Chapter 5

Exercise 2: Enhancing the Learning and Recall Process

This exercise requires you to explain how you would incorporate two of the six factors listed in this chapter for optimizing the learning and recall process as you complete a class project.

Your history professor expects you to write and present a paper on the topic "Thomas Jefferson's Relevance in the 21st Century."

Completing this assignment will require you to gather information, outline a plan for organizing the information, write a first draft, write several revisions, and write a final version to present to the entire class.

The professor has indicated that your paper should possess the qualities of clarity, conciseness, and concreteness. Two days before the due date, the professor announces in class that these three qualities will differentiate between strong and weak papers and presentations.

A. The two factors I would incorporate are

    1. _____

    _____

    _____

    2. _____

    _____

    _____

B. Explain how you would apply the two factors selected to complete this assignment. (You may apply the two factors selected to either the written part or the presentation part of the project, or both.)

(Continue your response on the next page.)

Learning Style
One's Distinctive Manner of Learning

6

Learning is an individual, creative process. Each person has a preferred way of doing things, a unique approach to gathering, assimilating, and retaining information. This approach is called your learning style and reflects your individual pattern of thinking and learning. You have an incredible capacity to learn. Do you take advantage of this innate ability? When you have information to process and learn, do you challenge your mind by utilizing the most effective and efficient learning strategies compatible with your particular pattern of learning?

In this chapter, we will explore how to use your learning strengths and how differences in personality, perceptual learning modalities, life experiences, environmental factors, and brain dominance influence the way we think and learn. There are several assessments in this chapter that can help you identify your personal learning style, or the various learning patterns that you engage in to think, recall, create, and solve problems.

Whole-Brain Learning

Did you know that most people lose around 90 percent of what they read and hear within 24 hours of being exposed to new information unless the information is organized and reviewed? Becoming more knowledgeable about how you personally use your brain to think increases the probability of developing more effective learning patterns and strategies for comprehension and retention.

The human brain weighs around three pounds (at 18 pounds, the sperm whale has the largest brain of any mammal) and serves as the command center for interpreting sensory input, coordinating bodily activities, and processing emotions and cognition. Most of the cranial cavity is occupied by the cerebrum, which is divided into two cerebral hemispheres: a right hemisphere and a left hemisphere. Connecting the two hemispheres is a large nerve track consisting of millions of nerve fibers, called the corpus callosum. These nerve fibers carry messages back and forth between the two sides of the brain, allowing the two sides to exchange information and provide us with a holistic, single perception of the world.

In the 1970s, the neurosurgeon Roger Sperry conducted groundbreaking research with patients who had experienced severe epileptic seizures and opted for surgery to have the corpus callosum severed to control the seizures. After this surgery, the two hemispheres of the brain could no longer communicate with one another. Because the right brain, which governs visual memory and spatial reasoning, controls the left side of the body and the left brain, which handles language and speech, controls the right side of the body, Sperry discovered that subjects forgot how to draw with their right hands and how to write with their left hands. Sperry was awarded a Nobel Prize in medicine for his research showing that the two hemispheres of the brain process information differently (split-brain theory).

Two interesting stories that illustrate the differences between how the left and right brain process information were reported by Oliver Sacks and Jill Bolte Taylor. The neurologist Oliver Sacks (1970) reported that he once worked with a well-known musician and teacher who was capable of recognizing prominent features and other details around him, but unable to grasp the whole picture due to damage to the right side of his brain. He suffered from what is called visual agnosia. He would walk down the street patting the tops of water hydrants and parking meters, mistakenly thinking they were children. Once when leaving Dr. Sacks's office, the client reached for his hat and instead took hold of his wife's head. The incident became the title of Sacks's book *The Man Who Mistook His Wife for a Hat*.

Jill Bolte Taylor is a neuroanatomist who experienced a severe hemorrhage in the left hemisphere of her brain. Within four hours, she lost her ability to speak, understand speech, and organize information into meaningful, timely sequences. She was left with the experience of living in the moment, with no concept of past or future events. At the time of her stroke, she was performing research and teaching at Harvard Medical School. In her book *My Stroke of Insight* (2009), Taylor recounts her stroke and the ensuing eight years of recovery. Although her left brain was damaged and she could not speak or understand speech, her right brain was functioning and could internally communicate whether or not a person was telling the truth and if their intentions were good. She was emotionally aware of who in her presence was being respectful, kind, or honest.

People characteristically display a predominant hemispherical preference. In other words, you tend to use one side of your brain more than the other. Our problem-solving skills, mental and physical abilities, and even personality traits are influenced by the way in which we use the right and left sides of our brain (Wonder & Donovan, 1984).

Right Brain The right brain thinks holistically and intuitively, creating moment-to-moment holistic impressions in the present moment, but is essentially unable to process language. Mental processes associated with the right brain register in our consciousness as feelings and hunches, based on visual-spatial reasoning (e.g., recognition of patterns including faces, drawing, dancing, and other movements). Information is often processed visually (and spatially), kinesthetically (through movement), and haptically (through touch). The right brain excels in abstract thinking and prefers to synthesize rather than analyze information, merging patterns of related and seemingly unrelated information together to form "the big picture." It is because of the right brain that we can make sense out of maps, recognize faces, and perceive our emotions. General overviews at the beginning of a chapter in a textbook can prove especially helpful to a right-brain-dominant learner. If you are using the right brain for problem solving, try following your hunches, daydream, brainstorm, and take long walks to mull over your ideas.

Left Brain The left brain thinks analytically and reductively by breaking information into parts, processing the information sequentially, analyzing all the details. The left brain helps us to make logical sense out of experience by stringing together all the moments experienced in the right brain into a logical, sequential, timely context. It is the left brain that brings us the ability to think of our moments in the context of the present, past, and future. Mental processes associated with the left brain include language (e.g., speech, written language, verbal memory, and reading) and mathematics. Unlike the right brain, which prefers to concentrate on a variety of issues and views, the left brain prefers to concentrate on just a single issue or point of view and look at the pros and cons of that view.

The lists found in Figure 6.1 summarize some of the main traits of right-brain and left-brain thinking. Which best describes the way you think?

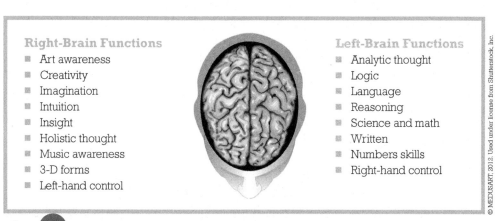

Right-Brain Functions
- Art awareness
- Creativity
- Imagination
- Intuition
- Insight
- Holistic thought
- Music awareness
- 3-D forms
- Left-hand control

Left-Brain Functions
- Analytic thought
- Logic
- Language
- Reasoning
- Science and math
- Written
- Numbers skills
- Right-hand control

© MEDUSART. 2012. Used under license from Shutterstock, Inc.

Figure **6.1** Characteristics of Left-Brain and Right-Brain Thinking

Although the left brain and right brain process information in distinctly different ways, the two hemispheres are connected, communicate with one another, and function as a whole, with each hemisphere contributing to a portion of our experiences. Obviously, willpower alone does not allow anyone to completely turn off or completely control either side of the brain, but you can increase your potential to learn by using a diversity of learning strategies that pull from both sides of the brain. Whether people are predominantly right-brained or left-brained, when mental areas of the brain once considered weak are further developed, a synergetic effect occurs in which all areas of mental performance improve (Buzan, 1976).

What can you do to better develop a whole-brain approach to learning? In class while listening to lectures, you can remind yourself to shift your body position, pay careful attention to the speaker's body language, outline your notes, listen for facts, and notice any patterns of information that emerge from the lecture. Above all, listen with an intent to learn. Always assume that you will learn something from whatever you are engaged in. Learn to shift back and forth between right brain and left brain whenever the style you are engaging in (right-brain or left-brain) is not working for you. For example, if you are right-brain-dominant and are working a math problem, you might see the solution but not the sequential steps to the solution. If you are only given credit if you show the steps, then there may be a problem. Consider another example: you are completing a history exam, and you have been asked to trace the key events that led up to the Voting Rights Act of 1965. Thinking from the right side of your brain, you might remember the events leading up to the Voting Act and understand the relationship among them, but not be able to recall significant dates, names, and pertinent legislation. In both situations, engaging the left brain more would help.

On the other hand, suppose you are left-brain-dominant and are working a math problem. You might remember the steps, but no matter how hard you try to solve the problem using the steps presented in class for a similar problem, you cannot arrive at the correct answer. You are probably having difficulty understanding the theory involved and seeing the overall pattern. In the history test example, you can remember all the dates and the names of key figures but not the overall pattern of events. Engaging the right side of your brain would help with both situations.

How do you jump back and forth from the right to the left and from the left to the right? You do this continually throughout the day as you make sense of the world around you. But if you are predominantly thinking from the right side and need to get the left side more engaged, start doing multiplication tables or figure out how much time you have left to complete the test. If you are processing information predominantly from the left side of the brain and want to move over to the right, daydream, visualize, meditate, or focus your attention on a visual point in the distance.

Most of the academic learning that occurs in colleges engages the logical, linear, orderly left brain. For students who use more of the right brain and think holistically and intuitively, learning can often be a frustrating experience. Since responsibility for learning rests with you, the student, it is essential that you become aware of your learning patterns and how to use the power of your brain more effectively for learning.

Brain Exercises

What other kinds of exercises can you engage in to capitalize on the power of your brain? Parlette (1997) suggests that you learn to exercise your brain as you do your body to improve concentration and motivation, and he challenges people to become more creative in their approaches to learning. It is through novel situations that the brain constructs and expands its neural pathways, increasing the capacity to learn. Complete Exercise 1 ("How Fit Is Your Brain?"), which appears near the end of this chapter. What is your score? _____. Do you think your brain could benefit from some exercise? Below are some general explanations given by Parlette about your brain evaluation to help you to reflect on your thinking patterns.

Questions 1 and 2 are questions about excitement and boredom. Boredom is indicative of a need for mental stimulation. Learning is an active, energizing process. If your brain is working up to its potential, then most of what you do feels exciting because your brain is having a workout. You are exercising by engaging in a strenuous mental application. The excitement is similar to a runner's high. Your brain needs stimulation to open new channels for learning.

Question 3 addresses stimulation. Your brain thrives on new situations and new problems. There are challenges throughout this text to cope with stress and anxiety, manage your time more efficiently, develop better communication skills, find a meaningful career, develop multicultural skills, and develop many other life-skills. Stimulate your mind. Do something different. Attend a lecture outside of class, go shopping at a different store, go to a different section in the bookstore, listen to a different radio station, visit an art gallery or a museum, attend a concert, read a book unlike what you ordinarily read, and engage in conversation with a wider circle of people. Engage the right brain by paying attention to your immediate surroundings, listening to music, or experiencing some form of art. Remember to visualize and daydream. Engage the left brain by working a crossword puzzle or even creating one. If you want to create one, start with an easy one and then work your way up to more complex crossword puzzles. Begin by following these simple steps:

- Make a list of 10 words with different lengths.
- Make up a clue for each word in the form of a rhyme, quote, or location. The clue can rhyme with the word, be a missing word from a quote (song, poem, play, well-known phrase), or a place associated with the word. If a chosen word turns out to be too difficult to work with, choose a different word and make up a new clue.
- Pick out the word with the most letters in it and write it down the middle of a blank piece of paper (graph paper makes the task easier).
- Pick another word that has a letter in common and place it. If you run out of easy connections, put the word somewhere new on the paper and begin another cross. Now you have a crossword puzzle.

Question 4 is about concentration. Do you have trouble concentrating on what is before you? Reread Chapters 2 and 4 and read Chapter 13 to see if you can diagnose the specific nature of your problem (e.g., motivation, listening, or stress).

Questions 5, 6, and 7 concern confidence and fear. We all experience fear and know that fear can paralyze us. Mistakes are important because they force the brain to reconfigure the process that led to the mistake, so we have a greater chance of success the next time around. The reconfiguration is the learning process. Remember that everyone is concerned at one time or another about looking stupid.

Question 8 focuses on artistic sensibility. Everyone has artistic ability. Whenever you base your likes and dislikes on how things look, smell, feel, sound, and taste, you are displaying your artistic sensibility. Do you think you can't draw? Get a pencil and a sheet of paper that is larger than your hand. Trace the outline of your hand and then fill in the details. Try the same with your other hand, or try placing your hand in different positions. Buy some modeling clay and start making your favorite shapes, foods, and animals. You are engaging your right hemisphere, and you are expressing your artistic sensibilities. It is good exercise for the brain.

Question 9 concerns problem solving. Did you know that artists engage in problem solving just as much as engineers, mathematicians, and scientists? Problem solving is good exercise for the brain. While the left brain is busy analyzing the problem from a logical stance, the right brain is busy creating alternative solutions. Suppose you want to multiply 604 by 25. You can approach the problem by writing it out and actually multiplying 604 by 25 to arrive at an answer of 15,100, or you can bring in the right brain and create a different sequence from which to work the problem. You could say that 25 is the same as 20 or two 10s, plus 5. To multiply 10 times 604, just add a zero. Now you have 6,040. Doubling that gives you 12,080. Now you have 5 times 604. Five times 600 is 3,000 and 5 times 4 is 20. Add the three numbers together (12,080 + 3000 + 20) and you have 15,100.

Question 10 asks if you ever have trouble making up your mind. Maybe the emotional right brain says one thing and the cognitive left says something else. Maybe you are having difficulty choosing the right response on a multiple-choice test, or choosing a major, or ending a relationship. Being indecisive is not a bad thing: it just means that your right brain is talking to your left brain. Consider this exchange of information to be good energy flow between the two sides of your brain. Instead of diminishing activity in either side of your brain, create more dialogue between them to explore your feelings and thoughts at a deeper level. When therapists tell their clients to get in touch with their feelings and to trust their feelings, what they are really saying is that the logical left brain is not getting enough input from the emotion-decoding right side of the brain.

Question 11 asks about memory. Memory is important. What would you be without your memories? How would this loss affect your personality? Do you take good care of your memories, filing them away where they can be easily retrieved? You can find many suggestions on how to improve your memory in Chapter 5 of this textbook.

Question 12 asks if you play enough games. Playing games is a form of exercise for the brain and serves many purposes. You engage the right part of your brain when you trust hunches. You engage the left part of your brain when you use strategies, engage in social interactions, and make judgments about the rules of the game.

Question 13 reminds us that when we can visualize, we can see possibilities. Do you have a difficult time visualizing? Try visualizing some aspects of the following things: favorite holiday, best vacation, future dream home, and ideal career after college. Visualizing can be a way to try something out to see if it fits our needs, wants, or goals.

Question 14 asks about physical coordination—getting our bodies to do what our brains want them to do. To exercise your brain, you do not need to engage in complex physical skills like figure skating or playing the piano. Do something different. It could be as simple as using the other hand for a day. If you are right-handed, use the left hand for the day.

Question 15 concerns how you organize and plan. Organizing and planning are good exercises. You need not spend a great amount of time on them, but do enough so you work your brain. Use organization and planning as a powerful means to solve a problem.

Question 16 addresses how you plan and initiate learning activities that keep your mind stimulated. All of us have natural talents that have not been exercised. Go to the library and choose three books on a subject you love, and then read them from cover to cover. Are you still interested in the subject? If so, think of other activities that you can engage in that feed your interests and help you to develop some untapped mental ability.

Does your brain need more exercise? Do you have a natural talent that has gone undetected due to a lack of brain stimulation? Chances are that you have the potential to be a lot more competent than you may have previously imagined.

From Parlette, S. (1997). *The brain workout book*. New York, NY: M. Evans & Company. Reprinted by permission.

Multiple Intelligences

Howard Gardner (1993), a developmental psychologist, proposes that we possess not only a multitude of talents but also "multiple intelligences." His research emerged from an inquiry on the topic of human potential in which he participated as part of a team of researchers from the Harvard Graduate School of Education. According to Gardner, there are at least seven different forms of intelligence: body-kinesthetic intelligence, verbal-linguistic intelligence, visual-spatial intelligence, interpersonal intelligence, intrapersonal intelligence, musical intelligence, and logical-mathematical intelligence. We are all intelligent in numerous ways.

Body-kinesthetic intelligence relates to fine-motor and gross-motor skills. People who excel in this type of intelligence have superior eye-hand coordination, are skilled in figuring out how things work, and may excel in a sport or in dancing. Playing sports, exercising, doing yoga, dancing, and engaging in other types of physical training can improve your body-kinesthetic intelligence.

Verbal-linguistic intelligence is an ability exhibited by linguistic processing. Creative writers, poets, public speakers, and others who are sensitive to language and meaning excel in the ability to use words effectively. To build your intelligence within this domain, read, write, work crossword puzzles, enroll in communication and speech courses, and learn new vocabulary words.

Visual-spatial intelligence relates to the ability to form a mental model and then mentally manipulate the model and use it. People who have a talent for sculpting, graphic design, abstract art, and other skills associated with mental imagery are thought to have well-developed spatial intelligence. Now might be the time to enroll in courses on photography, drawing, pottery, or landscape architecture to improve your visual-spatial abilities.

Interpersonal intelligence is the ability to understand people. Religious leaders, counselors, journalists, teachers, and others who spend much of their time interacting with others often excel in this area of intelligence. Take advantage of opportunities to work, volunteer, and socialize with different people to strengthen your interpersonal intelligence.

Intrapersonal intelligence refers to the ability to know one's self. Self-knowledge is being aware of and able to reflect on personal motivations for behaving, thinking, and feeling. Individual or group counseling, journaling, and other activities focused on self-exploration can improve your intrapersonal intelligence.

Musical intelligence is the ability to sing or play music well, but it also includes the ability to recognize rhythms and enjoy music and performances. To strengthen musical intelligence, enroll in a music appreciation course, learn how to play a musical instrument, take voice lessons, or take advantage of all the wonderful opportunities on campus and in your community to attend musical performances.

Logical-mathematical intelligence relates to the ability to think conceptually, solve problems, and calculate numbers. Is it easy for you to understand philosophy, math, or science courses? Do you enjoy solving problems? If so, you may excel in logical-mathematical intelligence. Enroll in courses in mathematics, logic, and critical thinking to strengthen your logical-mathematical intelligence.

Each person draws from a different combination of these seven intelligences, just as we use a combination of our senses in the learning process.

Courtesy of MATT GINTER

Example of Spatial Intelligence

Perceptual Learning Modalities

Modalities are preferred senses that one uses to gather information from the environment. Michael Galbraith and Waynne James identified seven specific perceptual modalities: print, visual, auditory, interactive, kinesthetic, haptic, and olfactory. These learning modalities are based on the five senses: seeing, hearing, touching, smelling, and tasting. Modalities that you use more effectively than others in learning are your strengths. The more modalities you use to learn, the greater your recall will likely be. For example, if you read something and then write it down or tell someone about it, you will have a better chance of recalling the information when you need it. Learn to take advantage of strong modalities and strengthen the weaker ones. You will be taking in information all around you. Complete the Learning Style Skill Assessment (Exercise 2). This inventory will help you discover your primary perceptual learning modalities.

What are your three primary learning modalities?

1. _____

2. _____

3. _____

Below are the descriptions of the seven perceptual learning modalities.

Print. If you retain information easily when reading, and when studying you tend to focus well on what you have read, then the print modality is a learning strength for you. Reading and writing are the primary ways that you process information. Print learners prefer written material and learn best when reading on their own. Underlining key terms and annotations written in your own words as well as summaries are good study strategies for a print learner.

Visual. When taking a test, do you ever try to remember the information from the upper right corner of your notes or from the middle of the page, or next to that fantastic doodle down the side of your notes? Chances are you are trying to locate the information visually and spatially, drawing on the visual-spatial memory center located in the right part of the brain. Visual learners learn best through observation. In conversations, a visual learner will often say, "I see," or "Picture that." For a visual learner, information is best processed when reduced and displayed in visual formats such as pictures, slides, diagrams, graphs, charts, and symbols. Color is also helpful to visual learners. When given directions, visual learners prefer that they be written down rather than spoken. Maps are even better.

Interactive. Do you like study groups? When you were younger, did you get a family member or friend to review information for a test by quizzing you? Do you try to get a discussion going in class if possible? People who learn best through using verbalizations, like discussions and group projects, and learn through teaching others, are said to utilize an interactive learning modality. If you are an interactive learner and you have no one to study with, you can still study interactively by making a question-and-answer study guide and then recording yourself reading the questions and answers. To start studying you only have to play the recording, listen to the first question, and then pause the recording so you can answer. You will have the opportunity to answer each question and then check your answer by stopping and restarting the recording.

Auditory. When taking a test or rewriting notes, do you hear your professor's voice in your head? Does listening to audiotaped summaries of your notes and explanations of specific concepts help you learn information? Auditory learners learn best from listening to lectures, reading aloud, and other auditory stimulation.

Haptic. In biology classes, if the teacher was using a model of the human skeletal structure to lecture, did you find yourself wanting to touch the model? Haptic learners learn best by doing; they prefer a hands-on approach to learning. They can benefit from building models where they manipulate objects or from using sticky notes, poster board, and magic markers. They will often take a trial-and-error approach to learning, using their hands to touch or feel. Note cards and computers can be great study aids. Haptic learners like concrete examples and often get more out of lab sessions than in-class instruction.

Kinesthetic. What are you doing when you study? Is your leg kicking back and forth? Are you moving about the room? Are you tapping or chewing on a pencil? Kinesthetic learners process information best through movement. While studying, they spend time recopying notes, writing lists, and outlining chapters. Note cards are helpful. They might separate the cards into piles, differentiating one pile from the other by how well they know the information. When writing a paper, they might write all ideas on note cards and then rearrange them as they synthesize and organize information to structure the paper. The next time you observe someone clicking his or her pencil or tapping it on the desk while thinking, realize that the person is not necessarily trying to drive you crazy. He or she may just be a kinesthetic learner using movement to retrieve information from long-term memory.

Olfactory. Did you know that olfactory learners just need to sniff their textbooks to prepare for an upcoming final? Just kidding. Some people, though, do have a strong sense of odor discrimination, so odors can affect their ability to concentrate and process information. We all associate some memories with particular smells and tastes. Students majoring in chemistry, animal science, and medicine often use their sense of smell to differentiate information. Many people use aromatherapy to relax. Could you study better in a room where scented candles were burning? Is it possible for you to study in an area that smells bad?

As a learner, you need to develop a repertoire of good study skills based on your own unique learning patterns and also learn to adapt your learning preference to the instructional style of the professor. Print and auditory learners have the best advantage in a university setting where you read, write, listen to lectures, and take notes. Interactive learners might excel in languages, whereas kinesthetic learners might do well in dance and physical education. Perceptual preferences affect success in certain academic areas. A visual learner who does not include charts, graphs, and other visual interpretations of information while learning may not learn to his or her full potential. Imagine you are a visual learner and someone gives you detailed directions to a location verbally. Will you remember the information if you cannot write it down or draw a map? The same is true for a kinesthetic or haptic learner who decides not to use note cards or similar means to study for class.

Personality

Each person is unique. Each person thinks differently, acts differently, has various wants and needs, finds different sources of pleasure and frustration, and conceptualizes and understands the world from a different perspective. The psychotherapist Carl Jung said that beneath the surface of all of these differences are preferences about ways of interacting with people, perceiving information in the surrounding environment, making decisions, and acting on decisions that give rise to various personality types. These different personality types influence the way you learn. Jung's theory about personality types is the basis for a personality assessment developed by Isabel Myers and Katharine Briggs named the Myers-Briggs Type Indicator (MBTI) (Myers, 1995).

The MBTI identifies 16 personality types based on individual preferences. Four dimensions differentiate personality types: introversion–extroversion, intuition–sensation, thinking–feeling, and judging–perceiving. Complete the personality assessment in Exercise 3 at the end of the chapter to discover your type. What is your type? _____ Now read through the following descriptions of the four dimensions to learn more about the influence of personality and learning.

Introversion-Extroversion

When solving a problem, do you prefer to talk with others or think it through alone? Do you tend to be more aware of what is going on around you or more aware of what you are thinking and feeling? The dimensions of introversion and extroversion are related to how people energize themselves in different situations, including learning.

Introversion (I). Introverts are reflective learners, scanning inwardly for stimulation. They become energized as they reflect and think about ideas. In an academic setting, introverts prefer working alone because they can comprehend better if they take the time to organize and think about the information before them. Introverts have a tendency not to speak up in class, as all their energy is spent on thinking and reflecting about ideas. Introverts plan out thoughts and words before writing, stop frequently to think as they write, prefer quiet places to study, and dislike interruptions. They spend so much time thinking and reflecting that they may start daydreaming about how things might be, and opportunities sometimes pass them by.

Extroversion (E). Extroverts are active learners who focus their attention outwardly for stimulation. They learn new information best when they can apply it to the external world. Extroverts are energized by people and thus prefer interacting with others while learning. They tend to participate in class, enjoying group projects, discussions, and study groups (similar to the interactive learners). Extroverts tend to jump into things enthusiastically, including writing assignments, and learn best in active learning situations that are filled with movement and variety. Because of this, they may get frustrated with long tasks that require a lot of reading and reflection.

Intuition-Sensation

Do you consider yourself to be more of a practical person or an innovative person? Is it easier for you to learn facts or concepts? This dimension tells you about how you perceive information in your environment.

Intuition (N). Intuition refers to use of the "sixth sense," or unconscious way of knowing the world. Intuitive people learn best when instruction is open-ended with a focus on theory before application. Intuitive learning can be characterized as a creative, right-brain approach to learning. Intuitive learners often work in bursts of energy that yield quick flashes of insight. They want and need to see how everything works together; they look at the big picture. They tend to engage in divergent thinking as opposed to convergent thinking. Creative approaches to writing are preferred, and writing tends to be full of generalities (and facts might not be too accurate!). On multiple-choice tests, intuitive learners follow their hunches but can make errors involving facts (too many details can bore them). If you happen to be an intuitive learner, it is a good idea to read each question twice to make sure you read it correctly. Intuitive learners may be negligent about details at times, but they are generally good at drawing inferences when reading. They prefer to read something that gives them ideas to daydream about.

Sensation (S). Sensing refers to the process of acquiring information through your five senses (sight, sound, smell, touch, and taste). Sensing people learn best when there is an orderly sequencing of material that moves slowly from concrete to abstract. Sensing people prefer to process concrete, factual information and can become impatient with theories or examples that are not oriented to the present. In an academic setting, they tend to work steadily and focus on details and facts. If not aware of this tendency when reading and taking notes, they can end up neglecting important concepts and miss the broader picture. When completing a writing assignment, sensing people prefer explicit, detailed directions. They prefer to read something that teaches new facts or tells how to do something. Sensing people are good at memorizing facts, and on multiple-choice tests they search for clues that relate to practical knowledge and personal experience. Because they rarely trust their hunches, they generally lose points by changing answers.

Thinking-Feeling

When you make a decision, do you tend to be more impersonal and objective or personal and subjective? We all use our cognitions (thoughts) and emotions (feelings) when making decisions, but we generally use one more than the other.

Thinking (T). Thinking people tend to discover and gather facts first and then make decisions based on logic. They enjoy problem solving, analyzing situations, weighing the pros and cons, and developing models for deeper understanding. In writing assignments, they are task-oriented, organizing thoughts and focusing on content. When reading, they tend to engage in critical thinking and can stay engaged in reading even if the information does not personally engage them.

Feeling (F). Feeling people tend to make decisions based on feelings, values, and empathy. Feeling types are motivated by personal encouragement, and in making decisions, they consider the effect of the impact of the decision on others. In writing they tend to rely on personal experience and focus on the message and how it will affect the reader. In reading, they prefer material that is personally engaging; otherwise, there is a chance they will become bored and quit reading.

Perceiving-Judging

Once decisions have been made, based on thoughts and feelings, how do you act on them? Do you seek closure and act quickly, or do you prefer to keep your options open and maybe even procrastinate?

Perceiving (P). Perceivers tend to be adaptable and spontaneous, preferring open, spontaneous learning situations. They like gathering additional information before acting on a decision, and because of their flexible, tentative nature, they are good at seeing multiple perspectives. Perceiving types tend to start many tasks at once and tend not to be good with deadlines. They prefer the process more than the completion of the task, can easily get distracted, and often need help in organizing. On multiple-choice tests, each answer can be a stimulus for more thought (gathering more information), so it is often difficult for the perceiver to choose the correct answer. When writing, perceivers tend to choose expansive topics that sometimes do not have a clear focus.

Judging (J). The judging type wants to get things settled and wrapped up. Judging types are goal-oriented and generally set manageable goals. Their first drafts tend to be short and underdeveloped. Judging types may be too quick to interpret various sections of a textbook they are reading. They tend to gauge their learning by how many pages they have read or how much time they have spent on it. They generally enjoy planning and organizing and prefer to work on one task at a time. Judging types prefer well-defined goals and get frustrated with a lot of ambiguity.

Personality clearly affects learning patterns. In Exercise 3, the score for each personality dimension suggests the extent to which that dimension affects your learning style. In the process of discovering your learning style, try to see if it matches your professor's teaching style. If your professor goes about lecturing in a roundabout way, using metaphors and analogies, trying to get you to see the big picture through theories and concepts, an intuitive teaching style is being used. If you are a sensing student who wants facts presented in an orderly, sequential manner beginning with concrete information, you may have to adapt your learning style to avoid feeling frustrated and discouraged. If your teacher presents a lot of facts and detailed information in a sequential, organized lecture format, a sensing teaching style is being used. If you are an intuitive learner who needs examples and theories first, you will need to adapt your learning style so as not to become bored and start daydreaming in class. Students who are sensing and judging (SJ) have a strong need for order and thus need a lot of structure in learning. Students who are intuitive and perceiving (NP) need more creative and autonomous learning situations. In a perfect world, teachers' teaching styles and students' learning styles would match, but as we all know, this is not a perfect world. The Swiss developmental psychologist Piaget wrote much about the power of adaptation. *Adaptation* is making adjustments to fit a new situation. We do it all the time as we assimilate new information into preexisting learning patterns. The more flexible your learning style, the greater your capacity to learn

Your Own Personal Learning Style

Learning styles are very individual. Your task is to take responsibility for your own learning and discover different ways of studying that work for you so you can take advantage of your brain's incredible capacity for learning. Your own personal learning style is based on brain dominance, perceptual learning modalities, personality, and also environmental factors.

Your learning environment also affects your ability to think and learn. What environment is most conducive to learning for you? Do you need a quiet place like an upper floor of the library where little noise is tolerated? Do you prefer a place where you know there will be people and lots of action? Did you know that some people find that they can concentrate best when music is playing softly in the background? The steady rhythms of baroque music from the 16th through 18th centuries (e.g., Mozart, Handel, Corelli, Pachelbel, and Vivaldi) seem to work best. This music tends to keep the body relaxed while the mind remains alert, ready to process new information (except for music majors who may be tempted to analyze the music!). At what time of the day are you most alert? What energizes you and what zaps you of your energy when studying?

Reflecting on your answers to these questions as well as becoming aware of all variables that affect your own unique learning patterns can enable you to become a more efficient, effective learner. Think and study in ways that match your learning style. Maximize your learning potential.

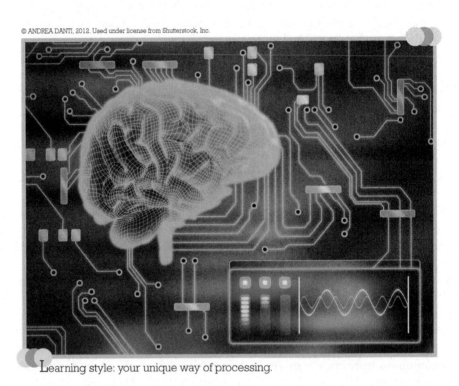

Learning style: your unique way of processing.

Sources

Buzan, T. (1976). *Use both sides of your brain*. New York, NY: E. P. Dutton.

Gardner, H. (1993). *Multiple intelligences: The theory in practice*. New York, NY: Basic Books.

Hampton-Turner, C. (1981). *Maps of the mind*. New York, NY: Collier Books.

James, W. B., & Galbraith, M. W. (1985). Perceptual learning styles: Implications and techniques for the practitioner. *Lifelong Learning, 8*, 20–23.

Keirsey, D., & Bates, M. (1984). *Please understand me*. Del Mar, CA: Prometheus.

Myers, I. (1995). *Gifts differing*. Palo Alto, CA: Davies-Black.

Parlette, S. (1997). *The brain workout book*. New York, NY: M. Evans and Company.

Sacks, O. (1970). *The man who mistook his wife for a hat and other clinical tales*. New York, NY: Harper Perennial.

Sperry, R. W. (1974). Lateral specialization in the surgically separated hemispheres. In F. O. Schmitt & R. G. Worden (Eds.), *The neurosciences third study programs* (pp. 5–19). Cambridge, MA: MIT Press.

Taylor, J. B. (2009). *My stroke of insight*. New York, NY: Penguin Books.

Wonder, J., & Donovan, P. (1984). *Whole-brain thinking*. New York, NY: William Morrow.

Chapter 6

Exercise 3: Discovering Your Personality Type

Put a check next to any statements that describe you.

EXTROVERT

_____ Enjoys interacting with others while learning

_____ Tends to jump into things enthusiastically

_____ Uses a trial-and-error approach to problem solving

_____ Enjoys group discussions and group projects

_____ Prefers active learning situations full of movement and variety

INTROVERT

_____ Prefers to work alone

_____ Likes to spend time thinking and reflecting before acting

_____ Thinks best in relative solitude

_____ Content working alone on lengthy projects

_____ Prefers to work with ideas

INTUITION

_____ Works in bursts of energy followed by not-so-productive periods

_____ Enjoys learning a new approach more than using it

_____ Tends to be good at solving novel problems

_____ Often impatient with routine procedures

_____ Prefers to focus on concepts and may neglect the details

_____ Wants to see the big picture

SENSATION

_____ Works steadily

_____ Learns best when starting with the concrete and moving to the abstract

_____ Prefers explicit, detailed directions

_____ Patient with routine procedures

_____ Tends to focus on facts and may miss overall concepts

_____ Values accuracy and precision

THINKING

_____ Tends to be logical and analytical

_____ Prefers to discover and gather facts before making decisions

_____ Weighs pros and cons of a situation

_____ Interested in what is just

FEELING

_____ Tends to make decisions based on feelings and values

_____ Considers others' feelings before making a decision

_____ Motivated by personal encouragement

_____ Interested in reconciliation

PERCEIVING

_____ Adapts easily to changes

_____ May tend to procrastinate

_____ Prefers open, spontaneous learning situations

_____ Tends to see all sides of an issue

JUDGING

_____ May not adapt easily to change

_____ Prefers to make decisions quickly

_____ Prefers to follow a path

_____ Remains on task

Evaluation

Answer the following questions by circling the appropriate letter.

Did you have more checks next to statements about extroverts (E) or introverts (I)?	E	I
Did you have more checks next to statements about sensation (S) or intuition (N)?	S	N
Did you have more checks next to statements about thinking (T) or feeling (F)?	T	F
Did you have more checks next to statements about perceiving (P) or judging (J)?	P	J

What is your personality type (write four letters)? ____   ____   ____   ____

Chapter 6

Exercise 4: Personal Learning Style

1. Do you think you are more right-brained or left-brained? Why?

2. Identify a specific problem (academic, personal, vocational). How would you solve this problem using a whole-brain approach?

3. What is your primary (strongest) and secondary (next strongest) perceptual learning modality?

    _____   _____

    What learning strategies can you use to capitalize on both modalities?

4. What is your personality type? ____ ____ ____ ____ (Refer to Exercise 3).

    How does your personality type relate to your perceptual learning modalities and your brain dominance?

5. Describe your perfect study environment.

6. Knowing how you process information can help you to select appropriate learning strategies congruent with your overall unique learning style. What changes do you need to make right now to become a more efficient and effective learner? (Since all students can improve upon the way they learn, "None needed" or some similar response is not an acceptable answer to this question.)

Winning Test Performance
Fine-Tuning Your Test-Taking Skills

7

Think about how much time you will spend in college preparing for and taking tests. Too much time? If you have been in college for a while, then you already know that a significant amount of your time revolves around tests—studying for them, taking them, or reviewing a past test to improve your performance. Developing effective test-taking skills is essential for achieving academic success in college. But why so many tests? Tests are valuable assessments that can offer feedback on how well you know the material presented in the course. Honestly, would you attend all of the class meetings and pay as much attention to lectures, read as attentively, or study as diligently if you were not going to be tested on the material? While you might not be one of them, without tests, many students would miss a significant number of class meetings and pay less attention when they were present. Taking required tests motivates some students to read and study more than they would on their own. You may be thinking, "Yes, but isn't there an easier way?" The answer is yes, and this chapter is devoted to enhancing test-taking skills to make the process of taking a test more efficient and effective.

How do you rate your test-taking skills? Complete Exercise 1 ("Test-Taking Quotient") at the end of this chapter to help you assess your test-taking skills. A high score of 100–120 indicates that you probably do well on tests most of the time, meaning you can still benefit from developing additional test-taking skills.

In this chapter, effective methods for managing test preparation, test-taking, test evaluation, and performance anxiety will be reviewed. There are specific steps you can take before, during, and after a test to maximize your performance.

Preparation before the Test

Preparation for a test begins the first day your class meets. Just as your weekly calendar is your road map for the week, your syllabus is a map for your course. Notice test dates and then work backward from test dates to schedule enough time for reading and studying, review sessions, meetings with professors, and perhaps tutoring. Schedule adequate time for test preparation. Preparation involves attending class, asking questions, paying attention, taking good notes, and engaging in effective learning strategies.

General Preparation Tips

- **Be organized and systematic about your studying.** Gather all your notes and handouts for each class and organize them in separate notebooks using a system that works for you. How do you know what works and what does not? Experiment and discover effective and efficient ways of studying. You want your notes to be manageable.
- **Manage your time.** Try not to get behind in your assignments. Review small sections of information at a time, conducting short reviews of the information on a daily and weekly basis. Ask yourself if you allow adequate time for preparation. If you have a problem with procrastinating, seek academic support from a counselor or other knowledgeable people who can help you to discover ways to overcome procrastination. Procrastination can make you feel trapped and unmotivated.
- **Participate in a study group or a review session.** Anticipate test questions. Ask yourself if you understand the most important topics covered so far in the course. Can you write a thorough summary of each topic or explain the topic to others? Have study partners create lists of possible test questions and then practice answering them.
- **Construct study guides for definitions, formulas, names, dates, and theories.** Think about what you may be asked to identify or define. Master the terminology used in the course. Be sure that you understand concepts. Some students find it helpful to research supplemental information over the Internet to develop a wider perspective and a deeper understanding of the material covered.
- **When preparing for a math test, keep in mind that math skills are based on practice and even more patience.** Schedule adequate time for reviewing. More difficult material will need to be reviewed more often.

Seek Information about the Test

Do you experience difficulty deciding exactly what to study for in preparation for the test? Gather as much information as you can about the test. Whether you are in a study group or not, talk to friends and acquaintances who have had the same professor and course. What do they remember about the length and format of the tests? Has your professor made available any old tests to study from? If so, where can you find copies?

Seek information about the upcoming test. Find out if a majority of the test questions will come from the lectures or assigned readings; what the format of the test will be; what percentage of the total grade the test represents; where, when, and at what time the test is to be given; and how much time will be given to complete the test. Do you know the types of questions that will be on the test or if there are any study guides available from the publisher of your text? You want to get as clear and accurate a picture of the upcoming test as possible. It may even be helpful to go by the professor's office if you still have some questions about the test.

Cramming

Be sure to get a good night's sleep the night before a test. The last 30 minutes before bedtime is a time to unwind, relax, and think positive thoughts about the upcoming test. If you must review, then review up to 30 minutes before you go to sleep. Review but do not cram the night before a test.

If you wanted to learn how to play tennis better, staying up all night to practice your tennis skills would not do much to enhance your performance on the court the next day. You would need to practice regularly over a long period of time to significantly improve your skills in tennis. Knowledge based on information presented through a course also takes a long time to develop. It takes time to analyze, synthesize, and evaluate information. If you have a test coming up and have not scheduled adequate time for organizing and reviewing information, you may find yourself cramming for the test. Instead of analyzing, synthesizing, and evaluating information, you will be reduced to memorizing information. Facts and concepts will simply be stuffed into your mind without making meaningful associations to previously learned information. Such information cannot be stored in long-term memory in the kind of organized, systematic way conducive to recall. Cramming is analogous to opening up a file drawer and throwing in a bunch of papers loaded with different kinds of information. If there is no organized file system, think of how difficult it would be to retrieve the information later.

Learning is about being able to take information and arrange it in a pattern that makes sense. When you cram unanalyzed, unsynthesized, and unevaluated information into your mind, the information cannot be utilized effectively as a foundation for future learning. This tends to make the process of learning slower and more difficult. Plan ahead to avoid cramming!

Taking the Test

You have prepared well for the test. You have eaten light, nutritious foods, being careful to avoid excessive sugar, caffeine, or other foods that can make your stomach queasy. Arriving on time for the test, you found a good test-taking place where you can sit and be less distracted. Your clothes feel comfortable, and you have all the necessary supplies needed to take the test (e.g., #2 pencils with erasers, black ink pens, an exam book, and calculator). You are wearing a watch to help pace yourself. (You know not to count on a clock being in the testing room, or keeping correct time if there is one.)

You feel relaxed yet alert as you prepare to begin the test before you. What do you do first? Write down your name, required identification number, and any other necessary information. Do not jump into the test. Before you respond to any question, survey the entire test. Notice the types of questions asked and various point values assigned. Devise a plan. How much time will you spend on each section? Pay attention to where most of the points are. You do not want to spend a lot of time on a bonus question worth ten points when you have yet to complete an essay question worth 40 points. Some students find it helpful to jot down memory cues such as formulas, dates, important concepts, and other information before they start answering test questions.

When you are ready to begin answering questions, it is a good idea to read directions twice. You will not necessarily begin with the first question. There is no rule stating that you must answer the questions in the order they are presented. Start answering the ones that are easiest for you, so you can feel confident. When you come to a question that you do not know or are unsure of, skip it and come back to it later. If possible, make a mark in the margin next to the skipped question so you can easily return to it later. As you work through the test, other information might jog your memory, enabling you to remember additional information that can help you to successfully answer the skipped question. Select the best answer; there may be more than one correct answer. When you are trying to answer test questions that you are not sure about, choose the answer that was your first guess. Use common prefixes, suffixes, and root words to help clarify meaning.

Try to pace yourself so you have some time at the end of the test to check over your answers. Look for any omissions and make corrections. Check over your answers to make sure they make sense. Be sure that you carried out any math problems through to the last step and check your signs, decimal placement, and numbers. Below are some specific test-taking strategies that can help.

Tips for Objective Tests

Objective tests assess your ability to recall and to compare and contrast information. Read all questions and answers carefully. Be careful not to overinterpret information and create meaning that is not there. Be cautious when changing answers, and double-check to make certain that your answers make good sense. There are different types of objective questions. Listed below are some tips for answering each type.

Multiple-Choice Questions. Read the question and then anticipate the answer before you examine all the choices. Always eliminate obviously wrong answers and avoid hasty conclusions. You can generally avoid answers that use absolutes (*always, never, absolutely*), but not always. Reduce the number of choices by eliminating any that are grammatically incorrect. If you see an answer with a lot of terms, beware! The professor may have put the terms there to confuse you. Do there seem to be two good answers? Chances are that one of them is correct. Go back and read the question again carefully, rephrasing the question in your own words. If you still cannot decide between two choices, then it is generally best to go with your original guess. You have no clue what the answer is? Select the answer that sounds familiar.

Be careful about changing answers on multiple-choice tests. Intuitive (N) types tend to trust their hunches but may not have read the question or answers carefully, perhaps missing some important information. Sensing (S) types pay attention to details but tend not to trust their hunches. They often express regret for having changed their original answers. Underline key words and remember, if you are clueless as to the correct answer, search for the answer in other test questions. Some last words of advice: Pay close attention to the choice with the longest answer (it just might be the right one), watch for those tricky double negatives, and if there is no penalty for guessing, then by all means guess!

True/False Questions. Answer all questions. Always keep in mind that if a statement is not completely true, that means it is false. You have a 50-50 chance of answering the question correctly. Did you know that there are usually more true questions than false ones? Read carefully, paying attention to details (i.e., qualifiers such as *never* and *always*). It is not unusual for students to miss important words that completely change the meaning of a question. Underline negative words and prefixes (*not, cannot, dis-, un-, non-*). Double negatives can be especially confusing.

Matching Questions. Students tend to do well on matching items. You are usually asked to recall definitions, terminology, dates, names, and other identifying information. Begin by matching the ones you know. Be careful about crossing out your options as you work through the columns. Can you use answers more than once?

Fill-in-the-Blank Questions. If you know ahead of time that you are going to be asked on the test to complete fill-in-the-blank questions, prepare for them by making study guides in this format. Look for embedded clues. Does the length of the line present a clue? In filling in the blank, have you made a grammatical error? Pay attention to whether your professor has chosen to use a singular or plural verb and whether there is an *a* or *an* before the blank. Fill in all blanks. Guess if you must.

Short-Answer Questions. Read, think about, and restate the question to make sure you know what is being asked; then write. Your answer will need to be complete and succinct.

Math Tests. Consider what is being asked, and what it is that you are being required to figure out. Make sure that you understand the question and your answer makes sense. Break down complex problems into simpler ones. See if you can visualize the problem, using diagrams or other visual aids. Human error accounts for many mistakes in solving mathematical problems. Check over your work several times for omissions and mistakes before turning in the test.

Tips for Essay Tests

You may be wondering why your professor would give the class an essay test when an objective test would be much easier to grade. Essay tests, as assessments, can give both your professor and you a more accurate view of what you know. An essay exam requires more than recognition of the course material: it requires recall, synthesis, and analysis of the information.

Begin an essay question or test the same way you begin an objective test. Look over the entire test to note the types of essay questions and the value for each. Read the questions and begin with the one that is easiest for you. Starting with the more difficult ones may erode your confidence and frustrate you. Before you begin writing, make certain that you understand the question completely. Here are some other helpful tips to complete an essay test successfully.

- Manage your time. How much time can you devote to answering each question? Be aware of time constraints, but avoid compulsively checking the time.

- Write clearly and neatly, making sure that everything you write is grammatically correct. Write legibly in ink, not pencil, which is difficult to read. Generally, the more legible and organized the answer, the higher the grade. First impressions do count.

- Leave blank lines between sentences. If you need to change an answer, draw a line through the statement and write above it.

- Before you begin to write, formulate a clear understanding of the question and the answer. Organize and outline your thoughts. Some students find it helpful to do a "memory dump." Quickly recall and jot down key facts, concepts, names, and perhaps some dates that are associated with the question you are answering. Then refer to these notes as you construct your essay.

- When constructing your answer, move from general statements to more specific statements. State your thesis in your opening sentence. Make your point and avoid wandering. Your answer should be logical and thorough. Generalizations must be supported by facts. Remember to include an introduction and a summary.

- If you begin to run out of time, jot down the rest of your outline, including the major points you intended to write about. (After all, grading an essay test is a subjective experience. Maybe the professor will take pity on you and give partial credit.)

- Identify and underline key words in the instructions and in the questions. Are you being asked to analyze? To compare and contrast? To explain? There is a difference.

Examine the different meanings of these commonly used direction words found in essay questions.

analyze: to separate into parts and examine closely and thoroughly

argue: to give reasons

compare: to explain similarities and differences

contrast: to indicate differences

criticize: to analyze, synthesize, and judge

define or identify: to present information that distinguishes it in some way and offers a clear meaning

discuss: to examine thoroughly and offer a conclusion based on facts

enumerate: to provide a list

evaluate: to give a logical, sequential summary of negatives and positives

explain: to interpret and clarify

illustrate: to give specific details and examples

justify: to defend by giving reasons for your position

paraphrase: to restate in your own words

prove: to show evidence to support a position

state: to provide the main points in a concise manner

summarize: to give the main ideas

trace: to provide and explain a series of events or steps

Evaluation of the Test

You have read some tips on how to prepare for and take a test. What about when the test is over? Is there anything you can do to improve future test performances? Yes, but first relax and then reward yourself for all the hard work you put into preparing for the test. When your test is returned, assess your performance. Evaluate whether or not you adequately prepared for the test. If you were not as successful as you had hoped, was it due to not knowing the material well enough or not having sufficient test-taking skills, or could it be that anxiety interfered with your test performance? People who are successful in life make mistakes like everyone else, but they take the time to learn from their mistakes. Complete a thorough evaluation of your preparation and performance and learn from your mistakes. At the end of this chapter is an objective exam analysis worksheet (Exercise 2) that you may want to use to analyze your next performance on an objective test. Study the example of a completed analysis in Figure 7.1 before you continue reading the text.

Reviewing Jane Doe's analysis worksheet, you should notice in the far-left column that Jane missed 19 questions on her exam. After analyzing each of her mistakes, Jane realized that 61 percent of them were due to poor exam skills and 39 percent were due to poor retention or lack of knowledge. Jane felt that her diet affected her ability to retain the information needed to answer question 1. Although she also selected poor retention as a reason for missing question 2, she felt that her ability to retain the information needed was related to the effect of a medication she had taken the night before the test.

The night before the test, Jane's sinuses were hurting, so she took an over-the-counter allergy medication that made her feel drowsy. She ended up sleeping later than she had planned because she still felt drowsy from the medication. When Jane woke up she was running late, so she ate a chocolate bar and drank a diet cola instead of having a light nutritious breakfast. Jane felt that both the medication and the breakfast affected her ability to concentrate while taking her test.

Continuing with her analysis, notice that when she analyzed question 4, she selected "failure to consider options carefully" as a reason for missing the question. In the far-right column, she stated that the reason she failed to consider her options carefully was not because she did not know the answer, but because she did not think first ("T.F.") before choosing her answer. She had selected a good answer but not the best answer available among the choices. Jane felt that she should have taken more time to think before selecting an answer. Having reviewed Jane's analysis of her test performance, what tips could you suggest to improve her performance on her next objective test?

Student: Jane Doe   Course: Biology 3300   Exam: #2 Grade: B–   Date: Oct. 30

Test item missed	Lack of Knowledge					English Skills				Exam Panic				Exam Skills						Other		Analysis Results Comments and Other Information
	Reading textbook	Inadequate notes	Application of knowledge	Poor retention	Other	Reading comprehension	Reading speed	Vocabulary	Other	Decreased concentration	Mental block	Forgot to use exam techniques	Other	Did not focus on question asked	Failed to consider options carefully	Poor use of time	Changed answer	Careless/clerical error	Other	Math	Other	A. 61% missed due to exam skills / B. 39% missed due to poor retention/lack of knowledge
1				X																		Diet
2				X																		Medication
4															X							Need to T.F.? (knew answer)
6																			X			Need to ask for clarification
12																			X			Did not read carefully
13				X																		
14														X								Did not note key word
16														X								Need to formulate own answer
19																X						Need to T.F.?
24														X								Failed to note key word
28															X							Need to T.F.?
30															X							Review Aphasia—pathophysiology
31				X																		Need to T.F.? ask for clarification
33				½												½						Review Parkinsonism
35				X																		Need to T.F.?
40															X							Practice "except" questions
41																			X			Medication
60				X																		Medication
85				X																		Medication
Items				7½										3	4½	1			3			
%				39										16	24	5			16			
% Totals	39%					0%				0%				61%						0%		

Figure **7.1** Sample Objective Exam Analysis Worksheet

Students can also evaluate their performance on essay tests. Ask yourself the following questions: Did I adequately prepare for the test? Did I formulate a clear understanding of the question and organize my thoughts before writing out my answers? Was I able to concentrate? Review the tips on how to take an essay test and then accurately assess your performance. What can you do to improve your performance on your next essay test? You may find it helpful to make an appointment to meet with your professor to obtain feedback on your last test performance. If your writing skills are not well developed, find out where on-campus tutoring is available to help you sharpen your writing skills.

Some students report that they prepare well for tests and know effective test-taking strategies to apply while taking a test, yet they still perform poorly on tests. Why? The problem may be performance anxiety.

Performance Anxiety

Anxiety is a pervasive sense of apprehension about something awful happening and the feeling that when that awful thing happens, there will be no way to cope with it. It is normal to feel anxious before any type of performance, and certainly a test is something that many students approach as a type of performance. In fact, feelings of nervousness can often contribute to feeling alert, energized, and eager to perform. But as we all know, anxiety can also make us feel fearful, overwhelmed, and filled with a sense of dread. The negative feelings associated with the experience of anxiety can interfere with optimal performance of any kind (e.g., making a speech, writing a paper, acting on stage, singing in a choral group, or taking a test). Millions of people suffer from some type of performance anxiety. The rest of this chapter will focus on physical, emotional, cognitive, and behavioral symptoms associated with performance anxiety and on how to effectively manage test anxiety.

How to Recognize Performance Anxiety

Performance anxiety can be experienced before, during, and after a performance. It is multifaceted in that it is experienced differently by many people. Stress is the pressure to cope, adapt, and adjust to new situations. It is a normal reaction to a novel situation. Your body is constantly preparing for new situations and challenges. If your body experiences too much stress, you may feel overwhelmed. If your body feels too little stress, then you may not have enough motivation to complete the task before you. Furthermore, if you perceive a situation as dangerous, your body is going to react as if that situation is dangerous, whether it is in reality or not.

If a person stands up before a group of people to make a speech and perceives that situation as dangerous, then without some sort of intervention, that person is going to feel threatened. The person may start shaking, feel sick to his or her stomach, be embarrassed, or even panic. If a student perceives a testing situation as dangerous, that student may experience the same dreadful feelings. Your thoughts about a situation influence your feelings and behavior. Fear can be a rational feeling, helping us to avoid a potentially dangerous situation, but fear can also be an irrational feeling that is debilitating.

Although the rest of this chapter focuses on how to recognize and manage one specific type of performance anxiety (test anxiety), strategies for dealing with test anxiety can be adapted to manage other forms of performance anxiety.

Test Anxiety

Before we take a close look at the symptoms and signs associated with test anxiety, complete the following assessment by checking the statements you tend to agree with.

Do you ever

_____ wish that tests did not bother you as much as they do?

_____ go blank during a test and not remember what you just studied?

_____ think that the more you study, the less you know?

_____ experience difficulty falling asleep the night before a test?

_____ find yourself feeling tense before, during, or after a test?

_____ worry about tests days or weeks in advance?

_____ find it difficult to stay focused while taking a test?

_____ feel your heart beating fast or experience difficulty breathing during a test?

_____ feel overly critical of your test performance?

_____ feel like running away from a testing situation?

If you put a check by many of these questions, you may have test anxiety. Students talk about feeling anxious about upcoming tests, being unable to sleep, worrying for days about tests, and feeling pressure. Test anxiety can be debilitating. Learn to recognize the signs and symptoms early on to prevent anxious feelings from snowballing into the feeling of being utterly overwhelmed. Listed below are some specific ways that anxiety manifests itself physically, cognitively, and behaviorally.

Physical symptoms can include an accelerated heartbeat, difficulty breathing, profuse sweating, nausea, dry mouth, loss of appetite, insomnia, stomachache, headache, muscle tension, cold hands and feet, shaky hands, and an overall feeling of nervousness.

Cognitive symptoms include all the irrational, exaggerated, self-defeating thoughts and worries experienced in conjunction with test-taking. You might experience racing thoughts or "go blank." We know that thoughts influence behavior. Be aware of your thoughts. They can be powerful. Look at the list of irrational, self-defeating thoughts below, and think of how they might affect someone's performance while taking a test.

Common Negative Thoughts Experienced While Taking a Test

This test is too hard. How will I ever pass?

My mind just went blank. I am doomed for sure.

I just want to finish and get out of here as soon as possible.

Everyone else is smarter than I am.

I just can't do multiple-choice questions. I will never finish in time.

I am the only one doing poorly.

I will lose my scholarship.

It doesn't matter how hard I try, I still do poorly. I think I'm going to throw up.

Have you ever had any of these thoughts? Below list some thoughts you have had that were associated with test taking (or another type of performance).

1. _____

2. _____

3. _____

4. _____

Behavioral symptoms can include procrastination, impulsive behavior, compulsive behavior, an inability to focus or concentrate, and avoidance behavior. When someone is anxious about taking a test, that person might avoid studying, decide to change majors impulsively, or engage in compulsive activities (e.g., checking again and again to make sure a door is locked, the oven is turned off, or his/her cell phone is on).

What can you do about physical, behavioral, and cognitive symptoms related to performance anxiety? The following section of this chapter focuses on how to manage test anxiety.

Managing Test Anxiety

Emotionally, people can begin to feel consumed by their anxiety, asking over and over, "What if this was to happen?" or "What if that was to happen?" Those "what ifs" can funnel into a sense of dread about an upcoming test that can fuel a paralyzing kind of fear known as a panic attack. A *panic attack* is a frightening experience that seems to come out of nowhere and is often accompanied by shortness of breath and feelings of disorientation, extreme fear, and loss of control. A person experiencing a panic attack feels a very real and present danger. Dealing with panic attacks is beyond the scope of this book. If you are experiencing some of these feelings, make an appointment with a competent professional (e.g., a counselor or other mental health professional) who can help you learn how to cope with your feelings.

The following suggestions offer advice on how to deal with thoughts, feelings, physical reactions, and behavior associated with test anxiety.

Dealing with Thoughts

In our roles as counselors and professors, we have often worked with students experiencing various forms of performance anxiety related to a number of different situations (e.g., taking math tests, making speeches, and writing term papers, theses, and dissertations). For example, one student had a 3.8 GPA in microbiology and had always performed well on tests for which she had adequately prepared. When she took the MCAT for admission into medical school, she "bombed" the standardized test. Although she had the skills to perform well on the MCAT, she let her fears of not getting into medical school overwhelm her to the point that when she was taking the test, all she could think about were thoughts like "What if I am really an imposter and not smart at all? What if I bomb the test and can't get into medical school?" Her thoughts became self-defeating and interfered with her performance on the test. She had to learn how to manage her thoughts and the accompanying feelings of anxiety in order to perform well on the next MCAT.

There are specific skills you can develop to reduce and control many types of performance anxiety. Changing the thoughts associated with your performance can help. Here are some methods for coping with anxious thoughts.

Reduce Negative Self-Talk. Become aware of the inner dialogue that you carry on in your mind. Do you engage in a lot of negative self-talk? Is it distracting when you are trying to concentrate and pay attention? If the answer is yes, you might want to learn about **cognitive restructuring**. Cognitive restructuring aims at reducing negative self-talk by replacing self-defeating thoughts ("I don't know the answer to this question, so I know that I will fail this test") with more positive, rational ones ("I may not know the answer to this question, but I am sure that I know the answers to many of the other questions"). A person's thoughts, beliefs, and ideas about a test affect his or her emotional reactions (fear and anxiety) to testing situations. Overexaggerating the importance of a test ("If I don't get an A on this test, I won't ever graduate from college") is an irrational thought that leads to negative self-talk.

Some people string a series of irrational thoughts together, forming a thinking pattern known as **catastrophic thinking**: "I don't know the answer to this question before me. I am going to flunk this test. I will never pass this class. I will never graduate from college. I will never get a good job. My friends and family will abandon me. I will be homeless." Watch out for these thinking patterns! Jumping to irrational conclusions is a disruptive thinking process that interferes with test performance. It can take a lot of effort to change thought processes. Learn how to recognize irrational thoughts as they form and how to change them into more realistic, rational, positive thoughts. Many of us feel that we should be more competent, smarter, better-liked, and harder-working than we are. We feel that we must perform at the highest level at all times. The famous psychologist Albert Ellis refers to this process as "musterbation" and warns of its abusive qualities.

Go back and look at some of the negative thoughts that you experience in a test-taking situation (or any other performance). List three of them.

Self-Defeating Thoughts

1. _____
2. _____
3. _____

Below, change your negative thoughts into more positive thoughts.

Positive Thoughts

1. _____
2. _____
3. _____

Separate Self-Worth from Performance. Do you see yourself as smart if you do well on a test and stupid if you do poorly? How much of your self-worth is based on test performance? Some students view grades as a measure of self-worth, which can be dangerous to one's self-esteem. Your self-esteem can go up and down like a yo-yo depending on how well or poorly you do in your classes from week to week. Avoid such either/or thinking. Charles Plumb has lectured across the United States about his years as a prisoner of war during the Vietnam conflict. He tells audiences that "whether you think you are a winner or a loser, you are right." Simply stated, beliefs you hold about yourself influence your behavior.

Creative Visualizations Such as Guided Imagery Can Help Reduce Anxiety. Visualizations help control negative thoughts and overwhelming emotions by creating a more positive space in which to perform. Directions for creating a visualization that can be used to alleviate or control anxiety during a test situation follow.

First, get in a relaxed state, and second, visualize yourself on the day of the test walking calmly over to the building where the test will be given. Notice specific details about your walk over to the building. Are there any special trees, benches, or other landscaping that you notice? Imagine walking into the classroom and finding a seat away from other students who might be discussing the test. Visualize yourself receiving the test and calmly looking it over, noticing the point values, the types of questions, and the directions. Then imagine yourself answering the questions. Tackle the easiest ones first, and then work through the test, remaining calm and relaxed. Be sure to include in your visualization an image of you checking your answers before handing in the test. As you create the visualization, add details about the room where you are taking the test, your seat, and other information about the test itself. Practice this visualization prior to actually taking a test, at a time when you are relaxed. That may be when you are lying in bed before you drift off to sleep or in the morning when you first wake up.

Dealing with Physical Reactions to Anxiety

There are ways you can change the way your body reacts to anxiety. The pattern of your breathing is important. When your body is relaxed, you breathe deeper, take in more oxygen, and can concentrate better. Deep breathing makes it easier to remain calm, especially while performing. If you can learn to control your breathing while taking a test, chances are you will perform better on your test. When we are anxious, our muscles tense and, as a result, we breathe at a more shallow level. Shallow breathing means that not enough oxygen is getting into the body. That is why a person may experience dizziness, cold hands, and frequent yawning.

One way to increase the amount of oxygen taken in is to engage in **abdominal breathing**. Try it. Get into a comfortable position. You might want to close your eyes. Concentrate on the air flowing in and out of your lungs. Breathe in through your nose and out through your mouth, using equal amounts of air. Now, slowly take in a deep breath, filling your lower lungs first (feel your abdomen expand), then the rest of your lungs. Hold your breath for just a moment, and then exhale very slowly. Try it again, taking in a long but comfortable breath, holding it for just a moment, and then exhaling slowly. Continue this pattern of breathing for no more than five minutes.

Breathing slows down the central nervous system. The Buddhist practice of mindfulness (living fully in the present moment) is the essence of Buddhist meditation. Conscious breathing, the process of taking a breath and being aware of how that breath of air moves in and out of your body, is a way to become more mindful, more relaxed.

Relaxation is important. You cannot be relaxed and tense at the same time. How do you relax? Do you exercise? Listen to music? Hang out with friends? List ten healthy things that you do to relax.

1. _____   6. _____

2. _____   7. _____

3. _____   8. _____

4. _____   9. _____

5. _____   10. _____

Visualize success.

Looking at Your Behavior

Some students feel anxious about taking tests because they do not use effective study and test-taking strategies or know how to manage their time. If you are experiencing anxiety about tests due to these factors, know that you can get some fairly immediate results if you are willing to change your habits and behavior. Everyone has the ability to change. Remember that you can change your thoughts and your physical reactions to test anxiety. You can also change behaviors you engage in that promote test anxiety. If you scored at the test-deficient level on Exercise 1 ("Test-Taking Quotient"), you may have some test-taking skills to develop. How do you manage your time? Is there any room for improvement? Effective study strategies, test-taking skills, and time-management skills are necessary for successful test performance. They can help to reduce anxiety in a testing situation. Let us review some of those.

- Prepare! Preparation involves constant, consistent reviews.
- Procrastination can increase test anxiety. Avoid cramming. Learn how to set realistic study goals, and reward yourself when you complete your goals, regardless of the outcome of the test.
- Engage in effective study and test-taking strategies. Assess your study habits and make necessary changes.
- Get help if you need it. There are behaviors that promote good test performance and behaviors that interfere with optimal performance. Learn the difference.

Sources

Ellis, A., & Grieger, R. (Eds.). (1977). *Handbook of rational emotive therapy*. New York, NY: Springer.

Kendall Hunt Publishing Company. (1999). *First-year experience sourcebook*. Dubuque, IA: Author.

Plumb, J. C. (March 5, 1996). *Making tough choices in challenging times*. Video taped at the 43rd Annual AORN Congress, Dallas, Texas. Sponsored by Exhibitor's Advisory Committee.

Reeves, J. (Producer), & Glauser, A. S. (Writer). (1997). *Test anxiety* [Videotape]. Athens, GA: GPTV.

Chapter 7

Exercise 2: Objective Exam Analysis Worksheet

Analyze your performance on a recent objective test using the form below. Refer to the sample discussed earlier in this chapter.

Course/Exam _____ Grade _____ Date _____

Test item missed	Lack of Knowledge					English Skills				Exam Panic				Exam Skills						Other		Analysis Results Comments and Other Information
	Reading textbook	Inadequate notes	Application of knowledge	Poor retention	Other	Reading comprehension	Reading speed	Vocabulary	Other	Decreased concentration	Mental block	Forgot to use exam techniques	Other	Did not focus on question asked	Failed to consider options carefully	Poor use of time	Changed answer	Careless/clerical error	Other	Math	Other	
Items																						
%																						
% Totals																						

From Funk, G. D., Bradley, J., Hopper, J. B., Hite-Walker, M., & Jerde, M. M. (1996). *Practical approaches for building study skills and vocabulary*. Dubuque, IA: Kendall Hunt. Reprinted by permission.

Critical Thinking
Developing Critical Skills for the 21st Century

8

" *To see if a plant could display a memory, a scheme was devised whereby Backster was to try to identify the secret killer of one of two plants. Six of Backster's polygraph students volunteered for the experiment, some of them veteran policemen. Blindfolded, the students drew from a hat folded slips of paper, on one of which were instructions to root up, stomp on, and thoroughly destroy one of two plants in a room. The criminal was to commit the crime in secret, neither Backster nor any of the other students was to know his identity; only the second plant would be a witness. By attaching the surviving plant to a polygraph and parading the students one by one before it, Backster was able to establish the culprit. Sure enough, the plant gave no reaction to five of the students, but caused the meter to go wild whenever the actual culprit approached. Backster was careful to point out that the plant could have picked up and reflected the guilt feelings of the culprit, but as the villain had acted in the interests of science, and was not particularly guilty, it left the possibility that a plant could remember and recognize the source of severe harm to its fellow. Do lawns recognize us? How about the weeds in a garden?*

THEODORE SCHICK, JR., and LEWIS VAUGHN, *How to Think About Weird Things*

he above experiment, actually conducted by a polygraph expert, is very curious and leads us to ask, "What are we to believe? What should we accept with reservations, and what should we

From Schick, T., & Vaughn, L. (1999). *How to think about weird things: Critical thinking for a new age* (2nd ed.). Mountain View, CA: Mayfield Publishing. Reprinted by permission of The McGraw-Hill Companies.

dismiss outright?" As we gather information about the world via the media (e.g., television, radio, the Internet, and newspapers and magazines), we tend to take much of the information at face value, ignoring the fact that the information has been selected and organized (shaped and edited) by the person or organization presenting it. People are often lulled into a false sense of security, believing that the sources of information they are basing their decisions on are objective and truthful (Chaffee, 1998). Discovering the answers to the six important questions that reporters are trained to answer near the beginning of every news article—*who, what, where, when, why,* and *how*—is not enough to allow us to think critically about complex and sometimes controversial topics. To engage in thinking at this higher level, one needs to know how to ask questions and think independently.

The authors of this textbook view critical thinking developmentally as a set of complex thinking skills that can be improved through knowledge and guided practice. Thinking skills are categorized in the problem-solving/decision-making set of life-skills. These skills include information assessment and analysis; problem identification, solution, implementation, and evaluation; goal setting; systematic planning and forecasting; and conflict resolution. Developmental thinking models, critical thinking and problem-solving models, and information about the construction and evaluation of an argument are presented in this chapter to help you strengthen your thinking skills and improve the quality of your decision making.

Thinking as a Developmental Process

Cognitive psychologists study the development and organization of knowledge and the role it plays in various mental activities (e.g., reading, writing, decision making, and problem solving). What is knowledge? Where it is stored? How do you construct mental representations of your world? The personal answers to these and other questions are often found for the first time in college when students focus their attention on what they know and how they know it.

Models of Knowledge

Different forms of knowledge interact when you reason and construct a mental representation of the situation before you, and different situations require different levels of thinking. How you learn and study chemistry is likely very different from the way you approach political science or calculus. Joanne Kurfis (1988) wrote about the following three kinds of knowledge.

- Declarative knowledge is knowing facts and concepts. Kurfis recognizes the considerable amount of declarative knowledge that students acquire through their college courses. To move students to a higher level of thinking, instructors generally ask students to write analytical essays, instead of mere summaries, to explain the knowledge they have acquired in the course.
- Procedural knowledge, or strategic knowledge, is knowing how to use declarative knowledge to do something (e.g., interpret textbooks, study, navigate the Internet, or find a major).
- Metacognition is knowing what knowledge to use to control one's situation (e.g., how to make plans, ask questions, analyze the effectiveness of learning strategies, or initiate change). If students' metacognitive skills are not well developed, students may not be able to use the full potential of their knowledge when studying in college.

William Perry

You read about the developmental theorist William Perry earlier in this textbook. In his research on college-age students, Perry distinguished a series of stages that students pass through as they move from simple to complex levels of thinking. Basically, they move from dualism, the simplest stage, where knowledge is viewed as a factual quality dispensed by authorities (professors), to multiplicity, in which the student recognizes the complexity of knowledge and believes knowledge to be subjective (e.g., he or she understands that there is more than one perspective of the bombing of Hiroshima or the role of the United States in the Vietnam War), to relativism, where the student reaches an understanding that some views make greater sense than other views. Relativism is reflected in situations where a student has made a commitment to the particular view they have constructed of the world, also known as *Weltanschauung*. Constructing a personal critical epistemology is an essential developmental task for undergraduates, according to Perry (Chaffee, 1998).

Bloom's Taxonomy of Thinking and Learning

Benjamin Bloom (1956) and his associates at the University of Chicago developed a classification system, or taxonomy, to explain how we think and learn (see Figure 8.1). The taxonomy consists of six levels of thinking arranged in a hierarchy, beginning with simple cognitive tasks (knowledge) and moving up to more complex thinking (evaluation). Thinking at each level is dependent on thinking skills at lower levels. One of the reasons that college students often experience difficulty learning and studying during their first semester is that the learning and study strategies from high school are not necessarily effective in the new setting. In high school you are generally asked to memorize, comprehend, and interpret information. In college you are asked to do all that and more. To be successful in a college setting, you need to learn how to apply, ana-

Figure **8.1** Bloom's Taxonomy

lyze, synthesize, and evaluate information. Let's look at Bloom's six levels of learning and thinking, beginning with the lowest level of thinking.

Knowledge Level. If you are cramming for a test, chances are good that you are thinking at the knowledge level, the lowest level of thinking. You are basically attempting to memorize a lot of information in a short amount of time. If you are asked on the test to identify, name, select, define, or list particular bits of information, you might do okay, but you will most likely forget most of the information soon after taking the test.

Comprehension Level. When you are classifying, describing, discussing, explaining, and recognizing information, you are in the process of interpreting information. At the bottom of your lecture notes for the day, see if you can summarize your notes using your own words. In doing so, you can develop a deeper understanding of the material just covered in class.

Application Level. At this third level of thinking, you are constructing knowledge by taking previously learned information and applying it in a new and different way to solve problems. Whenever you use a formula or a theory to solve a problem, you are thinking at the application level. Some words used to describe how you process information at this level are *illustrate*, *demonstrate*, and *apply*. To increase thinking at the application level, develop the habit of thinking of examples to illustrate concepts presented in class or during reading. Be sure to include the examples in your notations in your books and notes.

Analysis Level. When you analyze information, you break the information down into parts and then look at the relationships among the parts. In your literature class, if you read two plays from different time periods and then compare and contrast them in terms of style and form, you are analyzing. When you analyze, you connect pieces of information. You discriminate, correlate, classify, and infer.

Synthesis Level. When you are synthesizing information, you are bringing together all the bits of information that you have analyzed to create a new pattern or whole. When you synthesize, you hypothesize, predict, generate, and integrate. Innovative ideas often emerge at the synthesis level of thinking.

Evaluation Level. This is the highest level of thinking according to Bloom's taxonomy. When you evaluate, you judge the validity of the information. You may be evaluating opinions ("Is that person really an expert?") or biases. When you gather information from the Internet, how do you evaluate that information? Many college libraries offer guidelines for evaluating information found on websites. Cornell University's library offers criteria for evaluating the accuracy, authority, currency, objectivity, and coverage of such information; you can find this comprehensive guide at http://olinuris. library.cornell.edu/ref/research/webeval.html.

Answer the following questions to test your understanding of Bloom's taxonomy. According to Bloom's taxonomy of thinking, which levels of thinking would you be engaging in if you were asked to do the following?

- Read an article about an upcoming candidate in a local election and then summarize the candidate's characteristics?

- View a video about hate and prejudice and then write an essay about how you can confront hate and prejudice on a personal level?

- Read through the chapter in this book on learning styles and then determine the most effective way for you to study?

- Identify and define the parts of the forebrain?

- Judge a new campus parking policy created by your college's parking services?

Models of Critical Thinking/Problem Solving

Critical Thinking

One of the primary objectives of a college education is to develop the skills necessary to become an autonomous, independent learner. Critical thinking prepares you to be an independent thinker. Many models of critical thinking have been developed which can be used to develop strong critical thinking skills. One such model, developed by the authors of this textbook, is called **CRITICAL** (Glauser & Ginter, 1995). This model identifies important steps and key ideas in critical thinking: **C**onstruction, **R**efocus, **I**dentify, **T**hink through, **I**nsight, **C**onclusions, **A**ccuracy, and **L**ens.

Construction. Each of us constructs a unique view of the world. Our constructions, or perceptions, of the world are based on our thoughts and beliefs. Our cultural backgrounds influence our perceptions and help to form the basis of our assumptions. For example, you might assume that a college education can help you to get a better job. How do you know this? Did a parent or guidance counselor tell you so? If this is the only bit of information on which you are basing your assumption about the value of a college education, you have not engaged in critical thinking. If you had engaged in critical thinking, you would have analyzed and synthesized information that you gathered about the benefits of a college education. If you have based your decision to attend this college on good critical thinking, then you will know why you are here and will more likely be motivated to graduate.

Perceptions of information, behaviors, and situations are often based on unexamined assumptions that are inaccurate and sketchy. The first step in this model is to investigate personal underlying biases that are inherent in your assumptions about any issue before you. For example, let us say that you are with some friends and the topic of surrogate motherhood comes up. Maybe you have already formed an opinion about the issue. This opinion could be based on strong critical thinking, but if not, then your opinion is merely a strong, personal feeling. If you chose to look at surrogate motherhood from a critical-thinking perspective, you would begin by examining your own thoughts and beliefs about motherhood and surrogacy. No matter what issue is before you (e.g., the U.S. economy, the environment, abortion, genetic engineering), the process is the same: begin by examining your own assumptions. As you do this, look for biases and other patterns of thinking that have become cemented over time and are influencing the way you view the issue.

Refocus. Once you have acknowledged some of your own biases, refocus your attention so you can hear alternative viewpoints. Refocus by reading additional information, talking to people with opposing viewpoints, or maybe watching a documentary on the subject you are investigating. You are gathering evidence to support other views, trying to see other people's perspectives. Read carefully, and listen carefully with intent to learn. Can you think of any books that you have read or movies that have influenced the way you see a particular issue?

To illustrate the effect of refocusing, list three sources of additional information (e.g., book, movie, another person, newspaper, or experience) that changed your mind about an issue important to you. Explain how each changed you.

1. _____
   _____
   _____

2. _____
   _____
   _____

3. _____
   _____
   _____

Identify. Identifying core issues and information is the third step of critical thinking. After you have gathered additional information representing different viewpoints, think over the information carefully. Do any themes emerge that tell a different story? What does the terminology related to the issue tell you? Look at all the facts and details. We all try to make sense out of what we hear and see by arranging information into a pattern, a story that seems reasonable. When we do this, there is a tendency to arrange the information to fit our perceptions and beliefs. When we engage in critical thinking, we are trying to make sense of all the pieces, not just the ones that happen to fit our own preconceived pattern.

Think Through. The fourth step of critical thinking requires that you think through all the information gathered. The task is to distinguish between fact and fiction and determine what is relevant and not relevant. Examine premises and decide if they are logically valid. Look for misinformation. Maybe you have gathered inaccurate facts and figures. Check the sources for reliability. Asking questions is a large part of good critical thinking. Formulate good questions that call for clear answers.

This step of the model is where you analyze and synthesize information. You are continually focusing your attention in and out, similar to the way you might focus a camera. This step of the critical-thinking process can be very creative. You are using both parts of the brain. The right brain is being speculative and suspending judgment. The left brain is analyzing the information received in a more traditional style, thinking logically and sequentially. While thinking critically, have you detected any overgeneralizations (e.g., women are more emotional and less rational than men) or oversimplifications (e.g., the high dropout rate at the local high school is due to an increase in single-parent families)?

Find a story in your campus newspaper or another news source that covers a current, controversial social issue. Read through the story and then answer the following questions:

1. What is the main intent of the story?

2. What facts does the author present in support of the main premise of the story?

3. Which facts are relevant and which ones are not relevant?

4. How reliable are the sources that support the given facts?

5. Did you ferret out any biases or unsupported opinions of the author?

6. Are the premises logically valid? (Are the premises reasonable and do they support the conclusion?)

Insight. Once key issues have been identified and analyzed, it is time to develop some insight into some of the various perspectives on the issue. Sometimes some of the best insights come when you can sit back and detach yourself from all the information you have just processed. Often new meanings will emerge that provide a new awareness. You might find that you have developed some empathy for others that may not have been there before. When you hear the term *broken home*, what images do you conjure up? Analogies can act as powerful tools for gaining insight into our own perceptions. How do you think a child who resides with a single parent or alternates between divorced parents' homes feels when hearing that term applied to his or her situation? A lot of assumptions are embedded in such concepts.

Conclusions. If you do not have sufficient evidence to support a decision, suspend judgment until you do. An important tenet of critical thinking is not to jump to conclusions. If you do, you may find that you have a fallacy in your reasoning. A fallacy is an instance of incorrect reasoning. Maybe you lacked sufficient evidence to support

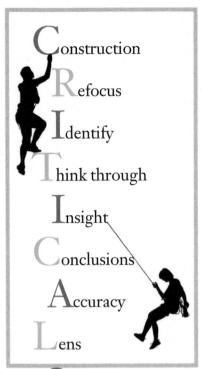

C onstruction
R efocus
I dentify
T hink through
I nsight
C onclusions
A ccuracy
L ens

Figure **8.2** Steps Required by the CRITICAL Model

Mountain climber going up © SABRI DENIZ KIZIL, 2012. Used under license from Shutterstock, Inc.
Mountain climber going down © SOLID, 2012. Used under license from Shutterstock, Inc.

your decision to major in biology, or maybe your conclusions about an issue related to the economy do not follow logically from your premise. Also look at the conclusions you have drawn, and ask yourself if they have any implications that you might need to rethink. Do you need to consider alternative interpretations of the evidence? Not every problem has a simple, distinct solution.

Accuracy. You are not through thinking! In addition to looking for fallacies in your reasoning, you also need to consider some other things.

- Know the difference between reasoning and rationalizing. Which thinking processes are your conclusions based on?
- Know the difference between what is true and what seems true based on the emotional attachment you have to your ideas and beliefs.
- Know the difference between opinion and fact. Facts can be proven; opinions cannot.

Lens. In this last step of critical thinking, you have reached the understanding that most issues can be viewed from multiple perspectives. These perspectives form a lens that offers a more encompassing view of the world around you. Remember that there are usually many solutions to a single issue. Finally, refer to Figure 8.2 to see a depiction of the steps in the **CRITICAL** Model.

Problem Solving

By this point in your life, you have encountered many difficult situations in which you had to engage in some sort of problem solving where you made decisions. Think of a fairly recent problem that you had to deal with—maybe a financial problem (e.g., a student loan, credit card debt), an academic problem (e.g., a change in major, low academic performance), an interpersonal problem (e.g., a roommate issue, lack of assertiveness), or a health problem (e.g., depression, a weight issue). How did you deal with this problem? Did you arrive at a satisfying solution? What decisions did you make or not make? Problem solving involves thinking creatively and critically. Are problem solving and critical thinking the same? Not really. Problem solving is about having the ability and skills to apply knowledge to pragmatic problems encountered in all areas of your life. It is the application of critical thinking to solve problems that involves creative thinking. If you were trying to solve a financial problem or decide whether or not to change roommates, you probably would not need a model of thinking as extensive as the one previously described. The following steps offer an organized and creative approach to solving less complex problems.

- Identify the problem; be specific and write it down
- Analyze the problem
- Identify alternative ways to solve the problem
- Examine alternatives
- Implement a solution
- Evaluate

Identify the Problem. In order to clearly identify the problem, you need to have a thorough understanding of what the problem is. What exactly is the problem you wish to solve? If the problem involves whether or not to move out of your dorm next semester, is it that your roommate is driving you crazy, or is it that you want to move into an apartment with your best friend next semester? Be specific. In defining the problem, look at the problem from different perspectives.

Analyze the Problem. Remember, analysis means looking at all the parts. It is the process by which we select and interpret information. Be careful not to be too selective or simplistic in your thinking. Break down the problem into manageable pieces and look at all the facts and details of the problem. Ask yourself specific questions. For example, suppose you want to move into an apartment with your friends. Do you need permission from anyone to do so? Can you afford to do this? Can you get a release from your residence hall? Your answer to all the questions might be yes, with the exception of being able to afford it. You want to move, so now the problem is a financial one. You need to come up with the financial resources to follow through on your decision.

Identify Alternative Ways to Solve the Problem. Use convergent and divergent thinking. You are engaging in **convergent thinking** when you are narrowing choices to come up with the correct solution (e.g., picking the best idea out of three). You are engaging in **divergent thinking** when you are thinking in terms of multiple solutions. Mihaly Csikszentmihalyi (1996) says, "Divergent thinking leads to no agreed-upon solution. It involves fluency, or the ability to generate a great quantity of ideas; flexibility, or the ability to switch from one perspective to another; and originality in picking unusual associations of ideas" (p. 60). He concludes that a person whose thinking has these creative qualities is likely to come up with more innovative ideas.

Lingo and Tepper (2010) reported that 84 percent of undergraduates surveyed in an ongoing national survey of creativity and academic choices identified creativity as an *important* or *very important* skill, and over half said that it was *important* or *essential* to find a career where they could express their creativity. Lingo and Tepper also point to recent research that suggests "creativity is not simply a product of personality or individual psychology, but rather is rooted in a set of teachable competencies, which include idea generation, improvisation, metaphorical and analogical reasoning, divergent thinking that explores many possible solutions, counterfactual reasoning, and synthesis of competing solutions" (p. A28).

Brainstorming is a creative problem-solving method. As you generate alternative ways to solve problems, you use both divergent and convergent thinking. Here are some steps to use if you decide to brainstorm.

1. Describe the problem.
2. Decide on the amount of time you want to spend brainstorming (e.g., ten minutes).
3. Relax (remember some of the best insights come in a relaxed state).
4. Write down everything that comes to your mind (divergent thinking).
5. Select your best ideas (convergent thinking).
6. Try one out! (If it does not work, try one of the other ideas you selected.)

Students have successfully used the process of brainstorming to decide on a major, select internships, develop topics for papers, and come up with ideas for part-time jobs. Being creative means coming up with atypical solutions to complex problems.

Examine Alternatives. How do you decide among the alternatives? Make judgments about the alternatives based on previous knowledge, the additional information you now have, and your goals. Consider possible outcomes for each alternative idea and visualize the solution with a mental movie.

Implement a Solution. Choose one solution to your problem and eliminate the others for now. (If this one fails, you may want to try another solution later.)

Evaluate. If the plan is not as effective as you had hoped, modify your plan or start the process over again. Also look at the criteria you used to judge your alternative solutions.

Think of a problem that you are currently dealing with. Complete Exercise 2 ("Creating Breakthroughs") at the end of the chapter. This is an opportunity to try to solve a problem using this six-step problem-solving model.

Critical thinking is essential.

Arguments

Critical thinking involves the construction and evaluation of arguments. An **argument** is a form of thinking in which reasons (statements and facts) are given in support of a conclusion. The reasons of the argument are known as the **premises**. A good argument is one in which the premises are logical and support the conclusion. The validity of the argument is based on the relationship between the premises and the conclusion. If the premises are not credible or do not support the conclusion, or the conclusion does not follow from the premises, the argument is considered to be **invalid** or **fallacious**. **Unsound arguments** (based on fallacies) are often persuasive because they can appeal to our emotions and confirm what we want to believe to be true. Just look at commercials on television. Alcohol advertisements show that you can be rebellious and independent and have lots of friends, fun, and excitement by drinking large quantities of alcohol—all without any negative consequences. Intelligence is reflected in the capacity to acquire and apply knowledge. Even sophisticated, intelligent people are influenced by fallacious advertising.

Invalid Arguments

It is human irrationality, not a lack of knowledge that threatens human potential.

Raymond Nickerson, in J. K. Kurfiss, Critical Thinking

In the book *How to Think About Weird Things*, Theodore Schick and Lewis Vaughn (1999) suggest that you can avoid holding irrational beliefs by understanding the ways in which an argument can fail. First, an argument is fallacious if it contains **unacceptable premises**, premises that are as incredible as the claim they are supposed to support. Second, if it contains **irrelevant premises**, or premises that are not logically related to the conclusion, it is also fallacious. Third, it is fallacious if it contains **insufficient premises**, meaning that the premises do not eliminate reasonable grounds for doubt. Schick and Vaughn recommend that whenever someone presents an argument, you check to see if the premises are acceptable, relevant, and sufficient. If not, then the argument presented is not logically compelling or valid.

Schick and Vaughn abstracted from the work of Ludwig F. Schlecht the following examples of fallacies based on illogical premises.

Unacceptable Premises

- **False dilemma** (also known as the either/or fallacy) presumes that there are only two alternatives from which to choose when in actuality there are more than two. For example: You are either with America or against us. You are not with America, therefore you are against us.
- **Begging the question** is also referred to as arguing in a circle. A conclusion is used as one of the premises. For example: "You should major in business, because my advisor says that if you do, you will be guaranteed a job." "How do you know this?" "My advisor told me that all business majors find jobs."

Irrelevant Premises

- **Equivocation** occurs when the conclusion does not follow from the premises due to using the same word to mean two different things. For example: Senator Dobbs has always been *patriotic* and shown a deep affection and respect for his country. Now, though, he is criticizing the government's foreign policy. This lack of *patriotism* makes him unworthy of reelection.
- **Appeal to the person** (*ad hominem*, or "to the man") occurs when a person offers a rebuttal to an argument by criticizing or denigrating its presenter rather than constructing a rebuttal based on the argument presented. As Schick and Vaughn (1999) note, "Crazy people can come up with perfectly sound arguments, and sane people can talk nonsense" (p. 287).
- **Appeal to authority** is when we support our views by citing experts. If the person is truly an expert in the field for which they are being cited, then the testimony might be valid. How often do you see celebrities endorsing products? Is an argument valid just because someone cites an article from the *New York Times* or the *Wall Street Journal* for support? You have to always consider the professional credentials of the "authority" whose expertise is being offered in support of an argument.
- **Appeal to the masses** is a type of fallacy that occurs when support for the premise is offered in the form, "It must be right because everybody else does it." For example: It's okay to cheat. Every college student cheats sometime during the undergraduate years.

- **Appeal to tradition** is used as an unsound premise when we argue that something is true based on an established tradition. For example: It's okay to drink large quantities of alcohol and go wild during spring break. It's what students have always done.
- **Appeal to ignorance** relies on claims that if no proof is offered that something is true, then it must be false, or conversely, that if no proof is offered that something is false, then it must be true. Many arguments associated with religions of the world are based on irrelevant premises that appeal to ignorance.
- **Appeal to fear** is based on a threat, or "swinging the big stick." For example: If you don't start studying now, you will never make it through college. Schick and Vaughn (1999) remind us, "Threats extort; they do not help us arrive at the truth" (p. 289).

Insufficient Premises

- **Hasty generalizations** are often seen when people stereotype others. Have you noticed that most stereotypes are negative? When we describe an individual as pushy, cheap, aggressive, privileged, snobbish, or clannish and then generalize that attribute to the group we believe that person belongs to, we are committing a hasty generalization.
- **Faulty analogy** is the type of fallacy committed when there is a claim that things that have similar qualities in some respects will have similarities in other respects. For example: Dr. Smith and Dr. Wilson may both teach at the same college, but their individual philosophies about teaching and learning may be very different.
- **False cause** fallacies occur when a causal relationship is assumed despite a lack of evidence to support the relationship. Do you have a special shirt or hat that you wear on game days to influence the odds that the team you are cheering for wins?

Crop Circles*

Crop circles are swirled patterns of bent-over plants, such as wheat, corn, or soybeans, which mysteriously appear in large fields. First noticed in southern England, crop circles have started to appear all over the world. They range from simple circular shapes to elaborate pictograms. Originally, some thought that the circles were produced by extraterrestrials or some other paranormal phenomenon. Others thought that they were produced by "plasma vortex phenomena" that consisted of a spinning mass of air containing electrically charged matter. Still others thought that they were produced by clever human beings.

In 1991, two pub mates in their sixties—Doug Bower and Dave Chorley—claimed to have produced many of the English crop circles by attaching a rope to both ends of a long narrow plank, holding it between themselves and the plants, and stepping on the plank to bend over the plants. To substantiate their claim, they produced a circle for a tabloid newspaper, which was later claimed to be of extraterrestrial origin by one of the believers in the extraterrestrial hypothesis. Since then, other crop circles thought impossible to hoax have turned out to be manmade. Apparently there is no reliable way to distinguish crop circles of terrestrial origin from those of extraterrestrial origin. Nevertheless, people continue to believe that crop circles are messages from outer space.

---

*From Schick, T., & Vaughn, L. (1999). *How to think about weird things: Critical thinking for a new age* (2nd ed.). Mountain View, CA: Mayfield Publishing. Reprinted by permission of The McGraw-Hill Companies.

Closing Remarks

Belgian physicist Ilya Prigogine was awarded the Nobel Prize for his theory of dissipative structures. Part of the theory "contends that friction is a fundamental property of nature and nothing grows without it—not mountains, not pearls, not people. It is precisely the quality of fragility, he says, the capacity for being shaken up that is paradoxically the key to growth. Any structure—whether at the molecular, chemical, physical, social, or psychological level that is insulated from disturbance is also protected from change. It becomes stagnant. Any vision—or any thing—that is true to life, to the imperatives of creation and evolution, will not be 'unshakable'" (Levoy, 1997, p. 8).

Throughout this textbook, you will read about how change affects you now as a student in college and throughout the rest of your life. Education is about learning how to look at and listen to what instructors, books, media, and other sources of information are communicating, and how to discover whether or not what they are communicating is true or false.

In reference to education and learning, the philosopher Jiddu Krishnamurti (1974) said that there should be "an intent to bring about change in the mind which means you have to be extraordinarily critical. You have to learn never to accept anything which you yourself do not see clearly" (p. 18). He said that education is always more than learning from books, memorizing facts, or the instructor transmitting information to the student. Education is about critical thinking, and critical thinking is the foundation of all learning.

Critical thinking is thinking that moves you beyond simple observations and passive reporting of those observations. It is an active, conscious, cognitive process in which there is always intent to learn. It is the process by which we analyze and evaluate information, and it is how we make good sense out of all the information that we are continually bombarded with.

Marcia Magolda believes that critical thinking fosters qualities such as maturity, responsibility, and citizenship. "Both the evolving nature of society and the student body has led to reconceptualizations of learning outcomes and processes. In a postmodern society, higher education must prepare students to shoulder their moral and ethical responsibility to confront and wrestle with the complex problems they will encounter in today and tomorrow's world. Critical, reflective thinking skills, the ability to gather and evaluate evidence, and the ability to make one's own informed judgments are essential learning outcomes if students are to . . . make informed judgments in a world in which multiple perspectives are increasingly interdependent and 'right action' is uncertain and often in dispute" (Magolda & Terenzini, 1999, p. 3).

Sources

Bloom, B. (1956). *Taxonomy of educational objectives: The classification of educational goals. Handbook I: Cognitive domain.* London: Longmans.

Chaffee, J. (1998). *The thinker's way.* Boston, MA: Little, Brown.

Csikszentmihalyi, M. (1996). *Creativity.* New York, NY: HarperCollins.

DiSpezio, M. (1998). *Challenging critical thinking puzzles.* New York, NY: Sterling.

Glauser, A., & Ginter, E. J. (1995, October). *Beyond hate and intolerance.* Paper presented at the Southeastern Conference of Counseling Center Personnel, Jekyll Island, GA.

Johnson, D., & Johnson, F. (2000). *Joining together.* Boston, MA: Allyn and Bacon.

Krishnamurti, J. (1974). *Krishnamurti on education.* New York, NY: Harper & Row.

Kurfiss, J. G. (1988). *Critical thinking: Theory, research, practice, and possibilities. Critical thinking, 2.* Washington, DC: ASHE-Eric Higher Education Reports.

Levoy, G. (1997). *Callings.* New York, NY: Three Rivers Press.

Lingo, E., & Tepper, S. (2010). The creative campus: Time for a "C" change. *The Chronicle of Higher Education*. Retrieved September 11, 2011 from http://chronicle.com/article/The-Creative-Campus-Time-for/124860/

Magolda, M. B., & Terenzini, P. (1999). Learning and teaching in the twenty-first century: Trends and implications for practice. In C. S. Johnson & H. E. Cheatham (Eds.), *Higher education trends for the next century: A research agenda for students' success*. Retrieved November 30, 1999, from http://www.acpa.nche.edu/seniorscholars/trends/trends.htm

Perry, W. (1970). *Forms of intellectual and ethical development during the college years: A scheme*. New York, NY: Holt, Rinehart and Winston.

Schick, T., & Vaughn, L. (1999). *How to think about weird things: Critical thinking for a new age*. Mountain View, CA: Mayfield.

Chapter 8

Exercise 1: Stranded in the Desert

Read the following description of a problem situation. Then answer the questions that follow.

You are one of the members of a geology club that is on a field trip to study unusual formations in the New Mexico desert. It is the last week in July. You have been driving over old trails, far from any road, in order to see out-of-the-way formations. At about 10:00 A.M. the specially equipped minibus in which your club is riding overturns, rolls into a 22-foot ravine, and burns. The driver and professional adviser to the club are killed. The rest of you are relatively uninjured.

You know that the nearest ranch is approximately 45 miles east of where you are. There is no closer habitation. When your club does not report to its motel that evening, you will be missed. Several persons know generally where you are, but because of the nature of your outing they will not be able to pinpoint your whereabouts.

The area around you is rather rugged and very dry. There is a shallow water hole nearby, but the water is contaminated by worms, animal feces and urine, and several dead mice. You heard from a weather report before you left that the temperature would reach 108 degrees, making the surface temperature 128 degrees. You are all dressed in lightweight summer clothing and you all have hats and sunglasses.

While escaping from the minibus each member of your group salvaged a couple of items; there are twelve in all. Your task is to rank these items according to their importance to your survival, with 1 being most important and 12 least important. Assume that the group has decided to stick together. How will you and your group survive?

_____ magnetic compass

_12_ book, *Plants of the Desert*

_10_ rearview mirror

_9_ large knife

_____ flashlight (four-battery size)

_11_ .38-caliber pistol

_8_ one transparent plastic ground cloth (6 ft by 4 ft) per person

_7_ piece of heavy-duty, light-blue canvas (20 ft by 20 ft)

_6_ one jacket per person

_3_ one 2-quart plastic canteen full of water per person

_____ accurate map of the area

_4_ large box of kitchen matches

From Johnson, D. W., & Johnson, F. P. (2000). *Joining together: Group theory and group skills* (7th ed.). Upper Saddle River, NJ: Pearson Education. Reprinted by permission.

1. Look over the top five items you selected as being most important. Why did you select these particular five? What is your reasoning?

2. Form groups of about five people (to be done in the classroom). You may assume that the number of club members is the same as the number of persons in your group. Read over the description of the situation again. What are the first decisions your group will need to make? As a group, come to a consensus on how you and your group will survive. What are some of the major problems that your group will have to overcome? Pay close attention to your reasons (premises) and your conclusions.

(After completing this exercise, turn to the solutions section at the end of this chapter to find out what the experts have to say.)

Chapter 8

Exercise 2: Creating Breakthroughs

Select a problem related to being a student at your college.

1. State the problem.

2. Analyze the problem (provide details).

3. **Brainstorm possible solutions.** (At this stage, **DO NOT ASSESS** the quality of the solutions you are listing. You are to write down whatever "pops into your head"—regardless of how silly or inappropriate a possible solution may first seem to you.)

4. Review your list of possible solutions. Pick the five best solutions from your brainstorming session and list them below:

(S1) _____

(S2) _____

(S3) _____

(S4) _____

(S5) _____

What three criteria do you want to use to assess the five possible solutions you listed above? Refer to Example 1 below before listing your three criteria.

Example 1

Stated Problem. Assume you state the problem as: ***I do not have enough money to cover my day-to-day expenses.***

Possible Solutions. From the brainstorming list of 15 possible solutions you select the following five as the best.

(S1) *Take Tuesday/Thursday classes and work the other days of the week*

(S2) *Beg my parents for more money*

(S3) *Take out student loans*

(S4) *Study hard, raise my GPA, and apply for a special scholarship*

(S5) *Alternate between going to school and working*

Criteria to Evaluate Solutions. The three criteria you select to assess the five possible solutions appear next.

(C1) *The solution must not add to my parents' current level of stress*

(C2) *The solution has to be genuinely feasible*

(C3) *The solution should not add to my present level of debt*

List three criteria you will use to evaluate the five possible solutions you listed at the top of this page.

(C1) _____

(C2) _____

(C3) _____

Now, using a rating scale from 1–5, rate each of the five possible solutions using your three criteria. A rating of 5 represents the highest rating you can assign. Review Example 2 before you assign any ratings.

Example 2

Criteria Used to Evaluate Solutions

(C1) *The solution must not add to my parents' current level of stress*

(C2) *The solution has to be genuinely feasible*

(C3) *The solution should not add to my present level of debt*

5 Possible Solutions (only two solutions are listed to illustrate the rating process)	Assign a rating from 1–5 for each criterion. For example, if Criterion (C1) is completely met for the solution listed for S1, then a rating of 5 would be appropriate.			Total Sum values assigned (C1 + C2 + C3)
	Criterion (C1)	Criterion (C2)	Criterion (C3)	
(S1) *Take Tuesday/Thursday classes and work the other days of the week*	5	4	5	14
(S2) *Beg my parents for more money*	1	1	2	4

Note. The above Total ratings (i.e., 14 and 4) indicate that (S1) is perceived by the student as the better of the two possible solutions.

---

5 Possible Solutions	Assign a rating from 1–5 for each criterion.			Total Sum values assigned (C1 + C2 + C3)
	Criterion (C1)	Criterion (C2)	Criterion (C3)	
(S1)				
(S2)				
(S3)				
(S4)				
(S5)				

5. What are your two best (rated highest) solutions?

_____

_____

6. Of the two best solutions, which solution will you choose to act on?

_____

7. What kinds of resources will you need to implement the solution you selected?
   (List at least four)

_____

_____

_____

_____

8. List some of your planning steps to carry out this solution.

_____

_____

_____

_____

_____

_____

_____

_____

9. **Evaluate.** Look over what you have listed as resources and planning steps, and decide if you forgot something important (if you left something out, please indicate what was left out that needs to be incorporated). Finally, indicate below if you believe the solution you have come up with is truly feasible, and give a tentative start date for putting your solution into effect.

Chapter 8

Exercise 3: Critical-Thinking Puzzle

Without lifting your pencil from the paper, draw six straight lines that connect all sixteen of the dots below. To make things more challenging, the line pattern that you create must begin at the X.

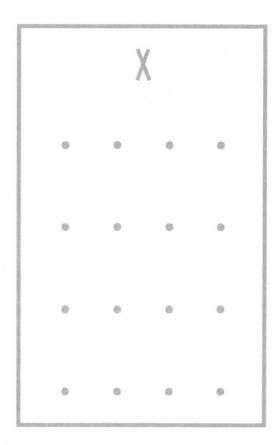

(The solution can be found on the last page of this chapter.)

SOURCE: DiSpezio, M. (1998). *Challenging critical thinking puzzles*. New York, NY: Sterling.

Chapter 8

Exercise Solutions

Exercise 1: Stranded in the Desert Exercise

The Expert's Ranking

 12 magnetic compass

 10 book, *Plants of the Desert*

 1   rearview mirror

 5   large knife

 8   flashlight (four battery size)

 9   .38-caliber pistol

 4   one transparent plastic ground cloth (6 ft by 4 ft) per person

 7   piece of heavy-duty, light blue canvas (20 ft by 20 ft)

 2   one jacket per person

 3   one 2-quart plastic canteen full of water per person

 11 accurate map of the area

 6   large box of kitchen matches

Rationale for the Expert's Ranking

The group has just been through a traumatic situation and most, if not all, of your group need to receive treatment for shock. Your group has five major problems to deal with: how to deal with dehydration, how to signal search parties, how to obtain as much drinkable water as possible, how to protect yourself from the cold at night, and how to gather food for the group if the group is not rescued within a few days.

If the group decided to walk out, traveling at night, all members would probably be dead by the second day. They will have walked less than 33 miles during the two nights. If group members decide to walk during the day, they will probably be dead by the next morning, after walking less than 12 miles. For the group to walk out, having just gone through a traumatic experience that has had considerable impact on the body, having few if any members who have walked 45 miles before, and having to carry the canvas and wear the jackets to prevent dehydration, would be disastrous. The group would also be harder to spot by search planes once they started to walk away from the site of the crash.

From Johnson, D. W., & Johnson, F. P. (2000). *Joining together: Group theory and group skills* (7th ed.). Upper Saddle River, NJ: Pearson Education. Reprinted by permission.

Exercise 3: Critical-Thinking Puzzle

Thinking "Outside the Triangle"

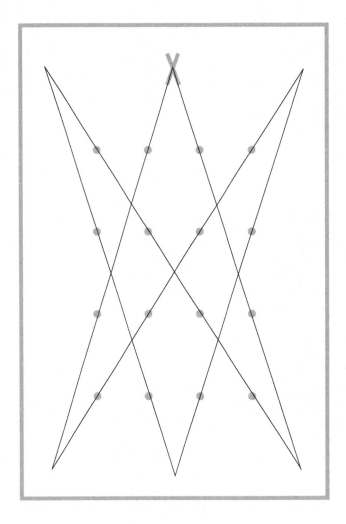

This problem is typically more difficult to solve if you imagine the dots marking the boundary of a geometric figure—a rectangle, for example. To arrive at the correct answer, you have to think "outside the box" (or in this instance, *"outside the triangle"*).

SOURCE: DiSpezio, M. (1998). *Challenging critical thinking puzzles*. New York: Sterling.

Acquiring Financial Skills
The Buck Stops with You

9

hatever name money goes by—dollar, euro, drachma, shekel, yen, ruble, baht, yuan, rupee, peso, tael, or rand—it was originally created to replace the early system of bartering used throughout the world at one point in time. Instead of changing goods or services for other goods or services (a system that was often burdensome and unwieldy), money could be used to pay for any goods or services desired, which made exchanges much easier. Historically, a variety of materials were used as money or to create money. Money has taken the form of clay tablets, cowry shells, lumps of salt, tea leaves, dried fish, stone coins weighing hundreds of pounds, and eventually, metal coins.

The technology necessary to produce metal coins caught on through much of the ancient world because metal coins eliminated many of the obvious problems associated with some of the earlier forms of money (e.g., salt-dried fish, compared to mental coins, deteriorated quickly). However, coinage was not entirely free of problems. The most significant problem introduced by the new currency was the weight of the metal used, especially in those situations where a considerable number of coins were required for payment. It was the Chinese who discovered a solution for this particular problem through the invention of paper money. The Chinese also experimented with other innovations, such as minting coins in the shape of what they were intended to purchase: for example, coins made in the shape of a human body were used to purchase clothing.

Money began to take on various meanings for those relying upon its use. While first seen as a medium of exchange, it soon served as a symbol for wealth, social standing, and power. It also became a way to send a message to others—by shaping and stamping their coins in a unique fashion, various civilizations intended to impress others with their right of authority and the degree of power possessed to assert that right. Clearly, money began to take on a meaning well beyond that of a means to facilitate acquisition of goods and services.

Of course, a civilization's coinage also involved practical considerations: for example, to deter people from scraping some of the gold or silver off before passing the coins on to another person, coins were eventually *milled*—that is, produced with ridges around the edge.

Contemporary Meanings of Money

Human Development: The Money Connection

There are two things we can say about the meaning of money that apply to everyone. First, because of the different tasks or expectations we face at each stage of life, money will have different meanings for us at various sequential points along the developmental trajectory. Simply stated, changes that unfold throughout our lives periodically require us to obtain different sets of financial skills and knowledge if we are to satisfactorily meet the financial tasks associated with a new stage of development. For example, it is reasonable to expect that a typical high school freshman would enjoy thinking about how to spend an unexpected gift of $100 on something he *wants* rather than *needs*. It is also reasonable to expect the same person at age 30, who was informed shortly after his recent marriage that he is one of those being laid off by his employer, to spend the same unexpected gift of $100 on a *family need* rather than a *personal want*.

Second, money has a range of different meanings within each age group. Obviously, not all 18-year-olds, or 78-year-olds, view money in the same way. In fact, we can expect to find significant differences among those within a particular age group. For example, while some 16-year-olds might experience money as creating a "burning sensation in their pockets," others the same age might see money as a step to obtaining something of greater value.

Years ago, one of the authors (Ginter) knew a fellow teen who was committed to saving all the money he earned through an assortment of summer jobs. At 16, he had amassed enough money to buy a small parcel of land and to finance the building of an automated car wash on the land purchased. He used the earnings from the car wash to pay for his college education. Prior to enrolling in college, Ginter himself spent all the money he had earned during three summers. Obviously lacking the skills of a frugal money manager, he soon found himself applying for loans to help pay for his college education.

Activity

Stop and Think

1. What does money mean to you?

2. Do you think money means the same thing to your friends as it does to you? Explain.

3. Does every member of your immediate family (brothers, sisters, and parents) view money in the same way? Explain.

Human Nature: The Money Connection

Money has figured into several major theories intended to explain human motivation and behavior in general. Karl Marx was a social theorist whose theory concerned the distribution of wealth within a society; his views had a significant impact on various political movements in the 20th century. Another theorist, the psychologist B. F. Skinner, proposed a comprehensive explanation for human behavior that led him to later outline the ingredients necessary to create a Skinnerian utopia. In this particular utopian community, the dwellers who received the most external rewards (dispensed in the form of "tokens") would be those who performed jobs that possessed little inherent reward. In fact, if the topsy-turvy rules proposed in Skinner's book *Walden Two* were applied to our world, business executives would receive salaries well below those of people employed to collect, haul away, and dispose of garbage. Finally, Sigmund Freud, the founder of psychoanalysis, focused on money's hidden meanings. In his *Interpretation of Dreams*, he speculated that dreams contained personal and universal symbols, and if one understood what these symbols meant; one would discover the secret message of the dream. Freud reviewed a client's dream that centered on the theme "payment for therapy" and believed the dream symbolically expressed a neurotic concern harbored by the client: specifically, this "repressed Victorian" client *unconsciously* viewed payment as a form of avarice, and essentially nothing more than a "filthy" exchange between her and Freud. As a result of working with this particular client and numerous others, Freud (1900/1965) realized that the concepts of *filth* and *objects of value* (which are concepts first linked together during an early stage of childhood) could be safely expressed in the form of symbolic dream stories of which the central theme is an insatiable desire such as greed (p. 233).

After considering the three theoretical positions briefly covered above, one could accurately conclude that money has many meanings: some meanings we are conscious of and some meanings remain out of our awareness, but the latter are still powerful enough to taint our view of the world. Even if you disagree with one or all of the theorists mentioned above, it is impossible to deny that people typically associate money with many different things in their lives. Money has even been linked to human activities such as humor (e.g., *"Money talks. It says good-bye."*), superstitious traditions or rituals, and common expressions that have found a place in our spoken and written language.

It should be obvious that these aspects of money can be easily illustrated by mentioning just a few of the many existing examples found in our culture. For example, some brides place a coin in a shoe on the day of their wedding for the purpose of obtaining future good fortune. New business owners display the first dollar received after opening their businesses. Visitors to Rome toss a coin into the Trevi Fountain to guarantee a return visit.

Many sayings and phrases about money have invaded our language and are frequently heard as we go about our daily activities:

"Show me the money."

"Shop till you drop."

"Share the wealth."

"Money can't buy happiness, but it helps."

"The buck stops here."

"Money makes the world go 'round'."

"A penny saved is a penny earned."

"That person has the Midas touch."

"You cannot be too rich or too thin."

"That person is morally bankrupt."

One indication that money has a strong psychological component is the way money keeps our mind focused on times other than the present (e.g., *"What bills should I pay next month?" "Investing in Company XYZ to create a retirement fund for retirement was a huge mistake for my parents!" "How can I get more money next year to go to college?"*). Interestingly, while money is frequently at the forefront of our thoughts, it also seems to pass through our hands easily and disappears much sooner than we expected.

In spite of the time we devote to thinking about money, the vast majority of people possess a superficial knowledge of paper money's characteristics. Most of us have poor memories concerning what appears on various denominations—even those we frequently use. To test your awareness of the identifying features of different bills, answer the questions appearing in the Question Box on the next page.

Managing Money to Achieve Academic Goals

Obviously money is important to us throughout our lives, but for the student experiencing the academic transition from high school to college, there is a major challenge pertaining to the use of money. The primary developmental task for students starting college is to handle their money in such a way that it allows them to stay in college. According to Lisa Goff (2009), investing in a college education is a good investment when one considers that college graduates, over their lifetime, will typically increase their earning power by an average of approximately $1,200,000 (or you can think of it this way: if you decide to drop out of college before you earn any college credit, you are likely to earn $1,200,000 less than if you had decided to stay and complete the requirements for an undergraduate degree). However, before a student can earn the "big bucks," the student needs to develop the skills required to utilize money as a tool that will enable the student to stay in college and graduate.

Question Box

Testing Your Knowledge about Paper Money

Whose *portrait* is printed on the $10, $20, $50, and $100 bill?

$10 _____

$20 _____

$50 _____

$100 _____

What *scene* is presented on the backside of the $10, $20, $50, and $100 bill?

$10 _____

$20 _____

$50 _____

$100 _____

What is the value of the largest denomination ever printed, and whose portrait appeared on the bill?

Value = _____

Portrait of _____

Since 1969, what is the largest bill issued?

Largest bill minted after 1969 _____

Answers appear in the Answer Box at the end of the chapter.

One aspect of managing money is learning exactly what you are spending your money on each semester. The following activity will help you determine where your money goes when it seems to "disappear."

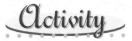

Where Is the Money Going?

Estimate how much you spend during the entire semester for each of the categories listed below. Then figure the percentage of the total amount that each category represents.

	$	%
Food consumed at residence	100 $	
Food consumed away from residence (eating out, food from vending machines)	20 $	
Nonfood groceries (e.g., cleaning supplies, laundry detergent)	50 $	
Residence (dorm, apartment)		
Clothing and shoes	50 $	
Utilities (electric, water, gas)	10 $	
Telephone (cell and residence phone)	150 $	
Garbage pickup	200 $	
Dry cleaning/laundromat		
Transportation (e.g., car loan, auto insurance, gasoline, auto repair, parking costs, oil change and maintenance, car license tag)	400 $	
Personal care (e.g., hair salons)	50 $	
Health care (e.g., medicine, membership at a physical fitness center, doctor and dentist visits, glasses/contacts)	60 $	
Newspapers/magazines	100 $	
Membership dues	500 $	
Postage		
Household items (e.g., furniture, cookware, repairs, decorations)	600 $	
Entertainment (e.g., basic cable hookup, movies, rentals, video games, etc.)	600 $	
Loan and debt payments (other than car)	500 $	
College expenses **covered by you or your family** (e.g., tuition, books, lab fees, etc.)	700 $	
Computer equipment, software, ink cartridges, paper, etc.	400 $	
Handheld electronic devices	300 $	
Internet service	200 $	
Tithing/charity		
Child care		
Insurance (other than car)		
Taxes		

total = 4,990

	$	%
Other categories not mentioned		
GRAND TOTAL		

INSTRUCTIONS: Use the space provided on this page to calculate percentages for each of the categories above. For example, if the GRAND TOTAL is $1,000 and you spent $300 on rent, then the Residence category accounts for 30% of the money spent during the semester (300/1000 = .30).

Area for Calculations

· ·

The percentages provided in Table 9.1 are based on figures from the U.S. Department of Labor, Bureau of Labor Statistics, Consumer Expenditure Survey. Compare your percentages to those for the age nearest your own. Are you satisfied with the way your money is being spent?

Table 9.1

	Age (average income)		
Category	25	50	70
Food at home	7.6%	6.5%	10.5%
Food away from home	5.0%	4.6%	4.4%
Shelter	7.6%	13.7%	14.9%
Utilities	5.7%	5.3%	8.3%
Clothing	5.3%	4.5%	4.8%
Transportation	15.5%	15.2%	15.3%
Health Care	3.4%	3.7%	10.7%
Personal Care	1.1%	1.0%	1.3%
Entertainment	4.6%	5.1%	4.9%
Other Spending	6.4%	8.8%	10.4%

Invest with personal values.

Whether you have financial assistance (e.g., parents paying some of the bills) or not, now is the time to develop some money management skills as well as explore some avenues for bringing in additional income. Certainly, one danger of being a student is acquiring too much debt. According to Fisher and Shelly (2009) and Goff (2009/2010), data indicate that somewhere between 50 percent and 66 percent of students graduating from college have borrowed money to finish their education. In addition, the average amount of debt acquired by undergraduate students ranged between approximately $21,000 and approximately $23,000 (it is much higher for those students who decide to remain in college to earn a professional or advanced degree). Lisa Goff believes undergraduate students should acquire as little debt as possible, but certainly no more than the amount they would earn their first year post-graduation. For example, if a student plans to enter a career with an annual starting salary of $40,000, then the student should aim to accumulate no more than $40,000 in debt by graduation day. (Lisa Goff recommends checking out sites such as **Payscale.com** to determine the starting salaries for various occupations.)

Steps for Obtaining Financial Control

While there are many important financial goals to consider (life insurance, retirement plans, investments, and so forth), our focus will be on four aspects of money management related to students: quick money tips, budgeting, financial aid and employment, and debt stress and credit problems.

Quick Money Tips

Banks

- When setting up a checking account, ask about options and determine which combination best fits your lifestyle.

  Common Options
  1. Overdraft privileges ensure that checks written will be paid.
  2. Direct deposit of income saves trips to a bank to make deposits.
  3. Some banks do not pay interest if the amount in the savings account goes below a certain amount. (According to Fisher and Shelly [2009], one can expect any interest earned to be low: recently the interest rate for checking accounts averaged 0.47 percent. While slightly higher in some cases, even savings accounts ranged an abysmal 0.37 to 0.57 percent.)
  4. Service fees can vary. Charges can run several dollars a month, but by keeping a minimum amount in the checking account, you may be able to obtain free checking.
- Avoid excessive use of ATMs. Plan so you can withdraw what you need for the week ahead rather than relying upon ATMs on a daily basis. While the fees seem small, they add up, and the trend has been for banks to increase this particular fee.
- Keep receipts, even if you simply drop them into a box or some other container. ATM receipts and deposit slips provide evidence to argue your case if an error occurs (while relatively rare, banks make errors, as do other businesses). Keep in mind that there is typically a time limit set for reporting an error. Ask your bank the length of time. The sooner you report an error, the better.

- Finally, banking has evolved over the decades and has taken on a number of forms: for example, one can now "bank" via Internet banks, mobile banks, commercial banks, credit unions, and thrifts. You might want to consider how these institutions differ in terms of receiving, lending, exchanging, and safeguarding your money before you make a final decision.

Credit Cards

According to Fisher and Shelly (2009), by the time beginning freshmen become seniors, they are likely to have acquired three times the number of credit cards. Also, on average freshmen carry a balance of approximately $1,600 from statement to statement, while seniors carry $3,000. Obviously, handling credit cards is far from a simple task.

It is very important to consider the various types of charges that come with any credit card you are interested in obtaining, and it is very important to compare it to other credit card offers so you can obtain the best possible fit for your needs. For example, credit cards sometimes charge an "over limit" fee when you exceed your credit line. In addition, it is common for late fees to be assigned when payments are past due. On many cards, even if the amount owed is small (say, under $20), you will be required to pay a minimum finance charge, which on a small amount owed can represent a relatively large percentage. Some lenders charge an annual fee, which is likely to be lower for regular cards than premium cards. Finally, interest rates on credit cards tend to be high compared to other loans.

Keep in mind there are various types of credit cards: fixed-rate; variable-rate; rewards; and gold, platinum, and titanium. Find the best deal, but do not be tricked by offers of low initial rates, which are often quickly replaced by much higher rates (see Table 9.2 to review a few of the credit card changes recently signed into law).

- Aim to pay off credit cards by each statement. This is considered one of the best ways to use credit cards. Avoid paying only the minimum on a credit card. The amount owed will never "go away," and you will ultimately pay much more due to the high interest rate.
- Avoid using a credit card for a cash advance, since they typically start charging interest (often at a higher rate) once the money is sent to the cardholder. In addition, a one-time fee may also be added.
- If your balance due has grown too large, consider cutting up unnecessary credit cards. Use the simplest means to see where your cash is going: buy with cash. Making purchases with cash prevents you from spending the "imaginary money" provided by credit cards. This imaginary money materializes later in the form of debt.
- Periodically check for what might be called "hidden services." You may discover that a monthly statement lists an automatic charge such as "credit life insurance"— notify the company that you did not ask for this service and you want it removed.
- If your credit cards are stolen, contact the lender. If the theft is reported soon enough, you will owe nothing; at worst, you will owe a small fee.

Table 9.2

Truth in Lending *(signed into law during 2009)*

- A credit card issuer has to wait until a person is 60 days behind in making a payment before it increases the interest rate.

- The issuer of a credit card must post on the Internet the full agreement that outlines what to expect when a credit card is issued.

- Instead of 14 days, the issuer must now allow 21 days to elapse between sending a statement and the due date for payment.

- Persons younger than 21 years old must provide proof of their ability to pay charges; otherwise parental or guardian assumption of responsibility for nonpayment is required before a credit card can be issued.

- Issuers of credit cards are no longer permitted to sponsor "giveaway campaigns" on college campuses.

- A "pay-to-pay fee" can no longer be charged when someone pays a fee over the Internet or by phone.

SOURCE: Starrs, C. (2009, November 8). Credit card changes. *Athens Banner-Herald*, pp. 1, 6.

Shopping

- If impulse buying creates problems, take steps to control your urge to buy. For example, take a grocery list with you when you shop and stick to the list.
- Shop at secondhand stores. These types of stores are typically referred to as thrift stores (e.g., Goodwill, Salvation Army) or consignment stores. Both types can provide bargains. Since new items appear almost daily, you might consider visiting such stores on a weekly basis to obtain the best bargains.
- According to Gregory Connolly (2011), the Better Business Bureau certifies two sites (Newegg.com and Tigerdirect.com) as businesses that offer various electronic devices, including laptops, at lower prices than one typically spends.
- Avoid shopping regularly at convenience stores (i.e., "gas-station stores"), since their prices tend to be higher, with a few exceptions (e.g., milk may be lower, but the lower price could represent an attempt to "bait and hook" you into going in and then paying higher prices for other items).
- When shopping at supermarkets, pay attention to unit prices displayed on the shelves, which allow you to more accurately compare the cost of different products.
- Avoid buying items from end-of-the aisle displays in supermarkets. In many cases, these do not offer the savings they appear to. Shoppers pause at the end of aisles, and store managers take advantage of this behavior to sell certain items.
- Try out generic brands for foods, spices, pet products, over-the-counter medicines, and so on. These store brands are frequently equal in quality, but cost significantly less.
- Make salads yourself instead of buying the bagged salads that are already made (the difference can be a 50 percent saving).
- Eat at your residence instead of eating out. If you decide to eat out, seek out bargains that advertise lower prices at non-peak times (e.g., dinner before 6 p.m.).

Miscellaneous Tips

- Zen Buddhists provide an excellent example of not becoming attached to worldly items. Simplify your life by reducing the number of items you buy. Review what you are paying for and ask yourself two questions:

Do I really need or want this? For example, do you need all the cell phone features for which you are paying? If the answer is no, get rid of some and save money.

Is there a less expensive (or free) way to get what I desire? If you really need or want something, consider alternatives besides paying for it. For example, join a car pool to reduce the cost of travel, bring your lunch with you rather than going out to lunch, and go to the college's library to read the newspaper instead of subscribing.

- Pay bills on time to establish good credit. Sending payments in on time builds a good credit history, which means you are worth the risk of loaning money to because you pay both the money loaned to you and the corresponding interest on schedule.
  - Avoid "friends" who borrow money, food, and so on without paying you back.

Budgeting

Debt is the worst poverty.

Thomas Fuller

Never spend your money before you have it.

Thomas Jefferson

Determine your monthly expenses. Compare the amount you are paying out to the amount of money coming in (income). In the beginning it is essential that you keep a daily record of expenses. Learn where the money is going. Once you establish the flow of your money, make suitable adjustments to gain better control if necessary. Establish goals and keep a budget to achieve them (e.g., "I will end each month with a few dollars, so I am not always asking my parents for help." "I will budget my money to have enough at the end of the semester to enable me to take a short three-day vacation." "I will cut back on nonessential spending to prevent situations like the time I had to get $500 with my credit card to pay some bills."). Keep in mind the difference between money spent on wants and money spent on needs.

Use the categories listed in the earlier activity "Where Is the Money Going?" as a model to set up a budget. Include all categories listed that are appropriate and add others that reflect your personal expenses. The greater the detail, the better you will understand where the money is going. Use this list to decide what you can cut back on, and then follow the budget you have set up. Adjust your budget after using it for a while; fine-tune it to fit your financial needs and personality.

Also, if you have to buy a big-ticket item while attending college, consider ways to reduce the costs. Take the example of a car. To keep cost down, consider buying a used car. Check reliable sources of information about used cars. A *Consumer Reports* investigation found the following used cars to have better-than-average reliability: Honda Civic, Toyota Corolla, Honda Accord, Toyota Camry, Acura TL, Acura RL, Mazda MX5 Miata, Honda CRV, Toyota RAV4, Toyota Tacoma, and Ford F150 2WD. (Search Google for an update.)

When it comes to used cars, be aware that some 20 percent of all vehicles that are considered totaled in accidents or other mishaps are rebuilt and sold as if they are simply pre-owned vehicles (Krebs, 2002). Krebs reports that in many cases, the history of the vehicle you are interested in can be checked through Carfax.com or AutoCheck.com for a small fee. You can also have your own mechanic check for previous damage and other problems. The cost of hiring a mechanic to check over a used car is well worth the money paid for such a service. Finally, for additional car buying tips, check out www.carbuyingtips.com.

Financial Aid and Student Employment

Budgeting should not simply be seen as an effort to cut back on spending. Budgeting also involves ways to increase income, looking for the amount of money available to cover certain costs. Remember, the word *budget* is inseparable from the word *income*. Supplementing one's available money might take the form of seeking employment or some type of financial aid. College personnel are available who can help students find employment and learn more about various types of financial aid, scholarship applications, confusing financial terms, publications devoted to financial aid information, and steps involved in obtaining financial aid. Financial aid advisors can answer many common questions over the phone, but if you are serious about obtaining financial aid, the sooner you set up an appointment to meet face to face with a financial aid advisor, the better off you will be. There are various sources of assistance: federal and state governments, banks, the college itself, and various private donations that are intended to assist students. Several examples of ways to help fund one's education are listed below (Goff, 2009/2010).

- **University Work Program (student employment).** In this case, you earn the money needed for various day-to-day expenses. Jobs are usually located on the campus. Sometimes the work is even tied to a student's career interest.
- **Aid for Military Personnel.** The campus's Reserve Officers' Training Corps (ROTC) provides both scholarships and living expenses (visit goarmy.com/rotc). Keep in mind that receipt of this form of assistance is tied to making a pledge to serve in the military.
- **Grants.** This form of financial aid does not require repayment. For example, federal Pell Grants are based on need and can provide several thousands of dollars for each child in a family.
- **Loans.** In this case, the student is expected to pay back the money borrowed. Typically, the repayment occurs after the student leaves the college, but the payment plan is based on a much lower rate of interest than is found with a non-education loan from a bank.
- **Private Programs of Student Aid.** A large number of organizations or individuals provide financial aid to individual students. Check with a campus financial advisor to learn more about this type of aid.
- **Special Programs Providing Aid.** In this case, funding is available for special groups of students (e.g., Donna Reed Foundation for Performing Arts, Women's International Bowling Congress Scholarship, Children of Deaf Adults Scholarship, Parke-Davis Epilepsy Scholarship Program, ESPN Scholastic Sports America).
- **Websites Worth Exploring.** Try these four websites to obtain additional information: (1) www.studentaid.ed.gov, (2) www.finaid.org, (3) www.foundationcenter.org, and (4) www.studentjobs.gov.
- **Predatory Loan Operations.** Several companies have appeared in recent years that are interested in making as much money as possible from students seeking financial help. If you are contacted by a loan company be sure to check with your college's financial aid office to determine if the company is trustworthy and fair in its dealings with students.

The actual list of possibilities in each of the above categories is long; students interested in obtaining up-to-date information should contact their college's financial aid office. In addition, various sources of information are available to help you learn more about ways to supplement the money you currently have to pay for a college education. Some examples follow. We recommend contacting the sources listed to determine if one or more of them can provide you with the type of information needed to achieve your financial and educational goals.

Financial Aid Guide. Source: Chronicle Guidance Publications. For more information, call 1-800-622-7284 or contact via www.chronicleguidance.com.

College Money Handbook. Source: Peterson's Online Bookstore. Contact via www. petersonsbooks.com.

Earn and Learn: Your Guide to In-School Educational Employment Programs by Joseph M. Re. Source: Octameron Associates, PO Box 2748, Alexandria, VA 22301 (703-836-5480).

Debt Stress and Credit Problems

Some students, such as beginning students with little family income and returning adult students who have given up (or lost) jobs to pursue a college degree, often find it difficult to make ends meet and might want to seek the advice of a consumer credit counselor (advisor). Usually one can find a service that is either free or only requires a small fee. Credit advising is designed to help individuals deal with financial problems. Typically, the advisor will meet with a person (or couple) to evaluate the financial situation and help the person develop a plan of action. The service will help the person establish a detailed budget, find the means to make payments, and even develop a plan for purchases in the future. Sometimes these services cooperate with the individual's creditors to get him or her back on a sound financial footing.

Finally, be aware of what is called *identity theft*. Identity thieves gather information about you that allows them to access your checking or savings account and to obtain credit cards and loans in your name. They acquire the needed information through a number of different avenues. They might submit a change of address form to a post office to have your mail sent to them, remove mail directly from your mailbox, or call your residence and trick you into revealing your Social Security number over the phone. In some cases, these thieves might have bought the needed information from unscrupulous restaurant servers who make a copy of your credit card number when you turn the card over to the server to pay a bill. Take measures to prevent the stealing of your identity (e.g., consider renting a post office box if someone in the neighborhood reports his or her identity was stolen). Authorities that have dealt with cases of identity theft recommend periodically checking your credit rating to uncover any problems resulting from identity theft. While credit checks can be obtained for no cost, frequent checking almost always results in you paying a fee. (Katie Crowe [2011] reports that CreditKarma.com provides credit scores at no cost and does so frequently enough to allow for close tracking.)

Closing Remarks

According to Kathy Chu (2009), overdraft fees have become one of the biggest avenues for banks to make money. For example, during the span of a recent year, banks were estimated to have earned $38,500,000,000 as a result of the fees they charged for overdrafts (on debit card use and ATM withdrawals) and insufficient funds (on checks). This amount was roughly twice the amount (i.e., $20,500,000,000) that banks earned through penalties tied to credit card use during the same time period.

These staggering amounts should make it clear that there are many important issues to consider when it comes to developing the skills necessary to manage money. In addition, while the authors of this textbook focused on those financial areas that have proven to be troublesome for students, there are other things to consider, such as savings accounts, financial plans, Social Security payments, investing, and taxes. We recommend that you seek additional information from an expert or one of the many published sources available about these other areas. As with the various other life-skills discussed throughout this textbook, financial skills will play a crucial role in your life *during* and *after* college.

Answer Box

Answers given in order:

Portraits are Hamilton, Jackson, Grant, and Franklin.

Scenes are U.S. Treasury building, White House, U.S. Capitol, and Independence Hall.

Largest bill printed was $100,000 and was embellished with a portrait of Wilson.

The largest bill printed since 1969 is $100.

Sources

Brill, H., Brill, J. A., & Feigenbaum, C. (1999). *Investing with your values: Making money and making a difference*. Princeton, NY: Bloomberg Press.

Chu, K. (2009, November 13). Fed requires OK for overdraft fees. *USA Today*, p. B1.

Connolly, G. (2011, August). Find a laptop bargain for student online. *USA Weekend*, p. 4.

Consumer Credit Counseling Services. (n.d.). *Client handbook*. Atlanta, GA: Author.

Crowe, K. (2011, May). Grads: Get help with your money. *USA Weekend*, p. 4.

Editors of Rodale Press. (1994). *Cut your spending in half without settling for less: How to pay the lowest price for everything*. Emmaus, PA: Rodale Press.

Emmett, R. (2000). *The procrastinator's handbook: Mastering the art of doing it now*. New York, NY: Walker.

Fisher, S. Y., & Shelly, S. (2009). *Personal finance in your 20s & 30s* (4th ed.). Indianapolis, IN: Alpha.

Fogarty, P. (Ed.). (2007). *Free money: Free stuff*. Pleasantville, NY: The Reader's Digest Association, Inc.

Freud, S. (1965). *The interpretation of dreams* (James Strachey, Trans.). New York, NY: Discus Books. (Original work published 1900)

Georgia Career Information System [Computer software]. (1998). Atlanta, GA: Georgia State University.

Goff, L. (2009, December/2010, January). The best way to pay for college. *Reader's Digest*, 146–153.

Hartman, H. (Ed.). (2001). *Time for kids almanac 2002 with information please*. New York, NY: Family Education.

Krebs, M. (2002, April). The best used cars ever: Kick the tires and go. *Reader's Digest*, 90–95.

Morris, K. M., & Siegel, A. M. (1992). *The Wall Street Journal: Guide to understanding personal finance*. New York, NY: Lightbulb Press.

Paris, J. L. (1997). *Money management for those who don't have any*. Eugene, OR: Harvest House.

Phillips, B. (1993). *Phillips' book of great thoughts and funny sayings*. Wheaton, IL: Tyndale House.

Pliskin, M., & Just, S. L. (1999). *The complete idiot's guide to interpreting your dreams*. New York, NY: Macmillan.

Prather, C. L. (1964). Money. In *World Book Encyclopedia* (Vol. 13, pp. 588–599). Chicago, IL: Field Enterprises Educational Corp.

Schemo, D. J. (2002, March 8). More graduates mired in debt, survey finds. *New York Times*. Retrieved from http://www.nytimes.com

Shearer, L. (2002, February 23). Identity theft rising threat, expert says. *Athens Banner-Herald*, p. A10.

Starrs, C. (2009, November 8). Credit card changes. *Athens Banner Herald*, pp. 1, 6.

Temper, S. (2002). Dealing with debt dilemma. *Athens Banner-Herald*, pp. F1, F3.

U.S. Department of Labor, Bureau of Labor Statistics. (1993). *Consumer expenditure survey*. Washington, DC: Author.

Chapter 9

Exercise 1: Money Management

1. Based on the material in this chapter, what area of money management do you believe you need to concentrate on the most? Explain.

2. How do you plan to work on this money management area? Be as specific as possible.

3. How does your personality affect your ability to manage money?

4. Describe how you see yourself financially in six years. What obstacles will you have to overcome to achieve your financial goals? What can you do during the next year to move closer toward these goals? How are these goals tied to your personal values (e.g., helping others, free time, power, creativity, stability, independence, security, personal freedom, and so forth)?

Exercise 2: Investing with Personal Values

Hal Brill, Jack A. Brill, and Cliff Feigenbaum's *Investing with Your Values* provides invaluable information that allows you to select and invest money in companies that operate in ways that are consistent with your personal values. Investing in keeping with your personal values allows you to make a positive difference in the world. The Council on Economic Priorities (CEP) uses a model of evaluation (reviewed in Brill et al.'s book) to grade companies in eight values-related categories:

Environment

Community

Charitable contributions

Minority advancement

Women's advancement

Workplace issues

Family benefits

Public disclosure

CEP assigns points for each category listed above. After each category is rated, all the points are used to calculate a grade for the company (4.0 is the highest possible grade). CEP places the top 40 companies on its honor roll. Several of these companies are listed below.

Adolph Coors Company

Avon Products, Inc.

Ben & Jerry's Homemade, Inc.

Dole Food Co.

Healthy Planet Products

Hewlett-Packard Co.

International Business Machines

Johnson & Johnson

Kellogg Co.

McGraw-Hill Co.

PepsiCo, Inc.

Starbucks Corp.

Sun Co.

Xerox Corp.

1. Based on what you believe is important, rank the categories used by CEP to evaluate companies.

   1) _____ (most important to you)

   2) _____

   3) _____

   4) _____

   5) _____

   6) _____

   7) _____

   8) _____ (least important to you)

2. Explain why you gave the highest and lowest rankings to the two categories you did.

3. Assume you have $50,000 to invest in a company for retirement. Your investment choice is either Company A or Company B.

   - Company A excels in the category you assigned the highest ranking. Investing in Company A will result in $300,000 at retirement.

   - Company B excels in the category you assigned the lowest ranking. Investing in Company B will result in $600,000 at retirement.

   Question: Would you invest in Company A or Company B? Explain.

4. Would you marry a person who assigned his or her lowest rating to any of the following categories: environment, minority advancement, or women's advancement? Explain.

5. Your responses to questions 1–4 probably tell you less about how you perceive money and more about your personal values. What did you learn about who you are by answering these questions?

SECTION 3

Interpersonal
Communication/
Human Relations
Skills

Relationships
The Bridges That Connect Self and Others

10

psychiatrist by the name of Harry Stack Sullivan believed that the defining feature of humans is that they are interpersonal beings. He made this assertion the foundation of his theory of human nature. For Sullivan, our personalities are what we display in our interactions with others. The interpersonal patterns we establish (how we relate to others and they to us) form what Sullivan called *dynamisms*. While Sullivan recognized the importance of basic needs (e.g., hunger), he was more interested in the need for emotional security and how this relates to our interpersonal nature. Sullivan believed that the interpersonal permeates our lives. For example, even the manner in which we eat has interpersonal components (e.g., a fork and knife are "social" inventions), and even the hermit who heads off into the wilderness to be alone still thinks of others and probably dreams about others.

Relationships Fill Our Lives

Regardless of how much time a student devotes to studying, a significant part of the college environment involves interpersonal opportunities. We believe that a balance should be sought between the academic world and the interpersonal world offered by attending a college. Knowledge is crucial to one's future career path, but so are interpersonal skills. Even in relatively isolated types of work, the ability to interact in an effective and satisfying way is essential. Sometimes getting involved in meaningful relationships with others is easy and just happens, but there are other times when starting or maintaining a relationship is anything but easy or pleasant. In this chapter we will discuss loneliness, effective communication and interaction skills, and injurious types of interactions.

© NEWART, 2012. Used under license from Shutterstock, Inc.

Communicate, communicate, communicate.

Loneliness

Beginning students (18-year-old freshmen and older students starting for the first time), transfer students, international students, and many others experience loneliness for a relatively long period (up to six months) before they come out of it. This is not surprising, since loneliness is to interpersonal relationships what the common cold is to sickness: everyone experiences bouts of loneliness. Attending college, with so many potential opportunities for social contact, may actually intensify feelings of loneliness because the lonely student can see people being together all around him or her. (A person can be very lonely in a crowd.) Interestingly, while we may tell someone else when we are stressed out, anxious, or even depressed, it seems more difficult to acknowledge being lonely. In spite of its frequent occurrence, the condition is stigmatized. Yet this does not mean it is not discussed or spoken about. If we listen, we find that loneliness is a common subject in poetry, literature, and songs.

The countless instances when the specter of loneliness has taken form in song include the question "All the lonely people, where do they come from?" posed by the Beatles, and the lyrical image of traveling along *a long, lonesome road* in verse four of Bob Dylan's "Don't Think Twice, It's All Right." In director Martin Scorsese's *Taxi Driver*, Robert De Niro's character remarks, "Loneliness has followed me my whole life. Everywhere. In bars, in cars, sidewalks, stores, everywhere. There's no escape. I'm God's lonely man." Finally, Walt Whitman's poem "I Saw in Louisiana a Live-Oak Growing" reflects the sense of fear and estrangement found with loneliness, as in this excerpt.

> I saw in Louisiana a
> live-oak growing, all alone stood it and moss hung
> down from the branches,
> Without any companion it grew there
> uttering joyous leaves of dark green,
> And its look, rude, unbending, lusty,
> made me think of myself,
> But I wonder'd how it could utter
> joyous leaves standing alone there without its
> friend near, for I knew I could not. . . .

Effects of Loneliness

Earl Ginter and Patricia Dwinell discovered that loneliness is a better predictor of grade performance than self-esteem. Specifically, while they found no relationship between self-esteem and performance in specific courses, they did find a relationship between loneliness and overall grades. Students who were lonely earned significantly higher grades. Ginter and Dwinell suggested the reason was that lonely students channeled their energy into studying. This is an intriguing finding because loneliness might serve to push us to seek activity, even if it is not social in nature—but more importantly, it tells us there is an important difference between depression and loneliness. Depression is associated with a reduction in activity; this is not necessarily true of loneliness.

While higher grades may be a positive outcome of feeling lonely, we believe it is better to aim to have both good grades and satisfying social relationships. In fact, the negatives associated with loneliness far outweigh any positives. Loneliness has been associated with physical illness, lower levels of perceived self-worth, and higher levels of anxiety, depression, and alcohol and drug abuse. When researchers Joseph Scalise, Earl Ginter, and Larry Gerstein studied emotional factors in loneliness, they found four dimensions to loneliness that people experience to differing degrees: depletion, isolation, agitation, and dejection.

- **Depletion.** The lonely person experiences a noticeable drop in vigor and resourcefulness. This condition is experienced as feeling drained, empty, hollow, and secluded.
- **Isolation.** The lonely person has a sense of "interpersonal segregation." He or she feels unloved, worthless, hopeless, and disliked.
- **Agitation.** This dimension reflects a tenseness or restlessness. Sometimes lonely individuals express a more aggressive attitude. They feel angry, nervous, humiliated, and guilty.
- **Dejection.** The lonely person is down in spirits. Unlike in depression, though, the feelings of despondency or discouragement associated with this dimension do not necessarily lead to a drop in general activity.

Before discussing what can be done about loneliness, we want to briefly discuss depression. It is not uncommon for college students to report periods of loneliness and depression, but the two conditions are not the same. Basically, while depression can also inhibit relationships, unlike loneliness, it usually has a profound effect on one's ability to perform.

Depressive episodes can range in intensity and symptoms, but typically a depressed individual will report the following: loss of appetite or overeating, insomnia, fatigue, low self-esteem, a feeling of hopelessness, and poor concentration during decision making.

Depression and Suicide

It is important to recognize that suicide and depression are linked. While not everyone who is depressed thinks of suicide as an appropriate solution, any mention of suicide should not automatically be dismissed as unlikely. Suicide is one of the leading causes of death in young adults. If a friend is depressed, help the friend seek assistance from one of the many resources on campus. According to Richard Warga, there are several common myths about suicide.

Myths about Suicide

- If a student speaks about committing suicide, he or she will not really do it.
- There are no warning signs that come before a student's suicide—so we should not expect any indication that something is about to happen.
- A student who attempts suicide is not ambivalent about dying—rather, the person is absolutely certain he or she wants to die.
- Suicide tends to be limited to the rich and poor segments of society, not middle-class, everyday people.
- Suicidal tendencies reflect a biological feature that "runs in certain families."
- A student committing suicide is *psychotic* because sane, normal people do not commit suicide.
- A suicide attempt permanently weakens a student's ability to handle future difficulties and as a result even relatively minor difficulties experienced later can trigger a suicide attempt.
- Psychological improvement immediately following a suicide attempt (for example, the person displays greater energy and involvement) is a clear indication that depressive thoughts are over and there is no danger of suicide.

The Truth about Suicide

The truth is that warning signs are usually present, many suicides are committed by people who are undecided about living or dying, just because a person had attempted suicide does not mean she or he will be this way for life, and a jump in energy does not necessarily mean the crisis is over. (In fact, the increase in energy may enable the person to plan and succeed next time.) Furthermore, suicide is found at all socioeconomic levels, and suicide in a family is not proof of certain families possessing an innate tendency for suicide. While depression is associated with suicide, the unhappy person committing suicide may or may not be suffering from a mental disorder. Separating fiction from fact is important, but possibly the most important thing to remember is this: If someone speaks to you about committing suicide, do not automatically assume the person is not serious. Listen carefully, be supportive, and take the most appropriate action that fits the particular situation. Finally, assistance with depression, a suicide attempt, or suicidal thoughts is typically available at a college's health center or counseling center.

Unhealthy and Damaging Relationships

As mentioned earlier, a significant part of the college experience involves forming new relationships—relationships that have the potential to significantly impact your life in numerous and positive ways. Establishing such college relationships can be easy, and sometimes they just seem to happen with no effort, but there are other times when starting or maintaining a relationship is anything but easy or pleasant. While the purpose of this chapter is to provide information about what constitutes healthy relationships, it is important to recognize there are certain types of relationships that it is best to avoid.

Everyone has experienced others who are very difficult to interact with, and while it takes at least two individuals to create interpersonal conflict, there are times when the primary cause for the conflict resides with the other person. It is important to emphasize that the types of difficult personalities discussed here differ in very distinct ways from other types of troublesome people we have encountered in life: for example, the person has displayed a certain pattern of speaking, behaving, and thinking that mental health professionals view as maladaptive because it interferes with establishing the kinds of healthy relationships we have come to expect in our culture. The term *personality disorder* has been used to categorize these types of unhealthy interpersonal patterns. Keep in mind, just because you might recognize some of these characteristics in someone else does not mean the other person is suffering from the personality disorder described (American Psychiatric Association, 2000). The five personality disorders listed below represent interpersonal extremes that are inflexible and pervasive in the person's life.

- **Narcissistic:** Their interactions are always tainted by self-centeredness. They are known for interacting in conspicuous ways designed to attract attention or admiration. In general, others are treated as if they exist to please and cater to the narcissistic person. Narcissistic personalities have a very difficult time accepting any form of negative feedback, even when the criticism was meant to be constructive in nature.

- **Histrionic:** They often become overly dramatic in their behavior or manner of speaking. These individuals seem to be motivated mostly by a desire to gain attention for what concerns them at the moment. They may even act in an inappropriately seductive way just so they can entice someone to focus his or her attention on them. While the emotions they express are exaggerated, they lack the kind of depth we would expect with such a strong display of feelings.

- **Dependent:** These individuals rely heavily on others, seeking advice, favors, and comfort. They are described by words like "clinging," because they seem to stay too close once they have established an interpersonal connection. They find it "impossible" to do anything without the other's support and may become like a shadow that follows the other person wherever he or she goes.

- **Passive-aggressive:** Their aggressive approach to relationships is often hidden and displayed in passive ways, such as procrastination or stubbornness. It is not unusual for them to display their irritation by a gloomy silence or becoming withdrawn for no obvious reason.

- **Antisocial:** While they can come across as very caring and concerned about others, this behavior often hides a strong interest in manipulating people for personal gain or satisfaction. In fact, these individuals are capable of generating considerable distress in others, but seem to experience their own lives without much or any anxiety. They lack empathy and are frequently driven to violate social norms and the rights of others (sometimes physically harming others).

Sexual Relationships

While sexual behavior is commonly undertaken for pleasure, pleasure is far from the only motive, since sex itself has a multitude of symbolic meanings. These symbolic meanings are tied to societal views concerning sexual behavior, legal standards, personal standards, and shared meanings held by two individuals who love one another. While sexual activity can be one of the most powerful forces to enrich a couple's relationship, some sexual behaviors, such as sexual harassment and rape, can have profoundly negative effects on people. Finally, the perpetrator of rape is almost always male, and while the victim can be a male in the vast majority of cases the victim is female.

Sexual Behaviors Gone Wrong

Sexual Harassment. The Office of Legal Affairs at the authors' institution distributes a pamphlet that summarizes its harassment policy, and the information it contains is typical of what is distributed on other campuses. According to the pamphlet, Title VII of the Civil Rights Act of 1964 and Title IX of the Educational Amendments of 1972 define sexual harassment as unwelcome sexual advances, requests for sexual favors, and other verbal or physical conduct of a sexual nature, when:

1. submission to such conduct is made, either implicitly or explicitly, a term or condition of an individual's employment or status in a course, program or activity;
2. submission or rejection of such conduct by an individual is used as the basis for employment or educational decisions affecting such individual; or
3. such conduct has the purpose or effect of interfering with the individual's work or educational performance; creating an intimidating, hostile, or offensive working and/or learning environment; or interfering with one's ability to participate in or benefit from an educational program or activity.

What is to be done if sexual harassment is suspected? Again, quoting from the pamphlet:

> All students and employees should report any sexual harassment that they experience, observe, or believe may be occurring, to the Sexual Harassment Prevention and Compliance Officer [on campus]. (Please keep in mind making a deliberate false accusation of sexual harassment can lead to the accused taking action. In such instances, the complainant will be subject to disciplinary action on the part of the college. However, failure to prove a claim of sexual harassment does not constitute proof of a false accusation.)

Acquaintance or Date Rape

The perpetrator of rape is not always a stranger. It can be the person seated next to you in your classroom, the person you met at the student union, the person you met through one of the college's many student clubs, and so forth. In fact, college women are more likely to be raped by a person they know than by a stranger.

The definition of rape is simple. *Rape = the use of force to obtain nonconsensual sex.* The word "force" is emphasized because while force may take the form of physical force, it can also take the form of emotional coercion that results in nonconsensual sex. An important distinction can be made between seduction and rape. According to the brochure *I Was Arrested for Date Rape*, distributed to students at the authors' institution:

One of the key questions in the issue of date rape is the difference between seduction and rape: the man feels he has merely seduced a woman; the woman feels that she was raped. **Seduction** *involves no force; it occurs when a woman is enticed into agreeing to have sex.* The key word is agreeing. Acquaintance rape often occurs when seduction fails and the man goes ahead and has sex with the woman anyway, despite any protests and without her agreement.

The brochure points out that acquaintance or date rape cannot be traced to a single cause, but usually involves several key elements.

1. **Myths and Misconceptions.** Growing up, men and women are exposed to a variety of messages about what their sex roles "should" be. Some of the messages and misconceptions listed below might contribute to date rape.
   - Some men are taught to "go for the win"—to be aggressive in sports, in careers, and in relationships.
   - Some women are taught to be passive and nice and accepting of people. They are taught they are "not supposed to make a scene."
   - Some men mistakenly believe that when a woman says "no" to sex, she really means "yes" in certain situations.
   - Some women are encouraged to look and act sexy. (Typically, at the same time they are told they are responsible for their reputations.)
   - Some women expect sexual attention from men, and might even be disappointed if men do not make sexual advances. They may think that something is wrong with them or with the male if he does not try something. Such behavior sends mixed messages and might cause confusion.

2. **Different Expectations Concerning Dates.** A man may expect sex to be part of a date because the woman had sex with him before, is wearing what he perceives to be sexy or provocative clothes, had sex with someone the male knows personally, and so forth. Such false expectations can contribute to a date rape situation.

3. **Alcohol.** Studies show that alcohol use or abuse is involved in over 75 percent of acquaintance rape cases.

4. **Poor Communication.** Studies show that men may interpret messages in a sexual way more often than women do. When a woman says, "Do you want to come to my apartment to study?" a male might hear a sexual message when none was intended.

The brochure also offers suggestions concerning what men can do to stop date rape. For example, **a male should always assume that "No" means NO!** If correct, the male has not offended or exploited his partner in any way. If the assumption was wrong, it is now her responsibility to open up the communication and reinitiate the encounter.

The following list represents the types of services that are typically found on or near most college campuses for victims of rape.

Medical assistance or consultation:

- The college's health center (check for special units, such as a women's clinic)
- The local hospital (emergency service)

For legal, judicial, or police assistance or information:

- Campus police
- City police
- Check telephone listings for relevant legal services

If the victim needs someone to talk with:

- Counseling/therapy services (often provided at a college's health center)
- Rape crisis line

The Key to Healthy Interactions: Communication and Human Relations Skills

Above all else, healthy relationships are built on clear communication skills. Table 10.1 outlines the three basic components of clear communication.

Table 10.1

Effective Communication Skills

Talking = Ability to openly express information to the other person in order to send a message. Most people do not have much difficulty expressing themselves, but some have never learned to share information.

Listening = Ability to actively listen to someone in order to receive the message being sent. In a college atmosphere, this is often difficult to do. Active listening requires you to tune in to what the other person is saying without interrupting. You must acknowledge your listening by giving nonverbal cues, put the speaker's ideas into your own words when you respond, and question anything that may not be clear.

Understanding = Ability to comprehend the message received, given the fact that actions and statements can take on different meanings for different people. The key is to recognize and accept differences in styles, and to adapt or adjust to such differences as needed.

From Conner, D., & Huguley, W. *The Auburn experience*.

One way students can feel they are participating more fully in college life is to achieve a better balance of work and play; connecting with others on campus is one aspect of this important balance. The best way to connect with others is through effective use of communication and relationship skills. A number of such skills have been identified, and they are relatively easy to learn.

You will encounter a wide cross-section of individuals while at college, including classmates, graduate teaching assistants, professors, administrators, and dorm personnel. Having an array of meaningful relationships within these groups can prevent or reduce loneliness. The following list represents a few of the qualities of healthy relationships.

- Mutual support is evident
- Displayed interest in one another
- Acceptance of the other person for who the person is
- Interactions marked by flexibility (e.g., the other person is okay with changes in plans that are beyond one's control)
- A willingness to compromise or work out conflicts when disagreements occur
- Interactions have an energizing quality (unhealthy relationships tend to leave us with a sense of being drained, as if we have encountered an *interpersonal vampire*)
- Feedback is truthful but tempered with consideration for feelings
- Respect is evident in how the individuals treat one another
- Empathy, or the ability to adopt the other's perspective, is present

Chapter 10

Exercise 1: Receiving and Sending Messages

While you answer the questions below, please keep in mind that this exercise is not focusing on the amount of skill building required—the point of this exercise is that everyone (including the authors of this textbook) can work on and strengthen their current skills.

1. Both **general communication skills** and **assertiveness skills** were covered in this chapter. Of these two areas, which would you pick to concentrate on to strengthen the skills you already possess? Identify the area selected and explain in detail why you selected this area over the other area.

2. Based on the information provided in the chapter (you can also use other resources, but cite your sources), develop a plan of action that will add to your existing repertoire of skills in the area you selected. Be as specific as possible when you discuss your plan.

3. What specific changes do you believe will occur when you implement your plan? (These changes will serve as your "measure of success.")

4. Pick a specific date to implement your skill building plan _____.

Connecting Common Threads across a Diverse World

11

We live in an increasingly complex world that requires us to be adept in many life-skills (interpersonal communication/human relations, problem solving/decision making, physical fitness/health maintenance, and identity development/purpose-in-life). In a pluralistic society, differences exist among and between various groups of people (e.g., ethnic, racial, religious, gender, sexual orientation, physical, and other groupings). While living in a pluralistic society can create tension as various groups attempt to sustain and develop their traditional cultures or special interests within the confines of a common society, the experience can also create a rich source of energy that can fuel the creative potential of a society and advance it culturally and democratically. To fully develop as a person requires one to be aware of both the common threads that hold people together as a community, a nation, and a world and the unique threads of various hues and textures that complete the tapestry called humanity. It takes focused awareness and a multitude of skills to negotiate a diverse world.

Multiculturalism

If we are to achieve a richer culture, rich in contrasting values, we must recognize the whole gamut of human potentialities, and so weave a less arbitrary social fabric, one in which each diverse human gift will find a fitting place.

Margaret Mead

Multiculturalism is a philosophical belief based on ideals of social justice and equity that recognizes not only that diversity does exist, but that it is a valuable resource in a community. Proponents of multiculturalism believe that it is to each and every person's advantage to acquire a competent set of skills to use when thinking about issues related to diversity. These life-skills are needed individually to help us achieve success in a multicultural world and collectively to move our society beyond a toleration of differences among people to a respect for cultural pluralism.

Multiculturalism challenges us to recognize multiple perspectives, and in doing so, we enhance our problem-solving and critical-thinking skills. While adopting a multicultural perspective can prepare us to live in a multicultural world, it can also create discomfort, fear, denial, guilt, and anger during the process. People often believe that their own standards are the right standards; this view is known as ethnocentricity. When you have different groups of people living close to one another, and each group believes it is functioning quite well by its own set of standards, conflict can arise as groups try to figure out what set of standards is right for the society as a whole.

College campuses are a part of this multicultural world and are challenged to respond to the needs of an increasingly diverse student population. Administrators on campus understand that change is inevitable and recognize the value of a multicultural education in helping students to develop multicultural competencies. Many colleges require students to take a multicultural class and, in addition, offer multidisciplinary programs (e.g., women's studies and African studies). As pointed out earlier, activities that challenge your mind expand the number and strength of neural connections that learning is based on. Engaging in activities that are unfamiliar or different (e.g., talking with people from cultures different from your own and engaging in diverse cultural experiences) helps to create a more complex system of thoughts, perceptions, assumptions, attitudes, feelings, and skills that can lead to greater learning potential.

The racial composition of the U.S. is based on immigration, and about a third of the total growth rate in the U.S. labor force is supplied by legal and illegal immigration (Marable, 2000). Pragmatically, students as well as others can benefit from developing a set of multicultural competencies because the world in which we live will continue to become more diverse. It is inevitable that among your neighbors, teachers, fellow students, coworkers, friends, and teammates will be individuals with backgrounds quite different from your own. As a college student, you are in a unique learning situation that offers numerous opportunities to increase your diversity skills. If you have not formed genuine relationships with people who have dissimilar backgrounds from you, now is your chance. People who ignore or resist opportunities may find themselves both vocationally and personally deficient in a global, multicultural society.

Demographic Changes

According to the 2010 U.S. Bureau of the Census report (U.S. Department of Commerce, 2011) there were an estimated 308,745,538 million people living in the United States, an increase of 9.7 percent since the 2000 census. About 72.4 percent identified themselves as white (only down from 75 percent in 2000 and 83 percent in 1990).

Projections for the year 2050 are that the percentage of white people living in the United States will continue to decline and the percentage of current minorities will increase. More than 47 percent of children under the age of five in the U.S. are Asian, black, or Hispanic. This number is expected to increase.

Over the last ten years, the people who identified themselves as Asian alone increased by 43 percent (equal to about 5 percent of the total population), which represents a growth of more than four million people. The Asian population in the U.S. grew faster than any other minority group. A small increase, 12.6 percent (up from 12.3 percent in 2000, but less than the 13 percent uncovered via the 1990 census), was found for those who self-identified as black or African American only. The American Indian and Alaskan Native population held constant at .9 percent of the total population, and people who identified themselves as Native Hawaiian and Other Pacific Islander rose from .1 percent in 2000 to .2 percent in 2010. In addition, 6 percent of the respondents identified themselves as a race other than ones listed, and about 3 percent selected more than one racial category.

In response to a separate question about ethnicity, 16 percent identified themselves as Hispanic or Latino; these respondents may be of any race (up from 13 percent in 2000 and 11 percent in 1990). The Hispanic and Latino population grew by 43 percent, which represents a change from 35.3 million in 2000 to 50.5 million in 2010 (in addition, the 1990 census reported a total of 22.4 million Hispanics and Latinos residing in the U.S.). The growth in the Hispanic and Latino population in the U.S. accounts for more than half of all the growth in the total population of the country between 2000 and 2010.

Geographically, most immigrants today settle in the western and southern parts of the U.S. More than 50 percent of the people who reside in Texas, the District of Columbia, Hawaii, and California belong to a minority group. While California is the state with the largest minority population (22.3 million), it was Nevada that experienced the greatest population increase of minorities (78 percent) between 2000 and 2010.

Along with the racial and ethnic demographic shifts that have occurred, especially among young children, the dramatic increase in the number of Americans 65 years old and older is important to note. The World Almanac (2002) refers to the U.S. as an "aging nation," a view supported by the U.S. Census Bureau's own projection that the population over 65 (12.9 percent of today's population) will increase to about 20 percent of the population by 2050. In addition, the number of people who are 85 or older (representing about 2 percent of today's population) will double to 4 percent by 2050. In fact, today the median age of the U.S. population is 36.8, which is the highest that has ever been reported.

Everyone represents diversity.

Living in a Pluralistic Society

Two primary goals of a college education are to help you develop lifelong skills for continuous personal growth and help you become a responsible community member. Today's college students do not believe that there are any quick fixes for our nation's social problems. A social problem facing many college students today on campuses throughout the United States is racism. Racism is a form of discrimination based on biased assumptions about what people are and are not. It is a powerful force throughout the nation, weaving in and out of cultures, institutions, and individuals. Racism, ableism, sexism, heterosexism, ageism, and classism are all powerful discriminatory forces. These "isms" have the power to include, exclude, legitimize, and marginalize groups of people. Assumptions about what people are and are not enable prejudices and discrimination to flourish.

Throughout the world, countries are becoming more pluralistic. Diversity encompasses differences in educational level, gender, ethnicity, race, age, sexual orientation, religion, socioeconomic level, physical ability, and many other personal characteristics. In the last 25 years, there has been a dramatic shift in population trends in the United States, and the demographics of this country will continue to shift. The pluralities and complexities that exist between and among groups of people will also continue to change as differences in language, politics, region, social class, religion, and nationality further subdivide groups. Marable (2000) calls for a new and critical study of race and ethnicity to understand the changes that are taking place around us. He believes that one of the reasons that discussions about race and social diversity are so difficult is the complicated relationship between ethnicity and race.

Terminology

The terminology associated with multiculturalism is continually changing to more accurately reflect changing attitudes about diversity. Currently you will read about "people of color" rather than nonwhites; gays, lesbians, and bisexuals rather than homosexuals; and people with disabilities rather than disabled or handicapped. Even though many people, through a process like stereotyping, choose to define other people rather narrowly, many people choose to define themselves in broad, diverse ways. What comes to mind when you think of a nontraditional student? A fraternity member? A gay student? A Hispanic student? An Asian student? A student with disabilities?

Culture refers to a way of being—the way we define ourselves. Culture implies a recognizable pattern of values and beliefs that is shared among a group of people who also share traditions. If someone asks you to define your culture, you might choose a narrow definition and respond that you are Catholic, Baptist, American, or German. You might also choose a broader definition of culture and respond that you are a musician, a Southerner, an athlete, or a member of a sorority.

What about race? Is it a social concept used to discriminate against groups of people, or is it a biological/genetic concept? There is a lot of controversy in the literature about the definition of race. Pedersen (1994) defines race as "a pseudobiological system of classifying persons by a shared genetic history or physical characteristics such as skin color" (p. x). Race is a topic that people struggle to talk about with one another. Talking about race can be especially challenging due to political and emotional misapplications of the term. For the first time in the history of the census, respondents in 2000 were given the choice of selecting one or more race categories to identify their racial identity, and about 2.4 percent (6.8 million) of the total population chose more than one racial category (Barron, 2002). According to the 2010 U.S. Census Bureau (2011)

92 percent of the nine million people (3 percent of the total population) who identified themselves as being more than one race selected two races. The greatest multirace combination selected was white and black. Questions about being Hispanic or Latino were designated in a separate category. As pointed out previously, there is often more diversity within a group of people who are regarded as having similar characteristics than there is between different groups.

Ethnicity exists within the broader category of race. Ethnic groups such as Japanese, Cambodian, Chinese, Korean, Filipino, Vietnamese, and Pacific Islander fall under the racial umbrella of Asian. Hispanics, or Latinos, as some people prefer, are generally descended from a country or culture where Spanish is spoken. Some Hispanic people may be from Puerto Rico, the Dominican Republic, Mexico, Guatemala, Cuba, Colombia, or Argentina. Hispanics are a very diverse group with varied customs, food, cultural patterns, and politics, and may prefer a more specific term such as *Puerto Rican* or *Guatemalan* rather than *Hispanic* or *Latina*. People who refer to themselves as black might look to Africa, Haiti, Jamaica, or the West Indies for their cultural heritage. People who identify with having a white ethnic background may look to Poland, Australia, Italy, Africa, Ireland, or Germany. Among the American Indian and Alaska Native populations, you will also find a multiplicity of cultural patterns.

What is your ethnicity? Exercise 1 at the end of this chapter is designed to help you to get in touch with your ethnic heritage. This exercise may be difficult for some of you whose relatives have moved away from the family's historical roots to assimilate into American culture. It may require making a few phone calls and doing some Internet research to put your heritage into an ethnic perspective. Before you read about suggestions for developing multicultural competencies, in the next section, take a moment to become familiar with some of the terms associated with diversity and multiculturalism.

Terms Associated with Diversity and Multiculturalism

ableism	prejudice or discrimination against people with mental, emotional, and physical disabilities
ageism	prejudice or discrimination based on age
anti-Semitism	hostility toward Jewish people
classism	prejudice or discrimination based on economic background
culture	group of people bound together by traditions (food, language, religion) and values
discrimination	an action or policy that differentiates one group from another in terms of treatment
ethnic	related to having shared cultural, national, or tribal origins
ethnocentrism	a belief that one's own culture is more correct, important, or superior
homophobia	an irrational fear of gay, lesbian, transgender, or bisexual people
prejudice	preconceived opinion for or against someone or something
privilege	unearned access to resources due to membership in a particular social group
racism	discrimination based on skin color and ethnicity; a belief that a particular race is superior or inferior
sexism	prejudice or discrimination based on gender
stereotyping	overgeneralizing about groups of people based on biased assumptions

Developing Multicultural Competencies

We know that our attitudes and beliefs influence our perceptions. We assimilate attitudes and beliefs throughout our lives, forming assumptions about the way things are and are not, including judgments about people. Unfortunately, we tend to filter out information that does not affirm, or align with, our perception of the world, so we tend to rely on many biased assumptions to guide us through life. Biased assumptions distort the truth and give rise to prejudices that keep us confined in narrowly defined spaces. Is there any way for us to get out of our own little boxes to see what is truly going on around us? The answer is, emphatically, yes! Biases can be intentional or unintentional. They might be based on cultural isolation or ignorance. When you form a belief about an entire group of people without recognizing individual differences among members of the group, you are engaging in stereotyping.

We are all guilty of stereotyping because of the way in which the mind stores, organizes, and recalls information to reduce complexity and help us make quick decisions (Johnson & Johnson, 2000). Johnson and Johnson report that the term *stereotype* was initially used in the 18th century to describe a printing process that duplicated pages of type, and it was not until 1922 that Walter Lippman used it to describe the process by which people gloss over details to simplify social perceptions. We tend to stereotype people to whom we do not pay much attention. The practice of stereotyping can lead to prejudice, which can lead to discrimination. Why does it endure? Read over the reasons given in Table 11.1.

Table 11.1   Reasons Why Stereotypes Endure

1. People tend to overestimate the association between variables that are only slightly correlated or not correlated at all, creating an **illusionary correlation**. Many people, for example, perceive that being poor and being lazy are associated. Any poor person who is not hard at work at the moment you notice him or her may be perceived to be lazy. Low-power groups can easily acquire negative traits in this way, and once acquired, the stereotype is hard to shed.

2. Having a prejudice makes people notice the negative traits they ascribe to the groups they are prejudiced against, and they more readily believe information that confirms the stereotypes than evidence that challenges them. People tend to process information in ways that verify existing beliefs. This tendency to seek, interpret, and create information that verifies existing beliefs is known as the **confirmation bias**.

3. People have a **false consensus** bias when they believe that most other people share their stereotypes. They tend to see their own behaviors and judgments as quite common and appropriate, and to view alternative responses as uncommon and often inappropriate.

4. Stereotypes tend to be **self-fulfilling**. Stereotypes can subtly influence intergroup interactions in such a way that the stereotype is behaviorally confirmed. People may behave in ways that elicit the actions they expect from out-group members, thus confirming the stereotype.

5. People often **dismiss** individuals who do not match a stereotype as exceptions to the rule or representatives of a subcategory.

6. Stereotypes often operate at an **implicit level** below people's conscious awareness.

7. People often develop a **rationale and explanation** to justify their stereotypes and prejudices.

From Johnson, D. W., & Johnson, F. P. (2000). *Joining together: Group theory and group skills* (7th ed.). Upper Saddle River, NJ: Pearson Education. Reprinted by permission.

What can you do to overcome biases that cloud your perceptions and create distortions? How do you move beyond intolerance and prejudice? These are questions that have no easy answers. **Examining your own attitudes, becoming more aware of other cultures, and developing a multicultural view** that will help you communicate with, appreciate, and respect people from diverse backgrounds are steps in the right direction.

Against Prejudice and Violence (NIAPV) record and report incidents of prejudice, discrimination, and hate crimes.

The Power of Prejudice

Ableism. Joy Weeber (1999), a person with a disability, has written about being discriminated against and described how painful it is. She wrote that her pain was caused by the unconscious beliefs of a society that assumes that everyone is, or should be, "capable of total independence and pulling themselves up by their own bootstraps" (p. 21). She defined ableism as a form of prejudice and bigotry that has as its core a belief in the superiority of being nondisabled and an assumption that those who are disabled wish they could be nondisabled—at any cost.

Laura Rauscher and Mary McClintock (1998) offer the following comments to help educate people about disability and oppression.

- Disability is not inherently negative.
- Becoming disabled involves major life changes, including loss as well as gain, but it is not the end of a meaningful and productive existence.
- People with disabilities experience discrimination, segregation, and isolation as a result of other people's prejudice and institutional ableism, not because of the disability itself.
- Social beliefs, cultural norms, and media images about beauty, intelligence, physical ability, communication, and behavior often negatively influence the way people with disabilities are treated.
- Societal expectations about economic productivity and self-sufficiency devalue persons who are not able to work, regardless of other contributions they may make to family and community life.
- Without positive messages about who they are, persons with disabilities are vulnerable to internalizing society's negative messages about disability.
- Independence and dependence are relative concepts, subject to personal definition, something every person experiences, and neither is inherently positive or negative.
- The right of people with disabilities to inclusion in the mainstream of our society is now protected by law, yet they are still not treated as full and equal citizens.

Heterosexism. Heterosexism is the belief that heterosexuality is the only acceptable sexual orientation. In recent years in the United States, there has been increased visibility, via news coverage, movies, advertisements, and television, of gay, lesbian, and bisexual people. Pat Griffin and Bobbie Harro (1997) point out that despite the increased visibility, most Americans continue to have contradictory feelings about gay, lesbian, and bisexual people, and educators have been uncommonly reluctant to address the issue of homophobia in the schools. Silence about issues that minimize particular groups of people can have devastating effects. The Department of Health and Human Services Report on teen suicide (1989) indicated that lesbian, gay, and bisexual young people were two to three times more likely to commit suicide. Prejudice and discrimination are powerful forces that isolate and marginalize people in society. The first step to getting beyond prejudice and intolerance is to examine your own attitudes and beliefs about people. The second step is to develop an awareness of other cultures.

Developing an Awareness of Other Cultures. The more experience we have with people from other cultures, the more likely we are to see individual differences among groups of people, and the less likely we are to stereotype people. Make an effort to get to know people from dissimilar backgrounds, with different life experiences. Most colleges host a variety of cultural events throughout the year to provide students with opportunities to learn about other cultures and meet a variety of talented people to form relationships with. Discover what different international organizations exist on your campus and in your community and be sure to check with your local Chamber of Commerce for local cultural celebrations. You are likely to find that international student organizations on your campus sponsor cultural nights, which students and the community are invited to attend. Discover where opportunities exist and make a commitment to be there. Develop an open mind, like an anthropologist who immerses himself or herself in another culture to learn about that culture. As you begin to experience other cultures, be aware of your own cultural filters and maybe your own prejudices that have kept you from making contact with certain individuals or groups.

Colleges offer numerous opportunities to study, learn, and travel abroad through programs that are often housed within offices of international education and service learning. You can also check with other colleges throughout the world to see what opportunities they have to offer. Whether you are participating in a global service learning program in Thailand or Costa Rica, studying in Italy, or attending a local Latino student celebration, ask a lot of questions and immerse yourself in the culture to develop a greater awareness of that particular culture.

You can also educate yourself about other cultures by watching documentaries and movies. Try viewing some international movies the next time you are looking for a movie to rent. Having to read subtitles cannot be used as an excuse! Your aim is to become more immersed in another culture. You might also try attending a different place of worship or interviewing other students about their experiences living in a different culture. The more personal information you have about another person or another culture, the less likely you are to stereotype that person or culture, and the more likely you will be able to interact in genuine, respectful ways in the future.

Developing a Multicultural View

The final step to getting beyond prejudice and intolerance is to develop a multicultural view. Developing a multicultural view requires the motivation to develop better diversity skills to interact with a wider range of people. For some people, the motivation to become multiculturally competent arises from a desire to become a social change agent in the community by helping other people develop more tolerant attitudes. Some people view this as a way of supporting their country, since democracy is a system based on mutual respect and equality of rights. There are things you can do to help build a healthier approach to living in a multicultural society: two of them are developing good critical-thinking skills and educating others about laws and policies pertaining to discrimination.

Develop Good Critical-Thinking Skills. When you are exposed to different perspectives on similar issues, you are challenged to think critically in the process of forming your own opinion. When thinking critically, you think through your assumptions about different groups of people. Remember that your assumptions are based on your experiences. Since you cannot experience everything in life, your assumptions are often going to have many biases where you filled in the gaps. The process of critical thinking can help you get beyond preconceived notions that have been formulated over the years and arrive at the truth.

Part of the process of developing good critical thinking skills is becoming aware of the influence you have on other people. Starting with yourself, think of how you influence friends and family, people at work and school, and your community. What actions could you implement within each one of these spheres to combat sexism, racism, ableism, and other discriminatory isms? Complete Exercise 4 at the end of this chapter to identify some of those spheres of influence. How can you change your environment to encourage a multicultural view of the world?

Educate Others about Laws and Policies. There are campus policies and laws to deal with acts of bigotry and discrimination. Become familiar with your college's non-discrimination and anti-harassment policy. In 1990 the Americans with Disabilities Act (ADA), a civil rights act for people with disabilities, passed into law. It states that all public facilities, including colleges, are required by law to make a serious effort to provide barrier-free access to all persons with disabilities. When you are eating out in a restaurant, do you ever wonder whether or not the restaurant is accessible to all? Many restaurants and public places are not.

Find out how your college responds to incidents of bigotry. Bigotry can appear in many forms: graffiti, physical violence, written and spoken remarks, and privileges. What about invited or uninvited outside speakers who come to campus to speak with students? Should what they say or the information they plan to distribute to others be censored? Should a student newspaper be allowed to run an advertisement that provides misinformation about a group of people and promotes racism, sexism, anti-Semitism, or any other form of intolerance? What about running a cartoon that is demeaning to people with disabilities or another group of people in a campus, local, or national newspaper?

The issue of political correctness (PC) has been debated on campuses and throughout society. Pedersen (1994) states, "Philosophically, PC means the subordination of the right to free speech to the right of guaranteeing equal protection under the law. The PC position contends that an absolutist position on the First Amendment (that you may slur anyone you choose) imposes a hostile environment for minorities and violates their right to equal education. Promotion of diversity is one of the central tenets of PC" (p. 5). Are you an advocate or proponent of PC? Why? If not, why not?

Closing Remarks

Various types of ecosystems—systems formed by a community of organisms interacting with their environment—are typically discussed in biology and ecology. The ecosystems that are most likely to remain viable are those with considerable diversity. It turns out that diverse systems are less likely to be decimated by a single illness, pollutant, predator, or some other unforeseen threat. A similar advantage can be found to operate on the societal level. Rather than weakening our society, the authors of this textbook firmly believe that diversity has the power to make the U.S. stronger in terms of motivation to achieve, developing novel and creative solutions for today's problems, and making us more resilient and capable of handling outside dangers and threats. Such positives can only be actualized if diversity is embraced and not shunned.

Sources

Barron, W. G. (2002). United States population: Census 2000—The results start rolling in. In W. McGeveran (Ed.), *The world almanac and book of facts 2002* (pp. 374–385). New York, NY: World Almanac Books.

Glauser, A. (1999). Legacies of racism. *Journal of Counseling & Development*, 77, 62–67.

Glauser, A. (1996). *Dangerous habits of the mind: Getting beyond intolerance and prejudice*. Presentation made at the 1996 World Conference of the American Counseling Association, Pittsburgh, PA.

Glauser, A., & Bozarth, J. D. (2001). Person-centered counseling: The culture within. *Journal & Counseling & Development*, 79,142–147.

Goodman, D., & Schapiro, S. (1997). Sexism curriculum design. In Adams, M., Bell, L., & Griffin, P. (Eds.). *Teaching for diversity and social justice: A sourcebook* (pp. 110–140). New York, NY: Routledge.

Griffin, P. & Harro, B. (1997). Heterosexism curriculum design. In Adams, M., Bell, L., & Griffin, P. (Eds.). *Teaching for diversity and social justice: A sourcebook* (pp. 141–169). New York, NY: Routledge.

Johnson, D., & Johnson, F. (2000). *Joining together*. Boston, MA: Allyn and Bacon.

Kendall Hunt Publishing Company. (1999). *First-year experience sourcebook*. Dubuque, IA: Author.

Life: *The year in pictures, 1998*. (1999). New York, NY: Time.

Marable, M. (2000, February 25). We need new and critical study of race and ethnicity. *Chronicle of Higher Education*, B4–B7.

Pedersen, P. (1994). *A handbook for developing multicultural awareness*. Alexandria, VA: American Counseling Association.

Princeton Language Institute. (1993). *Twenty-first century dictionary of quotations*. New York, NY: Dell.

Rauscher, L., & McClintock, M. (1997). Ableism curriculum design. In Adams, M., Bell., L., & Griffin, P. (Eds.). *Teaching for diversity and social justice: A sourcebook* (pp. 198–230). New York, NY: Routledge.

U. S. Department of Health and Human Services. (1989). *Report of the Secretary's Task Force on Youth Suicide*. Rockville, MD: Author.

Vincent, G. K., & Velkoff, V. A. (2010). The next four decades, the older population in the United States. *Current Population Reports*. U.S. Census Bureau. Washington, DC. Retrieved September 10, 2011 from http://www.census.gov/prod/2010/pubs/p.25-1138

Weeber, J. E. (1999). What could I know of racism? *Journal of Counseling & Development*, 77, 20–23.

Wijeyesinghe, C. L., Griffin, P., & Love, B. (1997). Racism curriculum design. In Adams, M., Bell, & Griffin, P. (Eds.). *Teaching for diversity and social justice: A sourcebook* (pp. 82–109). New York, NY: Routledge.

2010 Census shows America's diversity. (2011). *U.S. Census Bureau News*. U.S. Department of Commerce: Washington, DC. Retrieved September 12, 2011 from http://2010.census.gov/news/releases/operations/cb11-cn125.html

Chapter 11

Exercise 3: Why Do Stereotypes Endure?

Given below are several reasons discussed by Johnson and Johnson (2000) as to why stereotypes persist. What do you think are the most important reasons? Why? Explain your rationale on the second page of this exercise.

Reasons Why Stereotypes Endure

1. People tend to overestimate the association between variables that are only slightly correlated or not correlated at all, creating an illusionary correlation.

2. People tend to process information in ways that verify existing beliefs. This is known as the confirmation bias (the tendency to seek, interpret, and create information that verifies existing beliefs).

3. People tend to have a false consensus bias by believing that most other people share their stereotypes (e.g., seeing poor people as lazy).

4. People's stereotypes of others tend to be self-fulfilling. Stereotypes can subtly influence intergroup interactions in such a way that the stereotype is behaviorally confirmed.

5. People dismiss individuals who do not match their stereotype as exceptions to the rule or representatives of a subcategory.

6. Stereotypes often operate at an implicit level below people's conscious awareness.

7. People often develop a rationale and explanation to justify their stereotypes and prejudices.

Most important reasons:

1. _____

_____

_____

2. _____

_____

_____

3. _____

_____

_____

From Johnson, D. W., & Johnson, F. P. (2000). *Joining together: Group theory and group skills* (7th ed.). Upper Saddle River, NJ: Pearson Education. Reprinted by permission.

Explanation:

Chapter 11

Exercise 4: Spheres of Influence

Consider the different spheres of influence that you have. Beginning with yourself, explain how you can influence your environment in a way that is supportive of a more inclusive multicultural world.

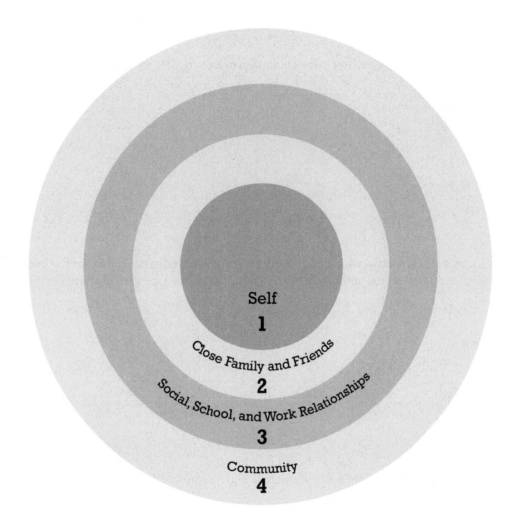

1. **Self.** Indicate how you could educate yourself, develop a deeper understanding of your values and feelings, and examine how you want to change.

2. **Close family and friends.** Explain how you could influence the people closest to you.

3. **Social, school, and work relationships.** Indicate how you might influence friends and acquaintances, coworkers, neighbors, classmates, and people with whom you interact on a regular basis.

4. **Community.** Explain how you could influence people with whom you interact infrequently or in community settings.

SECTION 4

Physical Fitness/ Health Maintenance Skills

Holistic Health
The Union of Mind, Body, and Spirit

ellness requires more than feeding and nurturing the physical body: it involves feeding and nurturing all the dynamic systems that make us human. Medical personnel (and other health experts) and the consumers of health-related services often perceive health as a thing that can be reduced to segments and parts. Such reductionism often creates the impression that these different segments and parts of health are independent of one another. They are not. Sometimes an aspect of health, such as diet, is segmented further into a bewildering array of possibilities. For example, the concept of a healthy diet has given rise to a confusing variety of diet plans published over the years (e.g., *The Zone, Dr. Atkins' New Diet Revolution, Sugar*

Busters, The Dukan Diet, Wheat Belly, Eat To Live, and *Forks Over Knives*) and exercise regimens with well-known celebrities competing for our health dollar through new books or audiovisual products.

Research in certain areas of human physiology is making significant advances (e.g., research projects applying what we have learned about humans' genetic makeup), while in other areas of health research advances seem to progress at a slower pace and sometimes even take a wrong turn. In the recent past, researchers studying an illness often used only male subjects and then applied the findings to both sexes, only to find later that gender differences limited or prevented such a generalization (this type of research error is much less common today). Furthermore, researchers studying human health frequently must rely on correlation studies. The problem is that correlation studies analyze data that is not collected under experimental conditions, where controls are in place to guard against contaminating influences that distort the data being collected.

The data collected in early correlation studies indicated that people who smoked cigarettes experienced higher rates of lung cancer, but the researchers in these early studies could not rule out other factors that may have been the cause. An early obstacle to studying the connection between smoking and cancer was the inappropriateness of subjecting humans to experimental conditions that were likely to induce cancer. Obviously, it is neither humane nor ethical to subject humans to a substance that may adversely affect health. However, just because a study is of a correlation type does not mean the results are wrong. Over time, correlation studies combined with other research approaches (i.e., infamous white mice) resulted in few individuals today claiming there is no cause-and-effect link between cancer and smoking.

Finally, we recognize that health-related information released to the public at various times is often contradictory (e.g., one day certain types of fats are bad and the next day another set of fats is the culprit). Sometimes, health-related information is so segmented or contradictory that we become immobilized and do nothing to enhance our health. At worst, we use the proliferation of suggestions, information, and contradictions as an excuse not to take action to improve our health.

Holism and Holistic Health

In spite of the difficulty of sorting through all the information about diet, exercise, and other health-related measures or activities, there does appear to be general agreement that certain types of diet are harmful and that not exercising does little to boost health. If you have specific concerns, we recommend that you consult an expert (more than one is best sometimes) to determine which diet and exercise program is best for you. Our intent in this chapter is to have you consider various factors that are associated with a healthy lifestyle.

We advocate an approach to health that is captured by the term *holism* (and the adjective *holistic*). According to the holistic approach, wellness is the result of a healthy body, healthy mind, and healthy spirit. It involves the whole person. There are physiological, psychological, and spiritual sides to health, and these areas overlap in such a way that they can never be isolated totally.

The spiritual aspect can be found in a wide range of activities and experiences. This spiritual side of a person can be nurtured by practicing the ways of Judaism, Islam, Hinduism, Buddhism, Baha'i, Shinto, Taoism, or Christianity, or in other ways such as communing with nature through mountain climbing or even intense involvement in a field of science that leads to a profound sense of awe about the universe's immense and wondrous nature. Albert Einstein possessed a deep understanding of the mysteries of the universe and frequently made comments that reflected this profound understanding. His often-quoted remark that "God does not play with dice" suggests that science can lead to a deeper awareness and connectedness that transcends the world known to the senses.

For many centuries, philosophies based on some form of holism have played a very important role in some cultures. The ancient Chinese practice of *feng shui* is an example. Happiness and good health in this philosophy are based on how we relate to the universe; ill health can be seen as representing an imbalance between the person and the universe. According to Lillian Too (1997), the Chinese concept of **chi** is an important concept to fathom if one is to practice feng shui seriously. Too wrote, "Chi has no form, no shape, and is invisible, yet through it, all things on earth that affect people's well-being manifest themselves. . . . Every room, every house, every building—all natural and manmade spaces—are believed to contain energy that has its own unique form of chi. . . . These types of chi, affect different aspects of the human condition and their subtle activation represents one of the most interesting dimensions of feng shui practice" (p. 7).

What can we learn from this particular Chinese worldview? We can learn that personal health involves us and everything around us, even things we are unaware of in our world (e.g., the factory in another county that is adding pollutants to the air we breathe). Poor diet affects not only our physical health, but also our mental ability to perform, and even our ability to reflect on the wondrous world around us. In addition, our poor health affects others. If you are in poor health, you might make decisions resulting from unclear thinking that could adversely affect others.

As you read this chapter, we encourage you to consider how each topic is connected to the physical, mental, and spiritual aspects of who you are. A healthy lifestyle is beneficial to all three areas, and all three areas are essential for a healthy lifestyle.

Overcome barriers.

Physical Benefits

- The immune system is positively affected, which shortens recovery time when ill and leads to faster healing if injured.
- Improvements in muscle tone, muscle strength, and flexibility occur. Physical appearance improves as a result.
- The chances of contracting a chronic disease are lessened.

Psychological Benefits

- We are able to better handle stress.
- A healthy lifestyle is associated with higher self-esteem.
- We are less likely to have an accident, as we are better able to focus on the present moment.

Spiritual Benefits

- A healthy lifestyle leads to greater energy and involvement with life.
- We are capable of maintaining a more positive outlook.

- Our creative ability is enhanced. As Abraham Maslow pointed out decades ago, self-actualization and its accompanying greater appreciation of all that is around us comes after basic health needs are met. (e.g., food, water, and warmth).

The Physical: Nutrition and Exercise

Nutrition

Tracking Portions. Over the last 20 years, the portions of what we consume at fast-food restaurants have grown in size. The activity below lists the amount of calories associated with each food item 20 years ago. You are to estimate the average number of calories currently associated with each item listed, and the amount of time it would take to burn off the extra calories using the physical activity indicated. (Answers are provided at the end of this chapter.)

Activity

Comparing Calories for Today's Portions to Yesterday's

Typical Portion from 20 Years Ago	Today's Typical Portion	The Time It Would Take to Burn Off the Extra Calories
Bagel = **140 calories**	Six-inch bagel = _____ calories	You would have to do **yard work** (rake leaves) for _____
Eight ounces of coffee with whole milk and sugar = **45 calories**	Mocha coffee = _____ calories	You would have to **walk** for _____
Cheeseburger = **333 calories**	Cheeseburger = _____ calories	You would have to **lift weights** for _____
French fries = **210 calories**	French fries = _____ calories	You would have to **walk leisurely** for _____
Two pepperoni pizza slices = **500 calories**	Two pepperoni pizza slices = _____ calories	You would have to **play golf** (walking and carrying your clubs) for _____
Popcorn served at a movie theater = **270 calories**	Popcorn (tub) = _____ calories	You would have to do **water aerobics** for _____

SOURCES: Department of Health and Human Services; National Institutes of Health; and National Heart, Lungs, and Blood Institute (2011 data).

For many adults in the United States, about 40 percent of the calories they consume in food come from fat. Obesity is often the combined result of poor diet and inactivity. Since many students have busy schedules, they tend to neglect their diets. However, taking time to improve your diet can improve your daily functioning and sense of well-being (Aubrey, 2005). The basic ingredients of a healthy diet are summarized in the food plate (see Figure 12.1).

A General Guide to Healthy Eating

- When it comes to fats and oils, you should aim to obtain these from fish, nuts, and vegetable oils (limit solid fats).

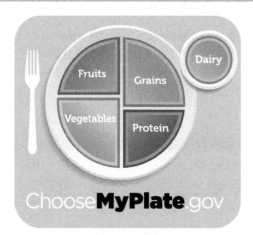

Approximate amounts for the five areas are listed below. Since amounts vary according to age and gender, go to MyPlate.gov for exact recommendations.

Grains: 5–8 ounces (i.e., whole grain breads, crackers, pasta, rice, or cereals)

Vegetables: 2 ½ cups

Fruits: 2 cups

Dairy: 3 cups of low-fat or fat-free (can substitute equivalent milk products)

Protein: Lean meats and poultry (vary with beans, nuts and seeds, peas, and fish)

Source for "MyPlate" food guide: United States Department of Agriculture (2011)

Figure **12.1** The Food Guide

- Reduce the amount of fat in your diet to less than 30 percent of your total calories, with less than 10 percent of the amount coming from saturated or animal fat. Cutting back on fatty meats, whole-milk dairy products, mayonnaise, and butter can have a significant impact on fat content. Many students fall prey to snacking. Start replacing potato chips with pieces of fruit or a healthy portion of popcorn without butter. The idea is to cut back on (but not eliminate) fats.
- Consume a variety of foods. Think in terms of the six food groups: fruit; vegetables; whole-grain cereals, bread, and other pasta; low-fat milk and other dairy products; lean meats such as poultry and fish; and certain types of oils.
- Eat a balance of foods, but try to eat more vegetables, fruit, and grain products.
- Be moderate in your consumption of table sugar (and other sugary items such as honey), as well as salt. Many students fall prey to consuming soft drinks and candy bars because of their availability on campus. Try substituting water and a small bag of low-salt or unsalted pretzels.
- Alcohol should be avoided. If it is consumed, moderation is the key: no more than one or two drinks in a 24-hour period. Binge drinking has become a concern at colleges across the United States. Laura Hensley (2001) found that college binge drinkers do not possess a value system that enables them to overcome the influence of other students. Hensley suggests that such students should seek counseling to build skills that would enable them to resist peer pressure. (Note: If you are attending college outside your home state, you should learn about local drinking laws, which may differ significantly from those in your home state.)
- Drink a lot of water during the day (six to eight glasses is recommended). Water is especially important during exercise.
- Eat breakfast and other meals. Skipping meals and catching up later is not a good approach to nutrition. A current recommended approach to losing weight is to eat less but to still eat; otherwise, the body thinks it is starving, and the body makes adjustments that are not beneficial to a healthy lifestyle.
- Finally, because *nutrition* in the broadest sense means "nourishing oneself by taking in some animal or plant product," we add to the list tobacco. We can nourish ourselves in healthy or unhealthy ways. Obviously, the authors view the use of tobacco as a form of unhealthy nutrition, and strongly recommend cutting back with the eventual aim of quitting for those currently smoking.

Nutrition Facts

Serving Size ½ cup (114g)
Servings Per Container 4

Amount Per Serving

Calories 90	Calories from Fat 30

	% Daily Value*
Total Fat 3g	**5%**
Saturated Fat 0g	**0%**
Cholesterol 0mg	**0%**
Sodium 300mg	**13%**
Total Carbohydrate 13g	**4%**
Dietary Fiber 3g	**12%**
Sugars 3g	
Protein 3g	

Vitamin A	80%	•	Vitamin C	60%
Calcium	4%	•	Iron	4%

* Percent Daily Values are based on a 2,000 calorie diet. Your daily values may be higher or lower depending on your calorie needs:

	Calories	2,000	2,500
Total Fat	Less than	65g	80g
Sat Fat	Less than	20g	25g
Cholesterol	Less than	300mg	300mg
Sodium	Less than	2,400mg	2,400mg
Total Carbohydrate		300g	375g
Fiber		25g	30g

Calories per gram:
Fat 9 • Carbohydrate 4 • Protein 4

More nutrients may be listed on some labels.

 *Figure* **12.2** A Typical Food Label

Learn How to Read Labels

Read the labels on food products. Understanding the information on labels will help you practice good nutrition. The parts of a typical label (see Figure 12.2) are described in Table 12.1, along with recommendations on how to use the information given.

Table 12.1

What the Label Means

Serving size. Is your serving the same size as the one on the label? If you eat double the serving size listed, you need to double the nutrient and calorie values. If you eat one-half the serving size shown, cut the nutrient and calorie values in half.

Calories. Look here to see how a serving of the food adds to your daily total. A 5'4", 135-lb. active woman needs about 2,200 calories each day. A 5'10", 174-lb. active man needs about 2,900.

Total carbohydrate. When you cut down on fat, you can eat more carbohydrates. Carbohydrates are in foods like bread, potatoes, fruits, and vegetables. Choose these often! Carbohydrates give you nutrients and energy.

Dietary fiber. In the past people simply called it "roughage," but their advice to eat more is still up-to-date. That goes for both soluble and insoluble kinds of dietary fiber. Fruit, vegetables, whole grains, beans, and peas are all good sources and appear to reduce the risks of heart disease and cancer.

Protein. Most Americans get more protein than needed. Where there is animal protein, there is also fat and cholesterol. Eat small servings of lean meat, fish, and poultry. Use skim or low-fat milk, yogurt, and cheese. Try vegetable proteins like beans, grains, and cereals.

Vitamins and minerals. Your goal here is 100 percent. Do not count on one food to do it all. Let a combination of foods add up to a winning score.

Total fat. Aim low for this category. Most people need to cut back on fat. Too much fat may contribute to heart disease and cancer. Try to limit your calories from fat. For a healthy heart, choose foods with a big difference between the total number of calories and the number of calories from fat.

Saturated fat. Saturated fat is part of the total fat in food. It is listed separately because it is the key player in raising blood cholesterol and your risk of heart disease. Aim to eat less.

Cholesterol. Too much cholesterol—second cousin to fat—can lead to heart disease. Challenge yourself to eat less than 300 mg each day.

Sodium. You call it "salt," the label calls it "sodium." Either way, it may add up to high blood pressure in some people. So keep your sodium intake low 2,400 to 3,000 mg or less each day. (The recommendation is no more than 3,000 mg of sodium per day for healthy adults.)

Daily value. Feel like you are drowning in numbers? Let the Daily Value be your guide. Daily Values are listed for people who eat 2,000 or 2,500 calories each day. If you eat more, your personal daily value may be higher than what is listed on the label. If you eat less, your personal daily value may be lower. (For fat, saturated fat, cholesterol, and sodium, choose foods with a low % Daily Value. For total carbohydrates, dietary fiber, vitamins, and minerals, your goal is to reach 100 percent of each.)

SOURCE: Food and Drug Administration. (n.d.). *How to read the new food label* (FDA 93-2260). Dallas, TX: National Center.

Bulimia Nervosa and Anorexia Nervosa: Nutritional Imbalances

Anorexia occurs when a pattern is established that reflects a refusal to maintain normal body weight. **Bulimia** is a bit more difficult to detect because the behavior itself (rather than a certain appearance) is prominent. Symptoms include excessive, inappropriate use of laxatives, periods of fasting, forced vomiting, and excessive exercise. Interestingly, obesity is not considered a problem in the same way as these two disorders: that is, while there is a specific psychiatric diagnostic category for anorexia and bulimia, there is none for obesity. To date, obesity is seen as a medical condition. Only in cases where there is evidence of psychological factors may obesity be labeled as a psychological condition or disorder. While there are other eating disorder conditions, such as pica (child repeatedly eating a non-nutritious substance) or rumination (regurgitating and rechewing food), in the case of young adults, it is anorexia and bulimia that have gained a great deal of attention. Certainly, these conditions can have a profound effect on health. Harmful physical effects include skin problems, kidney failure, heart problems, colon-related difficulties, ulcerated gums, and loss of bone density.

Anorexia is characterized by an intense "fear of becoming fat" even if the person is noticeably underweight and looks too thin or skeleton-like to others. In addition, persons with anorexia link their self-worth to body weight; regardless of the amount of weight loss, they do not see themselves as thin. In women, the symptom of *amenorrhea* may occur, meaning that menstruation does not occur for three or more consecutive cycles. *Bulimia* is associated with binge eating—eating excessive amounts of food during a period of a couple of hours and a sense of not being able to stop eating. The binge eating is associated with ways to undo the binge eating, such as vomiting, laxatives, enemas, fasting, and exercise marked by its excessiveness. Again, self-worth is tied to weight.

Treatment for such eating disorders can be lengthy. Typically, there are competent professionals at a college who can provide assistance (or an appropriate referral). The first step in reestablishing balance in a person's life disrupted by an eating disorder is to seek assistance.

Exercise

A primary key to establishing a healthy lifestyle is to exercise. Keep in mind that what may fit one person exercise-wise may not fit another, but do something! While maintaining a reasonable balance is important (somewhere between obsessive/compulsive routines and no routine), the optimum level of exercise you should aim for will vary according to your age and current health level. It is always advisable to involve a professional who can help you develop a program that meets your specific needs. With that word of caution, here are several exercise tips that are known to be generally beneficial.

- Walk instead of taking available transportation (e.g., car or bus) to get around campus. Consider getting exercise by bicycling around campus.
- Reduce or eliminate consumption of substances that interfere with your ability to exercise (e.g., cigarettes and alcohol).
- Get enough sleep. Being tired can interfere with your motivation to exercise.
- "Think exercise" by finding ways to incorporate exercise into your daily routine. Instead of riding the elevator in a campus building, take the stairs. Instead of having a pizza delivered, take your class notes with you and quiz yourself as you walk to the neighborhood pizza place. Also, recognize that while handball or basketball

may provide more exercise than golf or bowling, these latter types of exercise are better than inactivity.

- Get regular medical checkups and screenings. Part of your exercise routine should involve listening to a medical professional concerning your current state of health. Also, if a health problem has been detected, asking the medical professional to suggest what steps you should take to recover from or lessen the effects of the problem.
- Aim to do some type of aerobic exercise, such as walking, jogging, or swimming, for three 30-minute periods per week. (If you find it more convenient to walk or jog near your residence, do not do it alone, and let others know your routine: for example, tell a roommate you are leaving to run. Human predators are sometime attracted to campuses. To be safe, expect the worst.)

The Psychological: Stress and Sex

Seeing the words "stress" and "sex" together might seem strange, but both can be significant contributors to psychological concerns and thus negatively affect one's overall health. In addition, sex itself can be a powerful stressor in one's life. Certainly, everyone recognizes that sexual behavior has a physiological side, but for many the greater challenge pertains to the psychological aspects of sex.

Stress

Chapter 13 provides more in-depth information concerning stress. Here we offer a few stress-reducing suggestions as part of an overall approach to health.

- Reduce stress by taking greater control over your life. Be assertive with others who ask too much of you, and refuse to do anything more if you are already feeling overloaded.
- Set priorities and tackle top priorities in your life rather than be pulled in too many directions.
- As emphasized earlier—exercise. One benefit of exercise is that it significantly reduces stress levels. Even people who are not that interested in an exercise routine find themselves feeling less burnt out when they do exercise.
- Develop routines to wind down. Give yourself a time and place where you can unwind. Create an environment with objects that possess a nurturing quality. For example, having an apartment free of clutter (papers, books, clothes, and dishes have been put away) visually creates a sense of order that helps lower stress levels for some students. To leave a hectic, stressful academic environment only to return to a chaotic environment at your residence will hinder your ability to relax.
- Use techniques such as muscle relaxation and imagery to reduce stress (see Chapter 13).

Sex

Sex is more than physical: it has a whole array of personal, interpersonal, and familial meanings that have very little to do with the actual physiology of sex. Whether one's views about sexuality are liberal or conservative, knowledge of sexuality's various aspects is important. For example, individuals who choose to be sexually active are confronted with a wide array of birth-control methods from which to select (e.g., birth control pills, IUDs, condoms). Certainly, one sexual concern that can have profound health consequences and thus psychological consequences is sexually transmitted diseases (STDs). Table 12.2 describes the symptoms, possible consequences, treatments, and causes of common STDs. Remember that your campus's health center provides information and various types of services related to sexual health problems.

Table 12.2

Sexually Transmitted Diseases (STDs)

Chlamydia

- Many men and women do not experience any symptoms at all. Men may experience penile discharge or discomfort while urinating. Women infected in the cervix seldom have any symptoms and are infectious to men. Once it spreads to the fallopian tubes, some women report symptoms such as lower back pain, painful intercourse, and bleeding between periods.
- Untreated, chlamydia can cause swelling in the joints (similar to arthritis), urethritis (irritation of the urinary tract), or conjunctivitis (eye infection). Women have a one-in-eight chance of damaging fallopian tubes and causing infertility.
- Treatment: antibiotics
- Cause: several organisms, the most common being the *Chlamydia trachomatis* bacterium

Gonorrhea

- In men, the urethra tingles or feels uncomfortable, and burns while urinating. Thick, creamy, bad-smelling discharge drips from the penis. Untreated, gonorrhea leads to bladder infection, headaches or fevers, and swollen testes. In women, 30–50 percent have no symptoms; those who do experience a discharge or cervical (internal) redness, small bumps, and a burning sensation in the urethra during urination. They may also experience pain on one or both sides of the lower abdomen, vomiting, fever, or irregular periods. Both sexes can get gonorrhea in the rectum, throat, or eye through anal or oral sex or by touching infected areas and then touching the eyes.
- Untreated, gonorrhea leads to permanent sterility in men and women. Urethral constricting in men can cause painful urination permanently. Vaginal delivery of a baby may result in the infant being blind.
- Treatment: several commonly used antibiotics
- Cause: bacteria. New antibiotic-resistant strains of gonorrhea are emerging.

Human Papillomavirus (HPV) *(includes genital warts)*

- Small cauliflower-like bumps in the genital area or around the anus. In women, they can also show up inside the vagina or on the cervix. There may be one or several warts, or they may be so tiny they are invisible.
- Linked with precancerous changes of the penis, anus, vulva, and cervix.
- Treatment: freezing, laser burning, chemical solutions, or surgery.
- Cause: human papillomavirus (HPV).

Genital Herpes

- Males experience a small itchy area on the shaft of the penis; women, a small itchy area inside the labia majora. Both men and women may experience headaches along with the attack. Some just feel sick or as though they are getting the flu. About 24 hours later, the itchy area develops small reddish bumps that turn into blisters by the next day. Generally, the area is tender and painful. A woman may find urination painful. The blisters burst, leaving behind ulcers, or sores. The sores scab over in four or five days, and heal in a week or two.
- Can be spread to the mouth or eyes. Children born vaginally to mothers with active herpes have a 50/50 chance of getting herpes; 2/3 of babies who get herpes at birth die, and those who live suffer permanent brain or eye damage.
- Treatment: a number of drugs have been used to treat genital herpes. Acyclovir can be taken daily to help control herpes.
- Cause: virus known as herpes simplex. No present cure.

(continued)

Table 12.2 continued

AIDS

- No symptoms for six months to years. Symptoms can include swollen glands in the neck, armpits, or groin; loss of appetite or unexplained loss of weight; weakness in the legs; night sweats; a fever that lasts more than a week; chronic or long-lasting diarrhea; a dry cough; white spots or blemishes in the mouth; white sores or thickening in the mucous membranes of the mouth, tongue, or vagina; lymphoma; or shingles, which is characterized by skin eruptions and pain along the course of involved sensory nerves. In the final stages, one can expect to see herpes sores, abnormal thinness, pneumonia, tuberculosis, dementia, and cancer.
- Untreated, leads to death.
- Treatment: some drugs have been shown to slow the progression of the disease, and other drugs have been found to keep the condition in check. There are also cases where a person has experienced a temporary or permanent decrease in symptoms or remission of HIV-related symptoms has occurred.
- Cause: human immunodeficiency virus (HIV).

Note: Recent evidence indicates that some STDs are developing resistance to widely prescribed medications.

SOURCES: Adapted from Osher, B., & Ward, J. (1996). *Learning for the 21st century.* Reprinted by permission of Kendall Hunt Publishing Company.

Ryan, E. A. (1993). *Straight talk about sexually transmitted diseases.* New York, NY: Facts on File. Adapted with permission.

American College Health Association. (2006). *Making sex safer.* Baltimore, MD: Authors.

American College Health Association. (2007). *Sexually transmitted infections: What everyone should know.* Baltimore, MD: Authors.

AIDS, caused by the human immunodeficiency virus, deserves special attention because of its ability to kill; on a global level, it continues to be devastating. HIV-infected people have been exposed to infected semen, vaginal fluids, or blood: that is, it is by means of these sources that the virus enters the bloodstream. It can be expected that all infected individuals will succumb to AIDS (*acquired immunodeficiency syndrome*), although the range in time from contracting HIV (*human immunodeficiency virus*) to developing AIDS can be two years to over a decade. A person capable of spreading HIV may appear healthy for a number of years.

People with AIDS usually die from an infection that intensifies and/or Kaposi's sarcoma (blood cells that rid the body of cancerous cells are affected). Tables 12.3 and 12.4 contain additional information about HIV/AIDS and information about protecting oneself from infection.

Table 12.3

Facts about HIV/AIDS

Worldwide

- As of July 2008, an estimated 33 million people worldwide were living with HIV/AIDS.
- Approximately 67 percent of the 33 million adults with HIV/AIDS worldwide reside in sub-Saharan Africa.
- Since the beginning of the HIV/AIDS epidemic, millions of children younger than 18 years have been orphaned worldwide because of the premature deaths of HIV-infected parents. For example, in sub-Saharan Africa there are 11–12 million such orphans.
- On a daily basis, there are over 7,000 new infections reported.

United States

- In July 2008 there were 1.1 million people living with HIV/AIDS in the U.S.
- Over 53,000 new infections are reported each year.
- Of AIDS cases reported in 2008, 45 percent were among African-Americans, 35 percent were among whites, and 17 percent were among Hispanics/Latinos.
- Men account for 73 percent of the new cases reported and women account for 27 percent.

SOURCES: University Health Center. (n.d.). *AIDS: How to protect yourself & others*. Athens, GA: The University of Georgia, Division of Student Affairs.

Until There's A Cure Foundation. (2009). *Vital statistics*. Retrieved November 22, 2009 from http://www.until.org/statistics.shtml?gelid=CJyGna mnip4CFRQhnAodYVYdrA

Centers for Disease Control and Prevention. (2009). *HIV/AIDS fact sheets*. Retrieved November 15, 2009 from http://www.cdc.gov/hiv/ resources/factsheets/aian.htm

Table 12.4

HIV/AIDS: How to Protect Yourself and Others

Highest Risk of Infection

- Anal sex (penis in the rectum) without protection
- Vaginal sex without protection
- Sharing needles while injecting drugs, including steroids
- Sex with multiple partners
- Sex with someone whose sexual history you are not sure of

Moderate Risk of Infection

- Unprotected oral sex

Lower Risk of Infection

- Oral sex with a condom or dental dam
- Deep (French) kissing when blood may be present

No Risk of Infection

- Abstinence from sex
- Hugging, touching, and massaging
- Mutual masturbation (when persons involved have no cuts or sores on their hands)
- Any sex with a long-term partner who has never used injected drugs, is faithful, and is not infected with HIV

You Cannot Get AIDS From

- Using office equipment or a toilet after an HIV-positive person
- Being bitten by a mosquito
- Touching or embracing an HIV-positive person

SOURCE: University Health Center. (n.d.). *AIDS: How to protect yourself & others*. Athens, GA: The University of Georgia, Division of Student Affairs.

The Spiritual

A Western Philosophical Approach

The spiritual side is what allows us to transcend the normal boundaries of our existence. Existential thinkers have looked intently at the meaning of life and the pivotal role such meaning plays in our existence and health. According to existentialists such as Jean-Paul Sartre, Martin Heidegger, Karl Jaspers, Albert Camus, and Viktor Frankl, when we *experience a profound sense of emptiness* or *a profound sense of lacking direction*, we are struggling with a deep urge to establish a genuine meaning in our lives—a meaning that is rarely found in those things that we are told are so important, such as prestige, health, and fame. According to these writers, and others, there are central existential issues that confront us in our search for meaning.

- The world should be recognized as a place of uncertainty, especially in terms of our own death.
- Facing this all-pervasive uncertainty head-on eventually results in the realization that all we are left with is the ability to make choices and thus create our own meaningful action.
- While this realization of our ability to make choices is essential to establish meaning, it must be tempered with the additional realization there are limits to the types of choices we can make.
- We are responsible for the choices we make. In fact, this responsibility that is inherently ours is anxiety-provoking.
- How we deal with the anxiety of responsibility largely determines our personal identity.
- The "big task" in life to accomplish—to establish meaning out of chaos—is simple to achieve, but can also seem infinitely difficult to achieve.
- Life itself does not provide us with a ready-made meaning; the individual must establish this meaning. According to the existentialists, this meaning can be found in any number of pursuits.

An Eastern Philosophical Approach

Buddhism has close to 800,000 followers in the United States and hundreds of millions around the world. To find Buddhism's origin, you must travel back to Nepal approximately 2,500 years ago, when Siddhartha Gautama (later known as Buddha) achieved enlightenment, ending his personal journey of countless deaths and reincarnations (Ericker, 1995; Fargis, 1998).

There are many wonderful stories about the Buddha. These stories span his last life on earth. According to one of these stories, Buddha's mother knew he was destined for greatness because of what happened during his birth and immediately after. When Buddha was ready to be born, his mother, who was traveling at the time, stopped her journey to go into a forest so she could locate a safe place to deliver her child. The first sign that her child's birth was of importance to the world occurred when a tree bent over to provide her support during the delivery. Once the birth was over, the newborn was able to walk immediately, and as he walked, he left a trail of lotus blossoms: a lotus plant grew and blossomed wherever the newborn left a footprint.

Achieving enlightenment was not easy for Siddhartha Gautama (Ericker, 1995). It was only after many difficult years of seeking spiritual truth that he achieved the enlightened perspective that enabled him to break the cycle of life, death, and reincarnated life (which started the cycle over again). At the point of enlightenment, Siddhartha became known as Buddha, or the Enlightened One. Buddha's great spiritual insights into the human condition are known as the four noble truths:

- Humans live out a life that guarantees suffering and countless reincarnations back into the material world.
- Human desires are at the heart of suffering. Desires, combined with a belief in one's own self-importance, create the misery we experience throughout our lives.
- Obtaining nirvana, or breaking the endless cycle of death and rebirth to achieve true freedom, ends suffering.
- Nirvana is achieved through walking a righteous path that requires a certain type of thinking, behavior, and attitude.

The last step, achieving nirvana, is very difficult—it took Buddha countless reincarnations before he achieved nirvana. Even though a person may not become a Buddha in his or her lifetime, practicing Buddhism can be very rewarding in a large number of ways that satisfy the spiritual side of one's nature.

Closing Remarks

Religion and philosophy provide meaning for many people. Nevertheless, in some instances, the journey to find the meaning is more personal and only tangentially related to any of the established religions or philosophical approaches available to us all.

The spiritual connection, however it is obtained, allows a person to actualize his or her potential. For countless individuals, this spiritual aspect is as important to health as anything else discussed in this chapter; for some, it is even more important. We recommend that as a student, you take time to nurture not only the physical and psychological aspects of your existence, but also the spiritual side, which will better enable you to transcend immediate concerns to connect with something greater than any single person or thing. Health is the sum total of the physical, psychological, and spiritual. The authors believe that a deficit in any one of these areas can result in a life that is less complete than it could be. The exercise at the end of this chapter allows you to stop and consider how these three areas interact in terms of your own health.

Sources

Aubrey, A. (2005, April 19). *Government unveils revised food pyramid (NPR: Morning Edition)*. Retrieved June 14, 2005, from http://www.npr.org

Ericker, C. (1995). *Buddhism*. London: Cox and Wyman.

Facts about HIV/AIDS. (n.d.) Athens, GA: University Health Center, The University of Georgia.

Fargis, P. (Ed.). (1998). *The New York Public Library desk reference* (3rd ed.). New York, NY: MacMillan.

Hensley, L. G. (2001). College student binge drinking: Implications for a constructivist approach to college counseling. *Journal of College Counseling, 4*, 100–112.

Too, L. (1997). *Feng shui fundamentals*. Rockport, MA: Element.

Women and AIDS. (n.d.) Athens, GA: University Health Center, The University of Georgia.

Comparing Calories for Today's Portions to Yesterday's

Typical Portion from 20 Years Ago	Today's Typical Portion	The Time It Would Take to Burn Off the Extra Calories
Bagel = **140 calories**	Six-inch bagel = **350** calories	You would have to do **yard work** (rake leaves) for **50 minutes** to burn the extra 210 calories
Eight ounces of coffee with whole milk and sugar = **45 calories**	Mocha coffee = **350** calories	You would have to **walk** for **1 hour** and **20 minutes** to burn the extra 305 calories
Cheeseburger = **333 calories**	Cheeseburger = **590** calories	You would have to **lift weights** for **1 hour** and **30 minutes** to burn the extra 257 calories
French fries = **210 calories**	French fries (6.9-ounce portion) = **610** calories	You would have to **walk leisurely** for **1 hour** and **10 minutes** to burn the extra 257 calories
Two pepperoni pizza slices = **500 calories**	Two pepperoni pizza slices = **850** calories	You would have to **play golf** (walking and carrying your clubs) for **1 hour** to burn the extra 350 calories
Popcorn served at a movie theater = **270 calories**	Popcorn (tub) = **630** calories	You would have to do **water aerobics** for **1 hour** and **15 minutes** to burn the extra 360 calories

Note. The amounts of calories burned for today's bagel, coffee, and cheeseburger are based on a 130-pound person performing the exercise listed; amounts of calories burned for French fries, pizza, and popcorn are based on a 160-pound person performing the exercise listed.

SOURCES: Department of Health and Human Services; National Institutes of Health; and National Heart, Lungs, and Blood Institute (2011 data).

Chapter 12

Exercise 1: Achieving Balance

1. Of the three aspects of health (physical, psychological, and spiritual), which helps you the most in dealing with academic challenges?

2. How have you nurtured, or taken care of, the physical, psychological, and spiritual aspects of your health this semester?

3. Of the three aspects of health, which do you believe you need to strengthen or pay more attention to in your life? Explain. How might you strengthen or pay more attention to this particular aspect of your health?

Stress
Accentuate the Positive

13

Everyone knows when he or she is experiencing stress, and each one of us can discuss various stressors that confront us each week. A stressor, according to Hans Selye, is anything that produces tension in your life: it may be of a physical nature (e.g., starvation brought on by a drought in east Africa, restricted access to a friend's house caused by a broken leg in a cast) or a psychological nature (e.g., being involved in interpersonal conflict, being frustrated in a second attempt to pass a required course). Of these two categories, it seems that psychological stressors are forever present, even in the best of times, for most students. Psychological stressors confront us all regardless of how healthy, powerful, or rich we are, although these stressors differ in the degree to which they "stress us out."

Stress often arises when we have choices to make. In most cases we would rather deal with a choice between two goods than two evils, but conflict can still be experienced even when selecting one of two attractive outcomes. One example of such an **approach-approach conflict** (also called double-approach) situation might be having to choose between two high-paying, equally desirable jobs after graduating from college. While approach-approach conflicts are unlikely to end like the one in the example known as "*Buridan's ass*," where a donkey caught between two equally attractive piles of hay dies from being unable to decide which pile to eat, conflict is conflict, and even choosing between two desirables can be stressful.

Memories concerning our struggle to choose between two evils seem to be vivid and lasting. For example, a person choosing between taking out a student loan with a high interest rate or asking his or her parents for additional help knowing they can ill afford the assistance is in this situation. Having two dreadful choices is commonly referred to as being caught "between a rock and a hard place." In these types of situations, the person is experiencing what is known as an **avoidance-avoidance conflict** (i.e., double-avoidance). Situations that are defined by negatives often are frustrating because we find ourselves prevented from accomplishing some desired purpose. No matter what the cause, psychological frustration can be profoundly stressful and may even cause us to respond aggressively. We might scream at our roommate or even become physically violent if we experience a prolonged bout of high frustration.

Finally, the term **approach-avoidance conflict** is reserved for situations with an end goal that has both positives and negatives attached. For example, a new college graduate is offered what he considers to be his ideal job in the international company he was hoping to work for, but before he makes a decision, he learns that his immediate supervisor will be the same person who had incessantly picked on him in high school.

If asked, all of us could easily list stressful events or periods in our lives (e.g., the death of a pet, moving from one school or town to another, death of a close family member, divorce of parents, loss of some prized possession, enrolling in college classes for the first time). Stress can be defined as a personal experience of physical or mental strain that results in numerous physiological changes (e.g., heart-rate increases, increase in the force of one's heartbeat, digestive disturbance, blood-vessel constriction, elevated blood pressure, noticeable sweating, and rise in muscle tightness). In this chapter, we will discuss the causes and symptoms of stress and how you can develop effective ways to cope with stress.

What Is Stressful?

While we all experience stress, we are usually surprised to learn it has many faces and a subtle aspect that we are not always aware of, as if it is a companion that hides in the shadows. The following assessment will help to shed some light on the lifelong companion known as stress.

The Social Readjustment Scale

Indicate the number of times each event has occurred in the last year and multiply each number by the corresponding stress value.

Life Event	Stress Value		Number of Times You Experienced the Event in the Last Year		Score
1. Person you married (or equivalent relationship) dies	100	×	_____	=	_____
2. Divorce (or its equivalent)	73	×	_____	=	_____
3. The person you married (or equivalent relationship) agrees to a separation	65	×	_____	=	_____
4. Detention in jail or other institution	63	×	_____	=	_____
5. Death of a close family member	63	×	_____	=	_____
6. Major personal injury or illness	53	×	_____	=	_____
7. Marriage (or its equivalent)	50	×	_____	=	_____
8. Being fired from work	47	×	_____	=	_____
9. Reconciliation after experiencing a separation from the person you married (or equivalent relationship)	45	×	_____	=	_____
10. Retirement from work	45	×	_____	=	_____
11. Major change in health or behavior of a family member	44	×	_____	=	_____
12. In a relationship that results in pregnancy	40	×	_____	=	_____
13. Sexual difficulties	39	×	_____	=	_____
14. Gaining a new family member (e.g., through birth, adoption, grandparent moving in, etc.)	39	×	_____	=	_____
15. Major business readjustment (e.g., merger, reorganization, bankruptcy, etc.)	39	×	_____	=	_____
16. Major change in financial state (e.g., a lot worse off or a lot better off than usual)	38	×	_____	=	_____
17. Death of a close friend	37	×	_____	=	_____
18. Changing to a different line of work	36	×	_____	=	_____
19. Major change in the number of arguments you are having with the person you married (or equivalent relationship) (e.g., arguing a lot more or a lot less than usual regarding childbearing, personal habits, finances, etc.)	35	×	_____	=	_____

(continued)

From Holmes et al. (1967). *Journal of Psychomatic Research*, *11*(2), 214. Reprinted with permission from Elsevier Science. A few modifications were made to Holmes and Rahe's items to reflect current usage.

20. Taking on a mortgage for an amount that is about average compared to other mortgages (e.g., purchasing a home, business, etc.)   31   × _____ = _____

21. Foreclosure on a mortgage or loan   30   × _____ = _____

22. Major change in your responsibilities at work (e.g., promotion, demotion, lateral transfer)   29   × _____ = _____

23. Son or daughter leaving home (e.g., marriage, attending college, etc.)   29   × _____ = _____

24. Trouble with an in-law (or equivalent relationship)   29   × _____ = _____

25. Outstanding personal achievement   28   × _____ = _____

26. The person you married (or equivalent relationship) beginning or ceasing work outside the home   26   × _____ = _____

27. Beginning or ceasing formal schooling   26   × _____ = _____

28. Major changes in living conditions (e.g., building a new home, remodeling, deterioration of home or neighborhood)   25   × _____ = _____

29. Revision of personal habits (e.g., dress, manners, associations, etc.)   24   × _____ = _____

30. Troubles with boss   23   × _____ = _____

31. Major change in working hours or conditions   20   × _____ = _____

32. Change in residence   20   × _____ = _____

33. Change to new school   20   × _____ = _____

34. Major change in usual type and/or amount of recreation   19   × _____ = _____

35. Major change in religious activities (e.g., a lot more or a lot less than usual)   19   × _____ = _____

36. Major change in social activities (e.g., time spent at clubs, going out with friends, time spent visiting others, going to movies, etc.)   18   × _____ = _____

37. Taking out a loan of $30,000– $40,000 (e.g., using the loan money to help pay for college/graduate school)   17   × _____ = _____

38. Major change in sleeping habits (e.g., a lot more or less sleep)   16   × _____ = _____

39. Major change in number of family get-togethers (e.g., a lot more or a lot less than usual)   15   × _____ = _____

40. Major change in eating habits (e.g., a lot more or a lot less food eaten, or very different meal hours or surroundings)   15   × _____ = _____

41. Going on vacation   13   × _____ = _____

42. Going on a holiday break   12   × _____ = _____

43. A minor violation of the law (e.g., receiving a parking/traffic ticket, jaywalking, disturbing the peace, etc.)   11   ×   _____   =   _____

TOTAL (tally of above scores)   =   _____

Scoring

Using the original instrument, Holmes and Rahe found that one's level of stress is related to becoming ill (they studied participants over a two-year period). Past a certain level on the scale (150 points), the chance of becoming ill jumps dramatically, from 33 percent to 50 percent, and it rises to 80 percent once you hit a total score of 300. For Holmes and Rahe, the term *illness* includes diseases and bodily malfunctions; it also includes accidental injuries as well as emotional disorders. Thus, large amounts of stress seem to be related to experiencing illness. Perhaps a more productive outcome of the findings is to focus on those who, even with high levels of stress, function without becoming ill; these individuals may be able to teach us how we can better withstand stressful periods in our lives. If your score was high, bear in mind that you can learn how to resist and overcome periods of stress.

• •

What Is Stress Exactly?

The items listed on the assessment tool developed by Holmes and Rahe help us understand what the term *stress* encompasses in everyday language. Simply stated, **stress** is a reaction to the various things that happen to us, both negative and positive. Interestingly, while most of us readily think of negative events as stress-provoking (e.g., jail term, death of a close friend, being fired at work), in reality events that are very positive in nature can also be stressful (e.g., change in residence, vacation, marriage). Even though we might be able to cite exceptions, in the vast majority of cases one's wedding day is a joyful event marked by celebration. Marriage also introduces many changes for both people involved. Issues can range from who pays for which day-to-day living expense to the "correct" way to squeeze toothpaste from a tube. Changes associated with marriage can generate a lot of stress.

A meaningful and useful way to conceptualize stress is provided by this formula:

Number of Resources *minus* Number of Changes *equals* Stress

Thus, high levels of stress are due to changes exceeding resources, and low levels of stress are due to resources exceeding changes.

Holmes and Rahe's list of stressful events covers a wide range of the adult life span, although several of the items would not apply to many undergraduates. In a college environment, one would expect to find certain changes not listed by Holmes and Rahe to be just as stressful as those listed. These could include dropping or being withdrawn from a class with a "W," receiving a $20 ticket from campus police for a parking violation, changing from one major to another, not being able to enter a major because of one's grade point average, being withdrawn from a course with a "WF," joining a sorority or fraternity, transferring to another college (leaving this college or coming to this college as a transfer student), failing a course in one's major with a favorite professor, going on first dismissal from college, and being accused of academic dishonesty.

In the above equation, note that change plays a pivotal role in how much stress we experience. Frequently, we are forced to deal with changes that wear us down physically and psychologically because we lack the necessary resources at the time to cope.

Our stores of coping resources can fluctuate. Remember the last time you had the flu and experienced a drop in your ability to cope with the demands placed on you?

Not all change is bad; in fact, there is evidence to suggest that we need a certain amount of change to maintain our physical and psychological balance. Psychologists and other researchers have done sensory deprivation studies to examine the effect of relatively unchanging surroundings. Participants were required to wear blindfolds or the equivalent, to stay still by lying down in soundproof rooms or large containers, to have their arms restrained in special devices to avoid experiencing tactile sensations, and so forth. The effects were profound in some cases; several participants even reported hallucinations. It appears that while too much change is bad, too little can also be bad. Apparently, too few external changes result in the body creating self-induced changes (hallucinations). However, we are all individuals, and it is important to recognize that individuals differ in how much change they can tolerate.

Psychological Hardiness and Other Personality Differences

In *Man in Search of Meaning*, Viktor Frankl describes how an individual can confront a truly unusual degree of change (incarceration in a concentration camp) and not only survive, but come out stronger as a result. Perspective is very important in explaining such outcomes, and we all differ in the degree to which we like change, or seek change in our lives. Some people seem to be revitalized by changes, and some even seek out high-pressure positions because of the constantly changing demands. Many presidents of the United States likely fall into this category of stress-hardy individuals. People such as Jimmy Carter, Elizabeth Dole, John Glenn, Hillary Clinton, Dianne Feinstein, George W. Bush, and Barack Obama who are serving or have served in high-profile positions in politics probably all possess a high level of psychological hardiness. For example, when Senator Feinstein was asked whether she would consider running for president, she said:

> I've been the first [woman] four times now: once as president of the Board of Supervisors [in San Francisco], as mayor, as the first gubernatorial candidate in my state, the first woman Senator from my state. What I've learned is there is a testing period that goes on—particularly in an executive capacity. I think it [takes someone] with the ability to run a campaign well, put together a platform that resounds with the American people and someone with the stamina, the staying power, the determination and enthusiasm to carry it off. (Ciabatti, 1999, p. 6)

Psychological Hardiness

The quality of psychological hardiness is reflected in individuals who like and seek change and challenges, possess a clear focus or goal, and perceive themselves as having control. Stressful events can be short in duration (e.g., writing a speech) or long (e.g., a difficult job with a lot of responsibilities), but it is not always the magnitude of the event that determines how well we cope. The same stressors might be tolerable for one person but overwhelming to another. Our personal level of psychological hardiness is very important. In the mid-1990s, Salvatore Maddi and Suzanne Kobasa studied executives in stressful situations, primarily due to an organization undergoing reorganization with the possibility of losing employment. Such periods of reorganization are associated with ill health (increased colds, influenza, backaches, and migraine headaches). Maddi and Kobasa found that some individuals were not as susceptible to the reorganization stressor. These resilient individuals were able to maintain a sense of control over most events encountered in life and displayed few of the effects found in others. The researchers found that the psychologically hardy (PH) possessed these traits:

- An open attitude toward change, assessing change as a challenge rather than a threat to themselves.
- A high degree of commitment to what the person is involved in. This commitment is tied to goals and objectives. Subjects low in commitment tended to display evidence of being alienated—disconnected from work, people, and things.
- A sense of control over most events rather than a sense of helplessness. High PHs are convinced they can influence the course of their future. In their eyes, effort makes a difference at work, in school, and in relationships. Low PHs feel they have little if any power to influence outcomes. For this latter group, outside forces (a boss, bad luck, etc.) control their future.

One of the lessons to be learned from the work of Maddi and Kobasa is that individuals confronted with stress can meet it head on (take active steps) or let the situation roll over them (take a passive approach). In the latter case, the person does not see the situation as a challenge, but rather as a threat beyond his or her control. In some cases, rather than being able to call upon a sense of commitment to sustain them during a difficult period, individuals low on hardiness worry and try to escape; they may deny what is occurring or even blame others. The following list summarizes the differences between high PH and low PH.

High PHs	Low PHs
See change as a challenge	See change as a threat
Possess commitments that serve to strengthen them	Experience ongoing alienation that adds to their stress
Pursue active coping	Display forms of passive coping
Change tends to invigorate them (this is why they often seek change)	Change leads to them feeling helpless (this is why they avoid change in their lives)

State and Trait Anxiety

An individual's personality type can influence how much stress the person experiences. For example, while anxiety can be a symptom of stress and vary from day to day and week to week (called **state anxiety**), individuals also display an overall consistent pattern of anxiety (called **trait anxiety**). Charles Spielberger identified these two categories and uncovered some interesting findings. While the announcement of an important test can be expected to alter one's level of state anxiety, individuals differ in how much it affects them. These differences are related to the personality of the individual. Individuals with *low trait anxiety* usually seem calm and laid-back, while individuals with *high trait anxiety* typically seem high-strung and are frequently worried. Keep in mind that anxiety is not in and of itself bad—it serves to motivate us to study. Both high-anxiety and low-anxiety individuals may experience performance problems, but for different reasons: in the former case, the high level of anxiety hinders processing of information, and in the latter, there is too little anxiety to motivate the person to study adequately.

Type A and B Personalities

Another type of personality that has been linked to stress is the **Type A personality**. According to Meyer Friedman and Ray H. Rosenman, Type A personalities are stress generators, creating stress in addition to what is placed on them from the outside. Type A personalities are driven to work (often working long hours and on weekends) and very goal-conscious (frequently thinking of goals that need to be achieved and tasks that need to be completed), and find it very difficult to relax. This type of person always seems to be in a rush and may tend to finish others' sentences. Type A personalities find it very difficult to settle for less than perfection. Behind the wheel of a car, Type A personalities are likely to become agitated or angry because other drivers are "moving too slowly," preventing the Type A from getting to his or her destination. Finally, Type A personalities are known to take part in **polyphasic activity**—for example, making a list of things they must do that day while driving to work and trying to talk on a cell phone, all at the same time! The advantage of being a Type A is achievement (higher grades); the disadvantage is poor health (they tend to be more susceptible to heart attacks than Type B personalities). So what is a Type B personality? Essentially, the opposite of a Type A personality.

Learned Helplessness

Martin Seligman (1995) coined the term *learned helplessness*. Specifically, Seligman used the term to refer to situations where a person (or animal, since a lot of studies in this area used animal subjects) acts in a helpless manner if exposed to situations that are harmful or painful and cannot be avoided. The unavoidability of these situations seems to inhibit learning how to escape a harmful or painful situation in the future, even if the situation could be easily avoided.

In one early study on learned helplessness, dogs were placed in one of two treatments. Those in treatment A were confined to a harness and given electric shocks without any possibility of escape. Those in treatment B were exposed to the same exact conditions, except that if the animal struggled, it could escape. Treatment A led to the dogs becoming less competitive, less aggressive, and less able to escape painful situations in the future. Treatment B resulted in dogs that were more competitive, aggressive, and more capable of escaping painful situations in the future. Other animal experiments on mice and rats produced animals in the learned helplessness group that were less active, displayed greater difficulty learning, and gave up sooner when confronted with a challenge. Human participants in similar studies were found to be affected adversely in terms of problem-solving ability.

In general, from the numerous studies conducted, it appears that some humans, due to certain experiences in and outside the academic world, "learn to be helpless." The effects of learned helplessness follow:

- The ability to effectively solve problems is reduced. A drop in motivation, energy, and the will to struggle and survive occurs.
- Learning becomes much more difficult. People ignore or seem unable to profit from information.
- An elevation of emotional or physical distress occurs. Individuals are likely to show outward signs of anxiety and depression. If conditions are not altered, the person may become sick or develop an illness (similar to Holmes and Rahe's findings, this line of research also uncovered a relationship between stressful conditions and illness).

Prolonged Stress and Impairment of Functioning

Clearly, stress can be generated in many different ways, and we know from Holmes and Rahe's work that high levels of stress can result in illness and dysfunction. Does this happen overnight? The good news is no. The effects tend to accumulate over time, which means we have a period of time to take action to prevent the worst-case scenario from occurring. According to Hans Selye, when responding to stress, we go through a series of stages called the **General Adaptation Syndrome (GAS)**.

Stage 1: Alarm (Fight/Flight)

Stress leads to physiological changes in your body, a process that involves two phases. The **shock phase** occurs first and is associated with reactions such as a drop in blood pressure and body temperature. This is followed by the **counter shock phase**, which is associated with increased heart rate, respiration, adrenaline levels, and adrenocortical activity. The body is gearing itself up to either "fight" or take "flight," that is, run from a perceived danger.

Our "fight or flight" response has its origins in our early history as humans two million or more years ago. The problem is, we are no longer literally fighting or running from saber-toothed tigers. We can neither punch the rude, unreasonable professor nor run out of his required class. Often we must stay put, endure the stressors in our lives, and suffer the consequences. In the 21st century, the "fight or flight" response we are physiologically and mentally prepared to carry out is no longer appropriate in many situations, and the end result is that we remain stuck in a readiness mode.

Stage 2: Resistance

When we are stuck between fight and flight, the elevated physiological changes that occurred in the alarm stage are still active, but at a lower level. Even though the body becomes accustomed to this state of readiness, as it seeks to stabilize, the level of intensity is still strong enough to wear us down psychologically and physically. Over time, our condition worsens. If a person remains in the state of readiness long enough, the high blood pressure experienced can turn into hypertension (an outcome associated with the next stage).

Stage 3: Exhaustion

For many students, prolonged stress results in symptoms such as fatigue, irritability, loss of concentration, depression and crying, boredom, less restful sleep, loss of appetite (or eating much more), agitation, and becoming prone to making mistakes and having accidents. It is also associated with a drop in white blood cells, which impacts the immune system, increasing a student's chance of getting or suffering from a cold or the flu.

At this point, our resources are low and physical deterioration is starting to set in (possibly contributing to conditions such as heart disease, hypertension, asthma, colitis, and, according to several researchers, some forms of cancer). These *diseases of adaptation* or psychosomatic illnesses are the result of the person being blocked from reacting to a perceived threat in the manner the body was designed for. If fight or flight had been satisfactorily carried out, the body would have reestablished its equilibrium to the earlier pre-threat level.

Negative, Ineffective Ways to Handle Stress

Too often students (and others) respond to stress in self-defeating ways. For example, they use drugs and alcohol, withdraw from things that are important but cause stress, or rely on psychological defense mechanisms such as denial or projection to protect themselves (see Table 13.1). In fact, there are many things of a positive nature that can be done to relieve and prevent stress. The remaining sections of this chapter provide a number of suggestions and stress reduction techniques that we have found effective and relatively easy to apply.

Table 13.1   Five Examples of Defense Mechanisms

Denial: The student refuses to accept the reality of a situation that is creating pain, anxiety, or worry. For example, the student fails a course and then acts as if the event never occurred, even when speaking with someone who is aware of the failure.

Undoing: The student repeats certain actions that serve to negate something that was said or done. For example, a student steals $20 from another student and then attempts to negate the action by paying for the other student's lunch.

Projection: The student attributes unacceptable feelings and thoughts to someone else. For example, the student who fails a test because he decided to attend a party rather than study blames the professor for being irresponsible in putting the test together.

Reaction Formation: The student expresses the opposite feeling or thought than what he or she actually experiences because such thoughts or feelings are undesirable. For example, a student always compliments her roommate for the clothing she wears, but at the same time, she acts in ways that indicate she actually finds fault with the roommate's clothing.

Displacement: The student directs negative feelings toward a safe target rather than the person who fostered the negative feelings. For example, when a student's mother unjustly criticizes her over the phone, the student later directs the anger she feels toward her boyfriend rather than confront her mother.

Stress: What Can Be Done?

Everyday Techniques for Reducing Stress

Check Your Gauges (psychological/emotional, behavioral, and physical). Periodically stop and determine how much stress you are experiencing. Is it high or low? Whatever your level of stress, is the stress having a negative impact on your academic performance, your personal life, or your ability to just enjoy life? Sometimes such self-examination leads to the awareness that there are unnecessary sources of stress in your life. For example, perhaps an acquaintance is always putting you down in subtle ways but denies doing so; no one should go through life maintaining such an association. If confronting the person does not change the situation, it is probably better to break off the relationship.

Feed Yourself Psychologically and Emotionally. Read that book you have wanted to get to, listen to your favorite music, go to a movie or the local mall, start a hobby, or get involved in a community service such as Habitat for Humanity. It is important to take time to get away. While a stressed-out student may find it difficult to find the time to get away, such time-outs can replenish one's depleted energy and help break the cycle of lingering stress (i.e., GAS).

Feed Yourself Physiologically and Behaviorally. Exercise. Spend 30 minutes three times a week. Take advantage of the college exercise facility if one is available; play tennis, racquetball, handball, or basketball, or learn mountain climbing. Joining a team also helps to establish a support system. If you are on a tight schedule and cannot take time to travel somewhere, walk or run a mile or more a day near your residence (with a trusted partner so you are not out alone), or ride a bike on campus and climb the stairs in a campus building rather than riding the elevator. Not only is health improved by exercise, but exercise has been proven to reduce stress levels. Of course, adequate sleep and good nutrition are necessary ingredients in managing anxiety and stress.

Find time to relax.

Breathe Deeply. During periods of stress, take a moment to close your eyes. Breathe in two or three times in a slow and deep manner, allowing your stomach to rise as you breathe in. Slowly exhale through your lips. Increasing one's oxygen level in this manner can help relieve stress.

Divert Your Attention. Waiting for the professor to distribute a test to the class or to be called on to make a presentation can elevate your anxiety and stress level. Instead of sitting there thinking negative thoughts ("I am not sure I am prepared"), bump the negative thoughts aside with a pleasant image (visualize your favorite vacation spot) or focus on an available image (the tree outside the window that is swaying in the breeze). A simple refocusing from negative thoughts to something more pleasant in nature has been found to reduce anxiety and stress.

Visualize Success. When feeling anxious due to some stressor (e.g., a major course paper that is due), visualize yourself as being successful. Visualize the various steps necessary in a task and actually picture yourself being successful each step of the way. A student teacher might go to the classroom where he or she will be teaching and go through the lesson plan without students there. He or she might use the chalkboard, read from the text, and so forth, all the while imagining a positive outcome. Such an activity has proven to be effective in reducing one's level of anxiety and stress.

Apply Environmental Engineering Tactics. Make your apartment, dorm room, or house a relaxing environment. Decorate the walls with favorite posters or pictures, place objects around that elicit pleasant memories or feelings, or purchase a tropical fish tank, which can help to create a soothing environment. Have a place that can be your place to escape to and fill it with items that make you feel good.

Techniques for Periods of High Stress

During periods of high stress, we typically find it effective to develop an ongoing routine that involves cognitive restructuring, muscle relaxation, meditation, or sequential imagery. Such techniques are intended to be learned and practiced on a regular basis.

Cognitive Restructuring. Sometimes students are aware they are their own worst enemies because of negative self-talk—messages they repeat to themselves that negatively affect both performance and quality of life. Both test-anxious and non-test-anxious students say negative things to themselves (e.g., "I am going to fail this test!"), but test-anxious students make such remarks much more frequently and tend to believe them more. Albert Ellis, the creator of rational emotive behavior therapy, has had considerable success in having people tackle their stress-producing thoughts using an A-B-C approach to modifying behavior.

> **A = activating event**, which can be thought of as the stressor ("I have an important test Tuesday"). The event in and of itself is not the problem: it is how we perceive the event that is crucial.

> **B = belief** about the activating event. If my belief is that I will fail the test, then I will experience unnecessary stress.

> **C = consequence.** If I perceive myself as failing, I will experience stress and thus become anxious and not perform at my optimum level. We can alter the process at point B by forcefully injecting more positive thoughts to push out the self-defeating ones we have become accustomed to speaking silently to ourselves.

Ellis emphasizes that our irrational thinking generates a great deal of stress that simply does not reflect reality. This view is captured in the story of the man who discloses the following when reflecting back about his long life: "I am an old man who has had many worries in my life, few of which ever came true."

Imagery. Imaging exercises can also break the cycle of negative self-talk, but do so with images, not words. For example, a person may practice sequentially going through a certain set of positive images for ten minutes or longer. During a period of stress (e.g., waiting for a test to be distributed in class), the person can call upon one of the images used to reduce anxiety on the spot.

An example of an imaging exercise follows. Read over the following images and then close your eyes and imagine the scene described.

> It is a beautiful spring day.

> Out my window I can see a crystal-clear, deep-blue sky.

> Almost as in a dream I go to my front door and step outside.

> There is a gentle breeze.

The smell of flowers and the sound of singing birds are very pleasant.

I walk out onto the fresh, green grass.

I slowly kneel down and decide to lie back on the fresh spring grass.

The temperature is just right.

I start to daydream about a trip to my favorite beach.

I see myself on the beach and the sun is not too bright, just nice and warm.

The water is a beautiful aqua color that I can see through to the bottom.

The sand on the beach is a beautiful white, and coconut trees are spread out up and down the beach.

I start to walk on the beach.

The sound of the waves is very soothing. The saltwater smell is refreshing.

I stop when I notice a seashell embedded in the sand. It has many bright colors.

Reds.

Yellows.

Blues.

I bend over and pick up the beautifully colored shell. The feel of the water-worn shell is comforting.

The sun is going down and is near the horizon. I sit down on the sand to watch the sun set.

It is a beautiful sunset with various shades of reds, and I feel warm and at peace.

A deep sense of peace flows over me, and I have no fears or worries.

I return from my imaginary trip feeling both very relaxed and revitalized, as if I had just enjoyed a long, restful sleep, from which I open my eyes and feel great and optimistic about the world.

Deep Relaxation. For this exercise, it is recommended that you practice approximately 20 minutes per day for about two weeks to master the technique. In a quiet, disturbance-free location, you are to go through the following muscle groups, tensing and relaxing them. The technique teaches a person, without going through the whole procedure, to quickly scan the body in approximately ten seconds to locate pockets of muscle tension, which are then relaxed. The resulting state of relaxation can bring about a significant reduction in anxiety and stress, allowing the person to focus his or her attention without having negative thoughts intrude. Keep in mind that when practicing this technique, you should not strain any part of the body that has been injured or is recovering from injury.

Lie back in a bed (or on the floor). Place a pillow under your head. After taking three deep breaths as described earlier, do the following:

Close your eyes.

Clench both your fists. Study the tension.

Relax the fingers of your hands and study the difference. Enjoy the feeling of just lying there relaxed.

Again, clench both hands tighter and tighter. Study and focus on the tension you created in this part of your body.

Allow yourself to become relaxed all over.

Bend your elbows. Feel the tension created by bending your elbows. Dwell on the tension. Get to know how the tension feels in this part of the body.

Allow yourself to become very relaxed all over.

Become more and more relaxed. Imagine that you are so relaxed that you are sinking into the surface beneath you.

Straighten your arms out. Feel the tension created by pushing your arms straight out.

Now relax your arms and let them find their own place.

Wrinkle your forehead. Examine how the wrinkles feel and picture how they look.

Now relax. Let the wrinkles go and picture in your mind the way your forehead now looks without the wrinkles.

Squeeze your eyes shut. Experience the tension you created using your eyes.

Relax your eyes.

Relax all over.

Stay as relaxed as possible for about a minute.

Relax.

Relax.

Now clamp your teeth together. Study the tension created by biting your teeth together. Tension is being created in the jaws. Picture in your mind how the muscles in this area are tight.

Relax.

Now press your head back—push back on the pillow. Now stop and allow your body to become comfortable all over. Picture your body melting into the surface of the bed (or floor). Your body is so relaxed it is sinking down.

It is like you are a big rag doll just lying there. Relax.

Move your head down so it is now against your chest. Study the tension that this movement created.

Relax.

Bring your shoulders up. Study the muscle tension created when you try to touch your ears with your shoulders.

Relax.

Now pull in your stomach, tighter and tighter. Now relax.

Relax.

Create a small arch in your back. Feel the tension in your muscles when you arch your back. Relax and allow your back to settle into a comfortable position as you do when you go to sleep at night.

Point your toes up toward the top of your head. Maintain this for 20 seconds.

Now relax.

Relax.

Point your toes away from the top of your head. Maintain this position for about ten seconds. Now relax.

Relax.

Raise one leg. Keep the leg up until the tension starts to become uncomfortable.

Now lower that leg.

Relax.

Now lift the other leg. Keep it up for about the same length of time. Okay, now relax.

Become as relaxed as you are capable of becoming. Release all the muscle tension in your body. Relax more and more until you reach a very relaxed state—a very, very deep state of relaxation.

Lie there in a relaxed state for a while.

Now imagine getting up (do not move—just imagine getting up). Notice the change in muscle tension even when you just picture in your mind that you are getting up.

Go back to a deep state of relaxation. Let any tension you find pour out of your body as if you were a bucket with many, many holes and the tension were water.

After about a minute, permit yourself to come out of your relaxed state. You will feel refreshed upon getting up from where you were lying.

Meditation. There are various meditation techniques that can be used. A basic ingredient is to clear one's mind of thoughts and to concentrate on breathing. For example, as a person breathes, the person should count "one" for the breath in, "two" for the breath out, "three" for the next breath in, and so on. Continue all the way to the number ten. The trick is not to allow stray thoughts or images to occupy your mind. If this occurs, you must start over with the number one. It sounds easy—it is not. Try this exercise. It will take a period of practice (sometimes a long period) before you can reach the number ten without some sort of intrusion into your mind. Emptying one's mind is difficult.

In part, meditation is a way to slow us down. The mind is sometimes described as "a bunch of monkeys jumping from tree to tree," a metaphor to reflect how cluttered it can be with all the thoughts that enter its domain, disturbing its peace. As early as the 1970s, Herbert Benson and his colleagues at Harvard Medical School (see *The Relaxation Response*, 1975) found that when the mind is passively cleared during meditation, oxygen requirements drop, heartbeat slows, blood pressure lowers, and we experience a mental and physiological calmness.

Closing Remarks

According to Darlene Pedersen (2008), a previous U.S. Surgeon General stated that mental health is reflected in the type of mental functioning that enables a person to carry out productive activities, interact with others in ways that lead to fulfilling relationships, and most important of all, cope with adversity and change. For most students, it is not a single extremely stressful event that causes problems: it is the stress and anxiety they encounter on a daily basis that interfere the most with maintaining an effective level of functioning. We believe it is very important not to underestimate the accumulative impact of these day-to-day encounters that all students experience with stress and anxiety. As pointed out by Hans Selye (1976), without intervention, prolonged stress is not only disruptive to a student's academic performance, it can lead to illness and in extreme cases even death. We are convinced that adopting the various stress and anxiety management tactics found in this chapter will result in greater psychological health and an increase in the likelihood of optimal academic performance.

Sources

Barrios, B. A., Ginter, E. J., Scalise, J. J., & Miller, F. G. (1980). Treatment of test anxiety by applied relaxation and cue-controlled relaxation. *Psychological Reports, 46*, 1287–1296.

Benson, H. (1975). *The relaxation response*. New York, NY: Morrow.

Ciabattari, J. (1999, January). Women who could be president. *Parade Magazine*, 6–7.

Ellis, A., & Grieger, R. (Eds.). (1977). *Handbook of rational emotive therapy*. New York, NY: Springer.

Friedman, M., & Rosenman, R. H. (1974). *Type A behavior and your heart*. New York, NY: Knopf.

Glauser, A., & Glauser, E. (2001). *Cultivating the spirit of mindfulness in counseling and psychotherapy*. Presentation made at the 2001 World Conference of the American Counseling Association, San Antonio, TX.

Maddi, S. R., & Hess, M. J. (1992). Personality hardiness and success in basketball. *International Journal of Sport Psychology, 23*, 360–368.

Maddi, S. R., & Kosaba, D. M. (1994). Hardiness and mental health. *Journal of Personality Assessment, 64*, 265–274.

Pedersen, D. D. (2008). *Psych notes: Clinical pocket guide* (2nd ed.). Philadelphia, PA: F. A. Davis Company.

Seligman, M. E. P. (1975). *Helplessness: On depression, development, and death*. San Francisco, CA: W. H. Freeman.

Selye, H. (1976). *The stress of life*. New York, NY: McGraw-Hill.

Spielberger, C. D. (Ed.). (1972). *Anxiety: Current trends in theory and research*. New York, NY: Academic Press.

VandenBos, G. R. (Ed.). (2007). *APA dictionary of psychology*. Washington, DC: American Psychological Association.

SECTION 5

Identity Development/ Purpose-in-Life Skills

Vocation
More than a Job, More than a Career

*I*an Weber (2000) interviewed business psychologists Timothy Butler and James Waldroop about differences between the words *job*, *career*, and *vocation*. Although people tend to use the three words interchangeably, the words do not share a common definition. A **job** has to do with specific tasks and responsibilities that someone is employed to carry out. The word *career* "comes originally from the Latin word for cart and later from the Middle French word for racetrack" (p. 13). A career is a line of work such as teacher, nurse, botanist, or author. But one's career may not be one's vocation. According to Butler and Waldroop, *vocation* is derived from the Latin *vocare* (to call) and describes what one does that brings meaning and purpose to one's life via work. Some callings are to do something, while others are to be someone. Gregg Levoy, in his book *Callings* (1997), recounts how the mythologist Joseph Campbell reminds us that we are continuously having experiences that hint at our calling. If we listen to these hints and learn to recognize them, it is possible to choose the right vocation that can bring further meaning and purpose to our lives.

Vocational planning is a developmental process that involves self-exploration, career exploration, and occupational exploration. It can be an enjoyable, creative journey, but it does require purposeful planning to discover the kinds of opportunities needed to build life-skills for optimal growth. Zen masters inform us that every journey in life begins beneath our feet, even a 2,000-mile journey. Finding the right vocation is a journey that begins right beneath your feet. Choosing the right vocational path and identifying the college major and opportunities that can lead you to your calling are important steps in vocational planning, but not the only steps. The first step comes during the freshman phase of your college experience. This step's goal is to become more aware, through self-exploration, of your interests, values, skills, and aptitudes, and how your personality relates to career choice.

Self-Exploration

Who are you? What do you want? If you know the answers to these two questions, and are willing to put forth the time and effort needed to answer your calling, you are off to a successful start. The definition of success is a personal one. For some students, success is synonymous with making a lot of money, owning a business, having a prestigious career, or being elected to public office. For other students, altruistic endeavors and relationships may define success. Success can also be a combination of all these values and many more. Being able to identify precisely what you want in life is not necessarily an easy task.

Marsha Sinetar (1987) writes about discovering the right livelihood. She believes that choosing the right livelihood is based on making conscious choices. Sinetar acknowledges that this, too, is a difficult task because "unfortunately, since we learn early to act on what others have to say, value, and respect, we often find ourselves a long way down the wrong road before realizing we did not actually choose our work" (p. 11). Where you are today has a lot to do with decisions you have made in the past. Decisions that you make now create new directions that will determine your future. When you are conscious of the choices you make, you are choosing to be responsible. You are choosing to accept the consequences of decisions that you make, and in doing so, you learn to make better decisions.

At different periods in life, people make vocational decisions based on different sets of motivations. According to Butler and Waldroop, the decisions you make in your twenties are related to creating opportunities for yourself. You are trying to enlarge your world to find all the channels for getting what you think you need and want. In their thirties, people tend to make decisions based on the realization that there is limited time available to accomplish everything, so decisions become more focused. As you become aware of your own mortality throughout your forties and fifties, the gap between your dreams and reality narrows as you search for meaning and purpose. People tend to become more conscious of the choices they are making.

Why wait until later, until your forties and fifties, to discover meaning and purpose? It sometimes takes courage to make clear vocational choices that are reflective of who you are and what you want. The more you know about yourself, the easier the task of finding personal meaning and purpose in your life turns out to be. So be courageous—courageous actions can significantly lessen the amount of time required to find meaning and purpose, and the rewards are worth the risks involved.

Knowing your values is also an important piece of your vocational puzzle. Values are what ultimately guide our behavior and give us direction in life.

Values

Do you ever wonder why it is that you feel strongly about some issues, like abortion, the environment, or capital punishment, but not so strongly about other issues? The intensity of your feelings and thoughts on various issues is related to the strength of your values. **Values** are standards—reference points that guide your behaviors, thoughts, and feelings and are different from opinions and facts. They reflect what really matters to you. All your values together form your **value system**. Goals based on your value system will be stronger than ones that are not, and you will be more motivated to spend the necessary time and effort needed to reach them. If your career choice is firmly aligned with your values, you will be more enthusiastic and passionate about your career. Do you value competition, recognition, wealth, excitement, security, friends, volunteering, or success? Where do these values come from? Did they choose you (inherited), or did you choose them (assimilated over a lifetime)? Your values may be similar to ones held by significant people in your life, but values adopted without engaging in critical thinking are not as strong as ones that have survived being examined and then accepted as your own.

Do values ever change? Yes—experiences can modify and change them. For example, someone who values material wealth, prestige, and power may begin to value health, family, and spirituality more when faced with a life-threatening illness. A change in values will influence the decisions that a person makes about his or her career and about life in general. In college, as you meet new people, have new experiences, and are exposed to different perspectives, your values will most likely be challenged.

Considering the following questions can help you identify your own set of personal values. What is the most exciting thing you have done? What do you value most about another person? Who is it that you most admire? Answers to these questions may point to underlying values. Another way to identify values is to complete Exercises 1 and 2 at the end of this chapter.

Personality

When we talk about **personality**, we are referring to a set of motivations, beliefs, attitudes, traits, and response patterns that are consistent over time and distinguish one person from another. Each person is a unique composite of physical, biological, mental, emotional, and spiritual traits and potentials. In Chapter 6, you determined your personality type and learned about the effects of your primary attitude (extroversion or introversion). Additionally, you discovered some of the processes by which you make decisions (thinking and feeling) and how you act on those decisions (perceiving and judging).

Personality factors influence vocational exploration. *Thinking types* prefer to systematically gather facts about interesting majors, weigh the pros and cons of each major, and then make an objective decision. *Feeling types* tend to make subjective decisions based on how they feel about particular majors. If they do not feel personally engaged in the curriculum of a particular major, they are apt to switch majors to find one they feel more in tune with. When it comes to acting on the decision about a major and investigating various careers, *judging types* tend to reach closure quickly and begin to investigate specific career options, whereas *perceiving types* may resist closure and hesitate to become focused on one particular career path because they see so many options.

How does personality affect career choice? It is much nicer to be in an environment that affirms and supports you, rather than one where you have to continually explain and defend yourself. When your personality traits match up with a career, you will tend to find more support for challenges that you undertake and greater understanding for failed attempts. Let us explore some personality attributes associated with careers.

Extroversion and Introversion *Extroverts* tend to define themselves by how others recognize and respond to them, whereas *introverts* tend to be private and may not share what is significant and valuable about themselves with colleagues. In working situations, extroverts prefer to be around people and seek opportunities to interact with others. Introverts need time and space to think through their thoughts carefully before answering a question or giving an opinion. A person with an extroverted personality generally prefers a job that offers a lot of variety and activity and can become impatient with long, tedious tasks.

Intuition and Sensation. *Intuitive types* in the workplace want to be appreciated for generating ideas and theories, whereas *sensing types* want to be appreciated for all the details and facts they can bring to the work situation. People who rely on sensing prefer to use skills that they have already developed. They prefer work environments that have standardized procedures, and they do well in work that involves precision. Intuitive types are the opposite. They tend to dislike repetitive tasks and prefer careers that offer numerous opportunities to learn a variety of new skills.

Thinking and Feeling. *Feeling types* like to work in harmonious environments, generally enjoy pleasing people, and are genuinely interested in the people they work with. *Thinking types* respond more to ideas than people at work and are good at analyzing situations. They tend to be firmer in their decisions and seek careers that encourage the use of logical reasoning.

Judging and Perceiving. In a work situation, *judging types* are most productive when they have lists and plans to follow as well as the necessary resources (supplies, tools, and people) needed to begin work. *Perceiving types* are good at adapting to changes that arise at work and prefer to start projects rather than finish them. People who rely mostly on judging seek careers that require organization, whereas people who rely mostly on perceiving prefer work situations in which they can create their own schedule.

While no combination of preferences is inherently better than any other, knowing your personality type can help you understand not only your behavior in a work environment but also the behavior of those around you. Understanding how your values and personality influence your career choice is important when constructing a picture of your right livelihood, or calling. Next, let us connect some more dots and explore how interests influence vocational choices.

Interests

Most people are more likely to feel motivated to accomplish a task if they are interested in the task. Chances are good that if your interests are congruent with your occupational environment, you will achieve greater job satisfaction. A student we know attended a large college for a year, intending to major in psychology. After his first semester, he started feeling apathetic about attending classes and studying. At the end of his second semester, he returned home and began thinking about what he "would like to be when he grew up." He realized that his major interests focused on food: cooking, creating new recipes, observing people cook, reading cookbooks, and going to restaurants. He decided to become a chef. Now, having successfully graduated from a culinary institute, he is working as a chef and enjoying the work even though the hours are long and the work is demanding. What changed? He is now motivated to work hard because he is doing what he likes! Your interests can be a good predictor of job satisfaction. Think of times in your life when you were deeply engaged in what you were doing. It is during these times that your interests are activated, and you feel a sense of satisfaction and completion in what you are doing. Can you identify your interests and passions and turn them into a career?

What overwhelms one person in terms of challenge and supervision can stimulate and energize someone else. John Holland, a vocational psychologist, proposes that our interests define our personalities. He believes that different personalities cluster together in society, and that personalities can be differentiated from one another according to interests. Holland identifies six clusters of personality traits: realistic, investigative, artistic, social, enterprising, and conventional. According to Holland's vocational theory, career satisfaction and achievement are based on the degree of congruence between a person's interests and personality and his or her vocational environment (Holland, 1966). A popular career test based on Holland's theory of personality, which is found at most college counseling and career centers, is the Strong-Campbell Interest Inventory (SCII). It consists of 325 items concerning occupations, school subjects, activities, people, and characteristics. During the assessment, you make decisions about likes and preferences. The results provide information about occupations you might wish to pursue based on your profile of interests.

Assessing Interests

Read over the descriptions of the six personality clusters developed by John Holland. Then answer the questions that follow.

R = **Realistic.** People classified as realistic deal with their work environment in an objective and concrete manner. They prefer working with tools and machines rather than people and ideas. Realistic people are often characterized as being practical. They often enjoy working outdoors. Among the occupations that are primarily realistic in nature include those in athletics, military, construction, technical fields, forestry, agriculture, and skilled trades.

I = **Investigative.** Investigative types can be described as analytical, logical, scholarly, creative, and independent. Occupations characterized as being investigative tend to be related to scientific activities. Investigative people tend to be less conventional and less practical than realistic types. People closely aligned with this cluster would usually prefer to work alone rather than with other people. They prefer jobs where they can investigate and engage in critical thinking and logical analysis. Some specific jobs within the investigative cluster are ecologist, anthropologist, biologist, college professor, mathematician, physician, and computer programmer.

A = Artistic. Artistic types describe themselves as being independent, artistically inclined, creative, and unconventional. They dislike rigid situations with rules and regulations that are enforced. Some artistic jobs include actor, journalist, musician, photographer, media specialist, and interior decorator.

S = Social. Others generally see people who score high in the social cluster as sociable, nurturing, helpful, and responsible. These people have a lot of concern for human welfare and tend to be more optimistic than pessimistic. Social people tend to have good verbal skills and enjoy working with others in groups to solve problems. Jobs that involve these personality attributes include teacher, counselor, social worker, minister, travel agent, nurse, and recreational leader.

E = Enterprising. Enterprising individuals can be characterized as enthusiastic, assertive, and extroverted. They prefer occupations that involve sales or other situations where they are in a position of leading or persuading others. People who score high in this cluster are generally good at public speaking and interviewing. They prefer jobs in the fields of marketing, retail merchandising, health administration, real estate sales, law, television production, and politics.

C = Conventional. Conventional people tend to prefer jobs that are structured and predictable. They can be characterized as conscientious, neat, conservative, controlled, and persistent. They thrive on order and prefer systematic jobs such as banker, accountant, office manager, legal secretary, statistician, and dental assistant.

1. Which personality cluster fits you the best? _____

2. Rank the personality clusters based on how well each reflects your interests and personality traits, with 1 being the best fit.

   1. _____
   2. _____
   3. _____
   4. _____
   5. _____
   6. _____

• •

Skills and Aptitudes

The ability to acquire proficiency is called **aptitude**. Someone may have an aptitude to play the violin, but if that person is never given the opportunity to play, that skill may never be realized. Many students have the capacity to learn many things, but if the environment is not conducive to learning or students do not avail themselves of the opportunity, they may not learn. Do you have any aptitudes that you have not developed into skills? A **skill** is an ability to do something well. To develop a skill requires a lot of practice. Some people are able to take a well-developed skill and through intentional, directed practice, use that well-developed skill to perform at a highly competitive level (Colvin, 2008).

Colvin believes that people achieve excellence, not because they are born with a "talent" or a "gift," but because they purposely practice a skill set and are strongly motivated to move that skill set beyond its current level (even if the current level is recognized as being very good). In his book *Talent is Overrated: What Really Separates World-Class Performers from Everybody Else*, Colvin identifies behaviors to engage in before, during, and after practicing a skill set that will enable a person to achieve a level of excellence similar to that demonstrated by individuals such as Eli and Peyton Manning, Yo-Yo Ma, and Steve Ballmer.

Perhaps you are mechanically gifted, have good communication skills, are good at problem solving, or have a particular artistic skill like drawing, playing a musical instrument, or dancing. Some people have skills that are easily identifiable because they are observable. Others have skills that are harder to identify, like being able to analyze and synthesize information, mediate, and inspire others. Some people work better with data and information, while others work better with people. How quickly you learn and understand new information and engage in good critical thinking is based on skills.

When you have assessed your values, personality, interests, and skills, you have completed the first step in vocational exploration. Self-exploration will continue throughout your college experience (and life). As you become engaged in different activities and experiences, your beliefs, interests, values, skills, and even personality may change. You can expect that the picture or image that you have of yourself is likely to be revised during your college journey. Answer the following question: *"At this point in the journey, what picture or image of yourself forms when you connect all the dots?"*

_____

_____

Do you have a clear, accurate vision of what you want to do and who you are? Not only do you need a clear vision, but you also need a systematic plan for how to get there. Part of this plan is choosing the right major and the right career. The next stage of vocational exploration is career exploration.

Career Exploration

In addition to engaging in self-exploration, which you should begin as a freshman, get curious about all the possible career options out there for you. Talk with parents, professors, parents of friends, your career consultant at your campus career center, and whoever else might provide you with information about careers. Become familiar with the services offered through your college's career center, where you can generally find information about choosing a major and future career (e.g., information about interviewing, resume writing, campus recruiting, and career planning courses). Be sure to attend career decision-making workshops, take some vocational inventory tests, sign up for a class on choosing a major, sign up for internships, attend career fairs and seminars, and go on informal interviews. Also, make a list of careers that interest you and review it often.

Based on what you know about your values, personality, interests, and skills and aptitudes, what career do you think is the best fit for you?

_____

_____

What major will help you get there?_____

During your sophomore year, you should continue to obtain information about careers, seek out volunteer opportunities and work experience, talk to people about their work, and check out memberships in different clubs, committees, and organizations that can provide you with opportunities to develop leadership skills and other life-skills. Continue to visit the campus career center or go online and gather career information. Explore every career possibility that interests you. Consider taking an elective class in a major you are interested in. If you have not done so already, gather information about future employment and firm up your choice of a major. The following resources provide an enormous amount of information about careers and jobs.

Computer-Assisted Career Exploration Programs

State-Specific Career Information. Information relating to your state or the state where you will work after graduation can be used to match your interests and abilities with specific occupations. Current information is provided about occupations in different areas of the specific state, including working conditions, hiring requirements, and job outlook. For example, students in the state of Georgia have access to the Georgia Career Information Services (GCIS) database, which provides up-to-date information about specific fields of study, financial aid, military careers, and other colleges throughout the United States.

Type Focus is an online personality assessment that you can use to discover your personality type and find careers that match your personality strengths. This assessment or the Myers-Briggs Type Indicator (MBTI) might be available for students to use through the career center on your campus.

Interest Inventories can provide an understanding of the role that your interests play in the selection of a career. You can usually take the Strong-Campbell Interest Inventory online through a career consultant at the career center.

Books

Occupational Outlook Handbook (OOH). Published by the U.S. Department of Labor, Bureau of Labor Statistics, www.bls.gov/oco. This resource provides information on more than 300 jobs. Information is provided about training, qualifications, outlook, earnings, and working conditions. A good supplement to the handbook is the *Occupational Outlook Quarterly*, published about every two years, which has important articles and information about aspects of career planning. For more information about these publications and others, you can contact the Bureau of Labor Statistics through its website at http://www.bls.gov.

Dictionary of Occupational Titles (DOT). This resource is supplied electronically by the U.S. Department of Labor at www.occupationalinfo.org. The DOT offers descriptions of thousands of jobs, and is updated periodically. Jobs are organized into categories based on their similarities. A good use for this site is to look at the job clusters to see related occupations. It may be that you think of a career and want to know about related professions (counselor, social worker, and psychologist). The DOT can help you discover various job options.

Occupational Exploration

Is there a perfect job out there for you? Without the right career guidance, finding the perfect job might be akin to finding a needle in a haystack. Richard Bolles, author of *What Color Is Your Parachute? A Practical Manual for Job-Hunters and Career Changers*, hosts a free job search website (JobHuntersBible.com) that offers a variety of helpful resources directly pertaining to occupational exploration (e.g., articles, online job-hunting guides, and information about career assessments).

As a junior, there are specific occupational exploration tasks that you can engage in to increase your likelihood of finding that perfect job. You will want to increase your work experiences, continue attending career fairs, develop a resume, develop career contacts, network, take on leadership roles in organizations to which you belong, and do some serious research about careers (including learning about entry-level positions). Other steps you can take are to participate in cooperative education programs (co-ops) if possible, try to get jobs that are related to your major, do some mock interviews, and begin to gather information about graduate schools if you are planning to pursue a graduate degree. Check your campus career center to find the most comprehensive resources available. You will be able to locate information concerning cooperative educational experiences, internships, student employment, mock interviews, interviews with recruiters, and a variety of other experiences. Executive, managerial, administrative, and other positions can be highly competitive. Different kinds of work experiences, including internships and specialized training, can help you secure a position.

Having a good resume is essential to getting a good job. Many career centers can help you write a resume (and show you how to create an online version), set up a credential file, and educate you on how to secure government employment. Many campus career centers have a variety of books, as well as people, to help you write your resume.

Resume

There are plenty of books and free online resources about resume and cover letter writing. Besides your career center, check with campus and off-campus bookstores as well as libraries for online resources and books on resume writing.

The resume is a screening device intended to get you an interview. Remember, the receiver will probably invest very little time in looking over your resume; therefore, it must look great. Here are some general guidelines for developing a resume.

- Your resume needs to be well-organized, neat, and easy to read. (No smudges!) Make sure your grammar, punctuation, and spelling are correct. Use a good-quality paper in either white or ivory, and use a clear typeface and type size (10 to 14 point). Double-space above and below each heading.
- Learn how to format your resume to enhance specific information about yourself. The reader should be able to form a clear image of you and be motivated to meet you. When choosing a format for your resume, choose one that best suits your purposes. Become familiar with different formats. Know when it is best to use a chronological format (highlighting work history) and when to use a functional format. For example, if you have had little work history, you might want to focus on your skills using a functional resume format.
- Give identifying information at the top of your resume: name, address, and phone numbers where you can be reached. Be sure to get an answering machine or use voice mail to record messages if you are going to be away from your phone for long periods of time.
- Some people like to put an objective in their resume (e.g., "public relations position with a nonprofit agency"). If you include an objective, create it before you begin writing your resume. An objective can help you stay focused while developing your resume. Be sure that you support the objective throughout your resume.
- List your education in reverse chronological order. Make sure you include the year, type of degree (BA, BS), and name of the school you will graduate from. Include your overall grade point average if impressive, as well as professional affilia-

tions and training seminars. Also include career-related experiences: the name and location of the company, the titles of the positions you held, and the months and year you started and ended employment. List work experiences from most recent to least recent. You may also want to include school and community-related activities, honors and transferable skills, achievements, and a statement that references will be furnished upon request. Make statements specific, using words that convey action (e.g., *organized*, *supervised*, *developed*, *implemented*, *generated*, and *eliminated*). Each sentence should convey information about you that you want the reader to notice. Do not put down anything that you cannot later substantiate in an interview.

Occupational exploration tasks during your senior year include reviewing and updating your resume, requesting letters of reference, completing course requirements, signing up for interviews, sending out resumes, setting up interviews, taking qualifying examinations for your profession (e.g., a teacher exam), and participating in campus recruiting efforts. If you have not done so already, register with your career center to access a variety of career services. Check calendars to see what workshops and career fairs are being offered and when. Tell everyone you know that you are looking for a job and describe the type of job you want. This may also be the time to send out graduate school applications or begin buying a professional wardrobe.

Let's assume you have made your contacts, networked through your career center, sent out your resume, and have been asked to interview for a position. There are some general interview guidelines that are important to know.

Job Interview

A job interview serves two purposes. It is a way for the prospective employer to decide if you are the person for the job, and it is a way for you to see if you want the job. This may be an opportunity for you to get farther down the path to attaining your goals. Campus career centers often work with recruiters to set up on-campus interviews, which are usually screening interviews, with students. Spend as much time preparing for your interview as you did writing your resume. Additionally, here is a list of tips to help you successfully navigate your way through an interview.

- Dress neatly and appropriately.
- Be punctual and communicate your appreciation for the opportunity to meet with whoever is interviewing you.
- Job interviews generally start off with personal introductions and a bit of small talk. Remember to make good eye contact.
- During the interview try to appear confident and relaxed. You will probably be asked to describe yourself (qualifications including strengths and weaknesses) and your professional goals.
  - Explain how your education and experience are related to the particular job that you are interviewing for. (Whoever is interviewing you is most likely assessing you to see if your goals match up with their organization.)
  - Explain why you are interested in working with their organization. Knowledge of the organization is vital, so do your homework before the interview. Research the nature of the organization, where it currently is, and where it is heading. It will demonstrate your interest in the position.
  - Explain why you are leaving your current job, if you are doing so.
  - Ask questions. You can always ask about the organization's expectations for its employees as well as future challenges and directions.

- Communicate to the interviewer your skills and accomplishments. (Do not make outlandish claims. Dishonesty will not impress future employers.)
- Before you leave, ask when you can expect to hear from the interviewer again.
- After the interview, take time to make notes about the interview. Include in your notes people's names, ideas presented, further questions, and changes to make before the next interview.
- A few days after the interview, follow up with a note thanking the interviewer for the opportunity to meet with him or her and learn more about the organization. If you are interested in the position you interviewed for, say so, and state that you are looking forward to hearing from the interviewer should he or she have any further questions.

Employment Projections

Every year in the United States, millions of new jobs are created. Although not everyone in this country attends college, 68.1 percent of the high school graduating class of 2010 enrolled in a college or university, according to the Bureau of Labor Statistics (BLS). Employment that generally requires a college degree or other forms of postsecondary education is projected to grow faster than any other category of occupation. In fact, the fastest growth will be in occupations that require an associate degree. It is projected that the civilian work force in the United States will increase by 12.6 million between 2008 and 2018. In addition, the number of people aged 55 and older in the labor force will increase by 12 million during the same time period.

Even though the group known as "baby boomers" will continue to grow older, many are also expected to continue working. By 2018, they will make up a fourth of the labor force. The BLS projections reveal not only an aging labor force, but also a more ethnically diverse labor force due to increased immigration, a higher birth rate among people who currently are members of a minority group, and a greater number of Hispanics and Asians entering the work force over the next ten years. What conclusions can you reach about the civilian work force based on these projections?

The Bureau of Labor Statistics analyzes factors that influence economic trends in the United States (e.g., technology, foreign competition, demand for goods and services) to create projections about employment. The BLS projections for 2008–2018 are available and include the following:

Among the 30 fastest-growing occupations are network systems and data communication analysts, personal and home care aides, home health aides, computer software engineers, veterinarians, medical assistants, financial examiners, physical therapist aides, physical therapist assistants, physician assistants, skin care specialists, biochemists, biophysicists, dental hygienists, biomedical engineers, and athletic trainers.

Among the top 30 occupations with the largest employment growth are registered nurses, retail salespersons, physicians, surgeons, child care workers, postsecondary teachers, customer service representatives, combined food preparation and serving workers (including fast food), accountants and auditors, management analysts, medical assistants, computer software engineers, personal and home care aides, home health aides, post-secondary teachers, janitors and cleaners (but not maids and housekeeping services), and nursing aides, orderlies, and attendants.

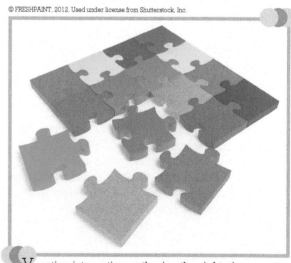

Vocation integration: gathering the right pieces.

Closing Remarks

The earlier you begin the process of vocational exploration, the more successful you will be in finding the perfect job, the right livelihood, your calling, or the answer to what you want to be "when you grow up." You will also be more likely to identify and take advantage of incredible opportunities that come your way during your college experience—opportunities that are aligned with your vocational choice. Table 14.1 summarizes some of the career-preparation activities that you can engage in throughout college. The right vocation is one that reflects your values, interests, personality, and skills. Marsha Sinetar writes about vocational integration, a term used to designate a person who is so completely congruent with and committed to his or her vocation that he or she has no doubts about whether or not to invest the energy required to get the job done. Some students feel that once they have chosen a major, that's it. In fact, many students change majors as their interests and values change. Remember that vocational exploration is a lifelong process. Most people change careers several times, retire, and engage in volunteer activities that bring meaning to their work and life.

Table 14.1

The Authors' Career/Vocational Suggestions: Steps to Take Each Year

Year One: Discover What You Need to Know	Year Two: Build on What You Have Learned
• Meet with a career consultant at your college's career center to discuss major(s)/vocation(s) that interest you *or* to explore the reasons you are undecided about your vocational future. • Use career assessments to identify how various personality factors, skills, values, and interests come together to suggest which type of work best matches who you are. • Use your college's career website to gather information about potential careers. Find out whether computer career programs like the *Type Focus* are available and whether they are accessible from your dorm/residence. • Attend your college's career fairs to obtain additional information; especially information about internships and co-ops (e.g., does the internship you are interested in require a one semester or an entire year commitment?). • Join email listservs in vocational areas you are considering (e.g., pre-med, psychology, pre-law). • Keep an open mind and adopt an ongoing creative approach to find out what major fits you best. For example, join campus organizations/clubs that personally appeal to you. • Continue to gather information about your potential major/vocation by speaking with those *most familiar* with the actual career/vocation: professors, family members, academic advisors, and other students who share your career aspirations. Discover what types of opportunities are provided by this area of work.	• If you are ready to declare a major (or you want to change) then meet with an advisor to declare a major. • Move from pursuing general information to more detailed information concerning your major/vocation by utilizing your career center's resources and personnel. • Explore with a career center consultant the possibility of doing a *job shadow* in those careers related to your major. This will require you to observe (i.e., shadow) a person carrying out his/her duties during a typical work day. • Assess your current level of skills: which are relatively weak and do they require strengthening? Decide how you might build up weak areas you identified. For example, if your college offers a seminar on "career exploration and preparation" you should consider enrolling in the class. Finally, we recommend you keep in mind two skill areas many employers have consistently reported over the last decade as problematic for new hirers: poor communication skills related to both speaking and writing (e.g., memos, business letters, documents, manuals, and so forth) and poor critical thinking/problem-solving skills. • Attend workshops devoted to writing resumes and cover letters. Even though you are not ready to apply for a job or attend a graduate/professional program of study, such workshops will alert you to what types of activities should be pursued to make yourself more marketable or competitive.

(continued on the following page)

Table 14.1 continued

- Pay more attention to those activities that will highlight your uniqueness. For example, use future semesters to decide how you will "build up your resume"—what should you pursue to fill in the gaps? You might decide it is important to: acquire leadership skills by working closely with a club advisor on your campus, volunteer your service to a professional state organization related to your major/vocation (professional organizations often offer membership to students at a reduced fee), strengthen your interpersonal and organization skills by taking classes known to provide students with opportunities to work with others on group projects, or create a strong network of people that can later assist you in getting a desirable job or in getting into your first choice among various graduate/professional programs (many students accomplish such goals by focusing on developing strong, positive relationships with professors and others related to their major area of study).

- Seek opportunities to work closely with professors on projects (if the college has no formal programs to connect students interested in working in a professional context with a professor you should take the initiative and seek out such a working relationship on your own). Co-presenting at a professional conference or being listed on a publication as one of its contributors will make a very significant and attention getting addition to your resume.

- Continue to attend job fairs, especially those that specifically offer opportunities in work-related areas that your major is preparing you for.

- If applicable, research pertinent graduate/professional school programs, and create a tentative list of professors and others from your career/vocational network who you believe will write recommendations best suited for certain programs.

- If you have elective hours remaining consider taking a course that will increase your marketable value.

- Sign up for the various placement services offered at your college.

- Participate in those career fairs that match those work areas that you hope to pursue.

- Use campus interviewing workshops to develop those skills necessary to better impress a potential employer or the faculty of graduate/professional programs.

- Continue to expand your career/vocational network by adding people from newly formed relationships.

- Seek recommendations from professors and others you have established relationships with. We suggest you maintain these relationships after you graduate by sending an occasional email update or holiday/celebratory card. Such on-going contact will greatly increase the likelihood these individuals will respond positively to future requests for letters of recommendation (be sure to send an up-to-date resume).

- Target those work settings or graduate/professional programs that match you well—three or more years of career/vocational preparation should have made you ready and more than capable of effectively accomplishing this task.

- Consider if there are any skills you might have overlooked that could help during an interview. For example, what if you were invited by interviewers to a formal dinner—would you know what each fork is used for? You might consider brushing up on such etiquette related skills so you are less anxious when you find yourself trapped in a formal setting.

- If you have decided to apply to a graduate/professional program give yourself enough time to prepare (use study guides, etc.) and take any exams necessary to complete your application packet. While you might schedule such exams early in your last year, it is probably best if the exploration of and preparation for such exams takes place a year in advance. Keep in mind that good time-management skills are required from start to finish in college.

Congratulate yourself for the exploration steps you have taken. Now, continue to find ways to motivate yourself to take the necessary steps to continue on your career path. Plan for your future and invest your time and energy deliberately.

Sources

Bolles, R. N. (2010). *What color is your parachute? A practical manual for job-hunters and career changers.* Berkeley, CA: Ten Speed Press.

Colvin, G. (2008). *Talent is overrated: What really separates world-class performers from everybody else.* New York, NY: Penguin.

Holland, J. L. (1966). *The psychology of vocational choice, a theory of personality types and model environments.* Waltham, MA: Blaisdell.

Kendall Hunt Publishing. (1999). *First-year experience sourcebook.* Dubuque, IA: Author.

Levoy, G. (1997). *Callings.* New York, NY: Three Rivers Press.

Occupational Outlook Handbook, 2010–11 edition: College enrollment & work activities of 2010 high school graduates. United States Department of Labor. Retrieved September 15, 2011 from http://www.bls.gov/newsrelease/hsgec.nr0.htm

Occupational Outlook Handbook, 2010–11 edition: Economic new release. United States Department of Labor. Retrieved October 1, 2011 from http://www.bls.gov/newsrelease/pdf/ecopro.pdf

Sinetar, M. (1987). *Do what you love and the money will follow.* New York, NY: Dell.

Webber, A. (2000, January). Is your job calling? *Fast Track*, pp. 13–16.

Chapter 14

Exercise 1: Values Clarification

Look over the list of values below and on the next page. Identify 15 values that are significant to you. Rank them from 1 to 15, with 1 being most important.

_____ Spiritual well-being

_____ Relationships

_____ Respect

_____ Empathy/compassion

_____ Generosity

_____ Sense of humor

_____ Autonomy

_____ Competition

_____ Integrity

_____ Security

_____ Wealth

_____ Good job

_____ Success and achievement

_____ Happiness

_____ Courage

_____ Strength

_____ Acceptance

_____ Appreciation of nature

_____ Adventure

_____ Learning/education

_____ Diversity

_____ Loyalty

_____ Freedom

_____ Intelligence

_____ Kindness

_____ Health

_____ Endurance

_____ Intimacy

_____ Creativity

_____ Love

_____ Challenges

_____ Altruism (helping others)

_____ Appreciation of beauty

_____ Recognition

_____ Ambition

_____ Pleasure and joy

_____ Fairness

Other

_____ a. _____

_____ b. _____

_____ c. _____

_____

1. What are your top three values?

   _____

   _____

   _____

2. How are these three values reflected in your life?

Chapter 14

Exercise 2: Work Values

Work values are qualities about a job that are most significant and meaningful to you. Without them, the job would not be satisfying. Identify ten work values that are important to you and rank them from 1 to 10, 1 being most important.

_____ Great salary		_____ Working outside	
_____ Recognition from others		_____ Having an office	
_____ Security		_____ Congenial workplace	
_____ Fun		_____ Challenge	
_____ Autonomy		_____ Competition	
_____ Variety		_____ Travel	
_____ Excitement		_____ Affiliation	
_____ Lots of leisure time		_____ Decision making	
_____ Leadership role		_____ Supervising others	
_____ Helping others		_____ Work flexibility	
_____ Prestige		_____ Public contact	
_____ Creativity		_____ Working alone	
_____ Improving society		Other	
_____ Influencing others		_____ a. _____	
_____ Continuity		_____ b. _____	
_____ Professional position		_____ c. _____	
_____ Flexible work schedule			

_____

1. What are your top three work values?

   _____

   _____

   _____

2. Describe why each of these values is important to you.

3. Will your career choice satisfy the three values you selected? Explain.

Chapter 14

Exercise 3: Greatest Achievements

Think about all the goals you have set for yourself thus far in your life and all of your achievements. List five *achievements* that you consider to be the most significant.

1. _____
2. _____
3. _____
4. _____
5. _____

Identify five *skills* that were used to reach your achievements.

1. _____
2. _____
3. _____
4. _____
5. _____

Identify five *interests* that are reflected by your achievements.

1. _____
2. _____
3. _____
4. _____
5. _____

Identify five *values* that are reflected by your achievements.

1. _____
2. _____
3. _____
4. _____
5. _____

Congratulations! You have completed the first step in vocational exploration: self-exploration. You have assessed and identified your values, personality, interests, and skills. Now look for patterns and themes among them all. What have you learned about yourself?

Chapter 14

Exercise 4: Career Decisions

Career decisions are influenced by what people learn about themselves and various professions. Research indicates that having a specific career goal in mind is related to a student's academic performance at a college. Uncertainty about a major has been linked to poor performance and frequency of dropping out.

Answer each question.

1. Review John Holland's six personality types: realistic, investigative, social, conventional, enterprising, and artistic. Discuss which type describes you best. Be sure to indicate traits or characteristics you have that make you believe this particular type fits you.

2. List occupations that match the type you selected above. Then explain why you think they match this type. Are there any careers you are interested in that do not exactly fit your personality type (e.g., your type is realistic, but you are interested in banking and accounting)? If the answer is yes, list these careers and indicate how you found out about the careers that do not fit your type (e.g., friend, family member, career assessment). Finally, explain what attracts you to the careers that do not match your type.

3. Select two careers that you are most interested in. Gather information about both careers using a career-exploration software program or printed source (e.g., *OOH, DOT*). The instructor of your course will specify whether he or she wants you to use a certain source.

How might you use the information you gathered concerning these two occupations to move closer to finding a career that will prove satisfying and rewarding? Refer to the list of work values given earlier. When you respond, discuss the work values that are of importance to you.

Campus and Community Connections
Development and Application of Life-Skills

15

This textbook emphasizes the development of life-skills necessary to master all the challenges presented by attending college, as well as other challenges that emerge throughout life. One of the basic assumptions underlying the importance of developing life-skills is that while one's ability to learn is somewhat dependent on innate factors, the maximization of life-skills is tied to external events, or life experiences. College can help you to maximize many of these life-skills by providing you with opportunities to develop the skills to become an autonomous learner, engage in continuous personal growth, seek and obtain a relevant career, and become a responsible member of the world community. All of this is possible, if you know where to look.

Community Connections

Your college is part of the community that surrounds it and most likely creates outreach services and promotes community service within surrounding schools, businesses, and government. Get to know some of these opportunities to serve your community. You can develop new skills and new relationship with leaders in the surrounding communities. Students often become involved in their community through work, volunteerism, internships, and other learning experiences. Begin your community exploration by reading one of the local newspapers or visiting your community's chamber of commerce to discover volunteer opportunities. When you become involved in your community, you are making a commitment and taking on responsibility. Simply stated, involvement in the community allows you to exercise responsible citizenship.

Service Learning

The difference that any of us will ultimately make in this world is equivalent to our throwing a stone into the sea. Science tells us that because the stone is lying on the bottom, the level of water must have risen, but there is no way to measure it. We must take it entirely on faith.

Gregg Levoy, Callings

Service learning is a form of experiential learning that promotes civic learning, the process through which students learn about their communities: how they function, the problems they face, and how students as individuals can enhance the community (Ehrlich, 1999). Discover which department on campus coordinates service learning opportunities. More than likely, your college offers a wide variety of courses and programs that integrate critical community service with academic work. In addition to becoming involved in your local community or state, you might choose to take your volunteer efforts into a more global arena by participating in a service-learning opportunity in another country. At the global level, you can immerse yourself in another culture and experience citizenship from a different perspective.

Whether you volunteer your time and talents to provide a service for your local community or a community halfway around the world, you will most likely be experiencing a situation that promotes learning and development in these four areas: interpersonal communication/human relations, problem solving/decision making, physical fitness/health maintenance, and identity development/purpose-in-life. More specifically, these experiences help you establish meaningful relationships, participate effectively in small and large groups, express opinions clearly, identify and solve problems, set appropriate goals, build critical thinking skills, clarify values, create meaning in life, and establish pragmatic moral guidelines.

In their book *When Hope and Fear Collide*, Arthur Levine and Jeanette S. Cureton report that colleges across America are having to provide students with remedial skills—not remedial in terms of reading, math, and writing (which they acknowledge that many students need), but remedial in terms of the following four attributes: hope, personal responsibility, appreciation and respect of differences, and self-efficacy. They found that many students are lacking in the ability to feel sincerely optimistic about the future (hope), often fail to take responsibility for the outcomes of their decisions and actions, are unable to recognize, accept, and respect differences among people and ideas, and are unable to feel that what they do would make a difference (self-efficacy). Gregg Levoy, author of the book *Callings*, cites former Czechoslovakian president Vaclav Havel, who said, "Hope is not the conviction that something will turn out well, but the certainty that something makes sense, regardless of how it turns out" (p. 4).

Service learning can provide you with opportunities that encourage the development of a sense of hope and meaning in life and an awareness of issues related to diversity, self-efficacy, and personal responsibility. Talk to people about their experiences volunteering for an organization whose mission they support. Volunteers often state that they feel their contribution made a difference in the life of someone else. People who volunteer also report feeling more hopeful about the future of their community and the country and world in which they live.

Building Community through Volunteerism

A nation is defined not by its people but by the ideas its people hold in common, not just in their laws but in their imaginations where ideas are born. A great nation, like a great idea, must be large enough for everyone to hope and dream and find new ways to come together to demonstrate the greatest idea of all, that it is not who we are but what we create between us that gives human life its real significance. We are not fully human until we are serving each other's destinies and can see our own dreams in each other's eyes.

Block by Block: Building Community in America's Cities
(PBS Video, 1997)

Community building is about strengthening communities using available assets and resources. As a volunteer, you are a valuable resource in your community. Sometimes the problems of the world, the United States, or our local community appear too overwhelming to tackle. Students may question what impact their volunteer work can make in alleviating the multifaceted problems facing societies today. Often after a traumatic event, people engage in an exploration of basic existential questions: What is the meaning of life? What is the meaning of *my life*?

Viktor Frankl lost his pregnant wife, mother, father, and other family members during the three years he spent in a concentration camp during the Holocaust. Once liberated, he wrote *Man's Search for Meaning*: An *Introduction to Logotherapy*, an influential book that has been read by millions of people and inspired countless others to alter the direction of their lives to create a personal meaning for their existence. Frankl's core message is that even under the most horrific conditions, a person can still choose to live a life of purpose and meaning. He believed this to be one of our primary motivational forces. To live a life of purpose and meaning, we need to seek out meaningful activities. For many people, volunteerism offers a meaningful experience.

Alexander W. Astin (1999) reported on the substantial decline in student participation in community service activities between high school and college. Two in every five students who participated frequently in high school never participated in college. In looking at factors in the college environment that encourage or discourage volunteerism, he found that interdisciplinary courses and student peer groups correlated positively to volunteerism. It appears that students who were enrolled in interdisciplinary courses participated more as volunteers. Astin surmised that this was most likely due to the fact that many interdisciplinary courses incorporate a service-learning component. Astin also found that if a student was involved in service projects, the display of involvement seemed to influence other students' future actions. Students were much more likely to volunteer if peers volunteered. Finally, Astin reported that the following three activities were negatively associated with volunteer participation: working at a job, living at home, and watching television. Among the effects of volunteer service on post-college education, Astin reported that volunteering during the undergraduate years produced positive effects on enrollment in graduate school, being committed to promoting racial understanding, and socializing across racial lines.

Students on campuses throughout the United States are becoming more interested in volunteering and are making various types of commitments in their communities. What kind of commitment have you made to your community? If you are thinking about volunteering, you might want to consider the following steps to make your volunteer experience more meaningful.

1. **Identify your own values.** What is significant and important to you? Values are a basic source of motivation.
2. **Identify your commitment level** (i.e., the amount of time and energy you are able to give), your skills, and objectives for your involvement.
3. **Identify a volunteer agency** that needs volunteers and fits your values, commitment level, the role you want to play in an organization, and your objectives for volunteering. Volunteer centers in your community or on campus can put you in touch with a volunteer agency that matches your availability and interests.
4. **Come up with a plan** for approaching the people who are actively involved in the agency you want to pursue. (You might want to use the interview guide at the end of the chapter to interview the director or assistant director of an agency to obtain additional information about the agency and specifics on how you can help.)
5. **Volunteer** if the organization or agency is a good fit, and you have the opportunity to participate. Find ways to share your skills and develop new ones.
6. **Identify and nurture relationships with community mentors.** Create and maintain community contacts for future personal, educational, career, and community service objectives.
7. **Participate in team building** within the agency. Determine how you can become an integral part of the team.
8. **Seek feedback** on your volunteer efforts.

To leave the world a better place—whether by a healthy child, a garden patch, or an improved social condition—that is to have succeeded. That only one life breathed easier because you lived—that is success.

Ralph Waldo Emerson

© SERGEJ KHAKIMULIN, 2012. Used under license from Shutterstock, Inc.

Create the right connections.

Campus Resources

The campus at your college encompasses all the students, professors, instructors, researchers, administrators, librarians, counselors, and other personnel who work for the college. It also includes all the academic programs and student services, as well as buildings, computers, books, and other resources. Whether you are a full-time student living on campus or a part-time student commuting to campus, you are a member of your college's community. Explore your campus, and become familiar with all that it has to offer. It can serve you well, if you know it and how to use it. Have you been on a campus tour? If you were unable to attend an orientation session before you started college, or attended the orientation but failed to pay attention on the campus tour, sign up for a tour. You might be surprised by what you learn.

Another good source for information about your campus and community resources is your college bulletin, which is generally your school's official resource for majors, courses, and academic information. Find it online and read it! You can learn about your school's policies and procedures, courses, student services, majors, departments, the organization of your college, and the multitude of services offered by different divisions and programs within your school. Before long, you will know where you need to go to change a grade, to seek advice about a major, and a lot more. You will also find information about the college bookstore, parks and other recreational sites, museums, libraries, student centers, and a multitude of other resources. You may become so knowledgeable that you might want to consider becoming a campus orientation leader—a job that pays money.

In the following section, you will find brief descriptions of some valuable resources available at most colleges. *Be sure to check the website of each office at your college for further information about student services.*

Academic Affairs

The office for academic affairs oversees research, instruction, public service, and outreach. This office makes sure that the educational objectives of the institution are met; it takes care of courses, majors, core curriculum requirements, admission standards, and instructional support. This includes various instructional units and programs across campus, such as an office of higher education, an office of financial aid, a registrar's office, an office of service learning, and/or an honors program.

An honors program generally provides students who participate in the program with honors sections of classes and seminars that are generally limited to enrollments of 20 students or less. Opportunities might be provided for students to work independently on a research project under the supervision of a faculty member. Check out your college's honors program website to learn about additional opportunities and eligibility requirements for enrollment.

Institutions of higher learning are invested in helping students succeed, and most students want to succeed, but students do not always come to college with the academic skills needed to achieve success. Many of the individual academic units at your college might offer tutoring in their discipline and even provide other support services for students who fail to meet their academic goals and want to become better students.

Many colleges have their academic support services centrally located in the form of a campus learning center. Such learning centers often provide a computer lab and various forms of instructional support where faculty, staff, and peer tutors work with students individually and in groups to provide tutoring in many core courses. Individual and group assistance in writing, mathematics, reading, and study strategies are typical services available at such learning centers. Additionally, counselors might be available to meet individually with students who have concerns related to academic success. There might also be one or more satellite offices located in the residence halls that offer free tutoring, test review sessions, academic counseling, and programs related to academic survival. Finally, check with your college to find out if there are courses offered that are specifically designed to help you fill in any educational gaps you may be worried about.

As a student, you will also want to become familiar with the undergraduate admissions office, which usually handles recruitment, undergraduate admissions, transfer credits, readmission, and orientation. Among the responsibilities of the office of the registrar are registration, maintaining academic records, reporting grades, and transcripts.

Student Affairs

Your college's division of student affairs is responsible for providing services and programs that promote the academic, social, and personal development of students. Within this office you will find a variety of resources in terms of people and programs to help students develop the life-skills necessary for achieving success. Some of the programs, services, and offices that will likely be found within student affairs include:

- A disability resource center guides your college in honoring its commitment to educate and serve students with disabilities who are admitted to your school. This center is generally responsible for coordinating academic and support services for students and helping to make the campus an accessible and welcoming environment for students with disabilities.
- An office of student support services generally offers individualized assistance to students, parents, faculty, and others who might be affected when a student experiences a hardship situation while attending college.
- A college health center will offer a wide range of medical, psychological, and prevention services. Among some of the clinics your health center might provide are a sports medicine clinic, a women's clinic, a mental health clinic, a vision clinic, and a dental clinic. A travel clinic for faculty and students traveling abroad is sometimes housed at the health center. Campus health centers operate proactively, presenting numerous programs and offering student services related to alcohol and other drug use, nutrition, and sexual health. Counseling and psychiatric services can provide numerous student support services including short-term individual counseling, group counseling, couples counseling, crisis intervention, psychiatric evaluations, and medication monitoring. Check out your college's website to learn about their services or to set up an appointment.
- A housing office is concerned with the housing needs of students and provides social and educational programs that promote the development of life-skills in a community environment. Check out their website to discover the most updated information about housing policies.
- A campus life office might oversee student organizations, a student union, and numerous other student-centered services. This is where you might also find information about being a part of a national student exchange program.
- An office of multicultural services and programs can weave together a variety of services for students and faculty that celebrate the culturally rich community at your college. Log on to their website and search for programs, community celebrations found on and off campus, and information about scholarships.

- **A recreational sports center** will coordinate intramural sports and organize a variety of recreational opportunities for students. Log on to their website to read about all the programs and fun ways to exercise.

Libraries

Get to know the library or libraries at your college. Learn the location of each, the hours they are open, the types of collections housed in each, the kinds of special services that are offered to students, the types of databases used, the electronic resources available, policies governing renewals, and other information that can help you use library resources to the fullest. There are usually well-known collections housed at college libraries. There might be impressive collections of letters from famous people or collections from political parties, public foundations, radio and television programs, the ACLU, and various individuals with special ties to your college. Get to know the quality of the resources available to you at your library. If you have not attended a library orientation, schedule one. The instructional and research librarians that you find at your college library are incredible resources for you to use as you learn to navigate the library system.

If you have more than one library, the main library might house material collected from the fields of social science, humanities, and business. You will find materials associated with physical and life sciences at a science library. Some colleges have a separate law library that may use its own online catalog (i.e., Gavel). A college can have hundreds of databases, tens of thousands of full-text journals, and thousands of books available electronically. At a student center, you might find computers that allow you to access an electronic library through GALILEO, or some other electronic means, to conduct searches for class projects.

Cultural Opportunities

Throughout the year, a variety of cultural events are offered on your campus to educate and entertain you. Not only do you not have to travel great distances to take advantage of all that is offered, but the events themselves are usually reasonably priced. Students generally pay reduced prices for concerts, speakers, and other performances. Season tickets often offer even further price reductions.

Have you been to your performing arts center or art gallery? They are often centrally located on campus. Take advantage of the intellectual and cultural opportunities that are available on your campus. Visit them online to discover what is happening on your campus.

Career Services

Your campus career center connects students with career opportunities (e.g., on-campus interviews, internships, student employment, career placement) and provides services (e.g., resume writing, vocational classes, workshops) to help you make a smooth, successful transition from college to work.

People as Resources

There are many people on campus who are available and eager to help you reach your goals. An important person on campus for you to get to know is your academic advisor. Your advisor can explain to you the difference between a national student exchange program and a study abroad program, and terms such as *minimum load*. He or she can provide you with information about majors, courses, registration, and graduation requirements. Even though you have an advisor, you are, and should be, responsible for knowing about courses and programs of study that are in your college catalog.

Another important person for you to find is a mentor. A campus is a wonderful place to find a mentor—a person who will take a professional and personal interest in you. Students generally look for mentors in fields that interest them. A mentor can provide opportunities and direction for you.

Leadership

Your college offers students many opportunities for developing leadership skills and other skills for lifelong learning. Check out what your college has to offer and take advantage of the services, resources, and opportunities. If you want some experience working in government at the local or state level, you can obtain an application from your career center, or maybe through a Governor's Intern Program. Generally, if you are enrolled in this program as a junior, senior, graduate, or law student with a 2.5 or higher GPA, you can participate in a full- or part-time internship experience through a state or local government agency or a nonprofit organization in your state.

Check to see if your college has a center for leadership and service or some other organization that provides opportunities for students to engage in leadership learning. Colleges offer all sorts of leadership development programs and experiences through campus organizations, various camps, and forms of mentoring. Students can also participate in various volunteer experiences through campus and community organizations that collaborate on service activities. *Alternative Spring Break* has become a popular campus program across the country for students to participate in: during spring break, students travel around the country to various communities where they actively engage in service projects.

If you put five people in a room together and ask them to perform a task, someone is bound to emerge as a leader. Would it be you? David Johnson and Frank Johnson (2009) concluded that the best predictor of leadership success is prior leadership success. Although studies have shown that there are certain traits associated with leaders (e.g., persistence, tolerance for ambiguity, internal locus of control, drive, and motivation to achieve), whether or not a person with those traits becomes an effective leader is dependent on timing (i.e., the right time and the right opportunity). Essentially, Johnson and Johnson concluded, good leaders emerge as leaders because they have the motivation and self-confidence to succeed, and because they will work as hard as necessary to reach available leadership positions. Skills needed to inspire, motivate, and guide other people can be developed through opportunities provided by your college and community. Institutes of higher education, local communities, and the world community need leaders, including student leaders, if these entities are to survive and thrive. Think of leaders whom you have admired. What qualities can you identify that helped these individuals be effective leaders? List five of these qualities.

1. _____

2. _____

3. _____

4. _____

5. _____

On the lighter side, Johnson and Johnson have identified five rules to carefully follow if you want a guarantee that you will never emerge as a leader. After reading over the five rules, see if any of them apply to you (including your behavior in class and elsewhere on campus).

- Be absent from group meetings as often as possible.
- When you do attend, be sure to contribute nothing.
- If you do participate, come on strong early in the discussion and demonstrate your knowledge of everything, including your extensive vocabulary of big words and technical jargon.
- Indicate that you will do only what you have to and nothing more.
- Read the paper (or do something unrelated to the meeting's purpose) during meetings.

Moral Learning

According to Charles Schroeder (1999), for students to become effective leaders on their campus and in their community, they must first develop a moral compass to guide them in making the right ethical and moral choices. This moral compass is a set of internalized beliefs regarding what is right and wrong. We are constantly engaged in the process of judging new experiences so we can make sense out of the world in which we live. *Moral learning* refers to the process by which we strengthen "the elements of character that lead to ethical actions. These elements include respect for the autonomy and dignity of others, compassion and kindness, honesty, integrity, and a commitment to equity and fairness" (Ehrlich, 1999, p. 6). A commitment to fairness and equality is dependent on awareness—being aware not only of the issues before you, but of your personal prejudices that may prevent you from being fair and just. Are you aware of the standards you use to make judgments?

Lawrence Kohlberg, a developmental theorist, developed a theory of moral development that describes stages of moral reasoning that people progress through as they grow from children into adults. According to Kohlberg (1981), young children make decisions about what is good and bad because they are told to do so by some authority figure (e.g., parent or teacher) essentially to avoid punishment. A higher level of moral reasoning is demonstrated when a person makes ethical decisions based on social obligation and a sense of duty. Kohlberg believed that most adults never reach the highest level of moral reasoning, which is characterized by a conscious respect for others and a genuine interest in their welfare. Moral judgment requires a person to think critically about what is right and wrong. Making a concerted effort to sort out the right from the wrong can lead to the creation of a moral compass that provides us with an internal guide that often serves us well in difficult times. Of course, following one's moral compass may make it difficult to live with others at times. At a minimum, a sound moral compass permits us to live with ourselves.

Taking an interest in your campus and community and engaging in a variety of activities that promote civic and moral learning can lead to the development of a multitude of skills that can serve you throughout life. Kohlberg believed that people could only progress in moral reasoning one stage at a time, and that people advance through these stages as they confront the disequilibrium, or sense of being out of balance, experienced at different times in their lives. (Disequilibrium is frequently caused by problems of a moral nature.) According to Piaget, another developmental theorist, the normal state of functioning is a state of disequilibrium, since we are always in the process of assimilating new experiences into preexisting cognitive structures.

In conclusion, experiences outside the college classroom can enable you to move to higher levels of human development and sophistication. While students come to college with a multitude of experiences, experiences such as volunteerism, internships, leadership positions in campus and community organizations, employment, and other kinds of service learning activities provide a holistic approach to learning. Think of how much of your time is spent away from the classroom. Make the most of your experience at your college by viewing the surrounding community as a type of classroom without walls, where your skills and abilities can be honed to prepare you to enter a complex world.

Sources

Astin, A. W. (1999). Involvement in learning revisited: Lessons we have learned. *Journal of College Student Development, 40,* 587–598.

Ehrlich, T. (1999). Civic and moral learning. *About Campus, 4,* 5–9.

Frankl, V. E. (1963). *Man's search for meaning: An introduction to logotherapy.* New York, NY: Simon & Schuster.

Gazda, G. M., Ginter, E. J., & Horne, A. M. (2001). *Group counseling and group psychotherapy.* Boston, MA: Allyn & Bacon.

Glauser, A. (1998). *Counselors are social change agents: Promoting the development of self-esteem and social competence in college students using community connections.* Presentation made at the 35th Southeastern Conference of Counseling Center Personnel, Jekyll Island, GA.

Johnson, D. W., & Johnson, F. P. (2009). *Joining together: Group theory and group skills.* Columbus, OH: Merrill.

Kohlberg, L. (1981). *Essays on moral development, Vol. I: The philosophy of moral development.* San Francisco, CA: Harper & Row.

Larson, K. R. (1999). *Female college students: Exploring how they manage affective and cognitive resources in response to heightened stress levels.* Unpublished doctoral dissertation, Kansas State University, Manhattan, KS.

Larson, K. R., Ginter, E. J., & Glauser, A. (2005). *Using existential constructs to foster greater student achievement.* Presentation made at the University System of Georgia 29th Annual Learning Support Conference, St. Simons Island, GA.

Levine, A., & Cureton, J. S. (1998). *When hope and fear collide.* San Francisco, CA: Jossey-Bass.

Levoy, G. (1998). *Callings.* New York, NY: Three Rivers Press.

Schroeder, C. (1999). Finding our moral compass. *About Campus, 4,* 1.

Virginia Wolf Productions in Association with Educational Media Institute. (Producers). (1997). *Block by block: Building community in America's cities.* [Videotape]. PBS Video.

Chapter 15

Exercise 1: Get to Know Your Campus Resources

Go on your college's website and explore resources associated with students at your college. You might look under student life, career center, financial aid, campus life, health and recreation, facilities, arts, athletics, campus resources, and academic resources. Find the location, phone number/website, and operational hours of each resource listed below.

Resource	Location	Phone Number and Website	Hours
Academic Support			
Advising			
Art Gallery			
Campus Bookstore			
Campus Life			
Campus Post Office			
Career Center			
Computer and Technology Support			
Counseling and Psychological Services			
Disability Resources			
Distance Learning			
Financial Aid			
Food Services			
Health Center			
Honors Program			
Housing			
Intercultural Affairs Office			
Intramural Sports			
Judicial Affairs			
Leadership Center			
Libraries			
Multicultural Services			
Parking Services			
Performing Arts Center			
Police/Campus Security			
Printing Center			
Recreation and Sports			
Study Abroad			
Volunteer Center			

Chapter 15

Exercise 2: Interview Guide

Identify an organization where you might want to volunteer. Arrange to interview the director or assistant director of the agency. Use the following questions as a guide.

History of the Organization

Can you tell me about this organization? Its history and mission?

What are some of the short-range goals (goals for the next 12 months) of this organization? What do you feel are some of the greatest accomplishments of this organization thus far? Is there a national program that your organization models itself after?

How do you and your colleagues deal with setbacks and barriers that are encountered? What are some of the current needs of your organization?

Community

What impact does your organization have on the community? In what tangible ways does this organization better the community?

How can people in the community best help to serve the mission of this organization? What resources in the community have you found to be of the greatest help?

What has your organization found to be the best way to inspire people to become more active citizens?

Direction

What are some exciting initiatives that you would like to see your organization take on or support, and what are potential roadblocks?

What is the outlook for an organization such as this?

What are some of the long-range plans of this organization?

Do you feel you have adequate resources in your organization to carry out its mission? If not, what else is needed?

What is the future direction of the organization?

What community needs does this organization currently meet?

Career

What led you to this profession?

If you could have any other profession, what would it be?

What would you recommend to a person who might be interested in pursuing a career in this organization?

Interview Report

Name _____

Class period _____

Organization _____

Name of person interviewed _____

Signature of the person _____

Office location _____

Summarize what you discovered through your interview experience.

Chapter 15

Exercise 3: Who Are You at This Point in Your Life?

Karen Larson (1999), who has explored the existential nature of people's lives, provides us with several different areas, or "domains," to consider when seeking an answer to the question *Who are you at this point in your life?*"

Level of engagement

Degree of goal direction

Sense of expectancy

Understanding of capacity

Sense of purposefulness

Perception of psychological resources

You will respond to each of these areas later in this exercise, after the warm-up portion of this exercise is completed.

Part A: Warm-Up

Read and visualize the following. Do not rush; devote several minutes to visualizing or reflecting on what you read.

1. Where are you in life? What comes to mind when you read the following words?

Career	Interactions
Self	Student
Attitudes	Tasks
Energy level	Professional
Internal frame of reference	

2. As you navigate through your day, what is the nature of your movements (the way you walk, move your arms, move as you interact with your boss, friends, family, significant other, etc.)?

Visualize yourself moving in each of the ways listed below. Are any of these words a good description of the way you move throughout the day? Can you think of other words that might describe you better?

fluid	uncomfortable
rigid	formal
harmonious	awkward
wooden	rapid
forceful	confident
dancing	calm
blocked	steady
graceful	clumsy
ungraceful	musical
smooth	struggling
stuck	

3. Are there any changes going on in your life now? What stressors are present? Are you experiencing any transitions?

4. Are you moving toward any changes, stressors, or transitions? If you are, do you feel enriched or depleted?

Can you see the thing you are moving toward? Identify and name this thing.

5. Are any changes, stressors, or transitions moving toward you? If there are, do you feel enriched or depleted?

Can you see the thing that is coming toward you? Identify and name this thing

Part B: Domains of Inquiry

Read the explanation of each domain. Then explain how each domain affects how you are living your life.

1. **Level of engagement.** Includes involvement in your career, professional development, social or recreational activities, family life, organizations, or any other activity that indicates a sense of energy, connectedness, or values-congruence.

2. **Degree of goal direction.** Refers to whether or not you are able to articulate short-term, mid-range, and long-term objectives.

3. **Sense of expectancy.** Your level of optimism and hopefulness about the future.

4. **Understanding of capacity.** The degree to which you perceive yourself as "responseable," empowered, or able to maintain a sense of control and accountability.

5. **Sense of purposefulness.** The degree to which you perceive your own life as valuable, rewarding, and meaningful.

6. **Perception of psychological resources.** Your ability to effectively navigate the emotional territory of your world and to adapt and maintain psychological resilience during periods that test your resources.

Conclusion

Do you recall what these Egyptian symbols mean (from Chapter 1)?

If the seemingly countless questions appearing throughout this textbook could be reduced to a single, encompassing question, it would be *"Who are you at this point in your life?"* This course essentially has provided you with a pathway to uncover a more complete answer to this very important and complicated question.

Exercise 4: Creating a Personal Mandala

There are many ways to answer the question *"Who are you at this point in your life?"* A right-brain approach to answering this question is drawing your answer. In Jungian psychology, drawing a mandala provides a unique means to symbolically represent the unifying aspects of one's own self (i.e., your complete individuality).

In this exercise, you will draw a personal mandala to answer the question "Who are you at this point in your life?" While a mandala is frequently depicted using a concentric configuration of geometric shapes, you should feel free to depart from this traditional form.

Complete the steps and questions that follow.

1. Use page 329 to draw your personal mandala. With your eyes closed and a pen in your left hand (right hand if you are left-handed), draw for about a minute or two on your paper. When you finish, look at what you have drawn. Briefly describe what kinds of images came to you.

2. What might these images represent in your life?

3. Now draw a circle around your drawing. Create additional images out of what you have already drawn. What are some of the images that you have further created from your original drawing?

4. What do these new images represent in your life?

5. To what extent does your personal mandala represent your values? Are any of the images tied to something you want to explore at a deeper level?

6. Is there anything that resonates powerfully within you (something you feel strongly about) that is associated directly or indirectly with your personal mandala?

7. Is there anything you want to do as a result of drawing and then viewing your personal mandala?

8. Briefly describe what it felt like to draw and view your personal mandala.

Chapter 15
My Personal Mandala

Use this page to draw your personal mandala.

INDEX

A

Abdominal breathing, for stress, 147
Absence policies, 79
Academic honesty, 84–86
Academic motivational orientation
    assessment, 49–52
Acquaintance rape, 208–210
Ageism, 225
Agitation, with loneliness, 205
AIDS, 252, 252–253
Alarm stage, of prolonged stress, 267
Alcohol use, 209
AMOA, 49–52
Amotivation, 34, 51
Anorexia nervosa, 249
Anti-Semitism, 225
Anxiety, 143–145, 153–154
    managing, 145–147
Apathy toward topic, 80
Aptitudes, 288–289
Arguments, 164–166
    defined, 164
    fallacious, 164
    insufficient premises, 166
    invalid arguments, 165
    irrelevant premises, 165–166
    unacceptable premises, 165
Arrangement of information, 85
Artistic personality trait, 287
Assertiveness, 214–215
Associations, organizing information
    into, 85
Astin, Alexander W., 309–310
ATMs, use of, 188
Attention, faking, 80
Auditory learning, 122
Autonomous learners, 98–99
    developing skills, 8
Autonomy, development of, 14

B

Banks, 188–189
Behavioral symptoms, 145
Benefits of college education, 8–9
Bloom, Benjamin, 157–159
Bloom's taxonomy of thinking, 157–159
Body-kinesthetic intelligence, 119
Boosters to maintain motivational
    level, 42

Bradford, Leland, 97
Brain
    fitness, 127–128
    left side functions, 105
    right side functions, 105
Briggs, Katharine, 123
Budgeting, 191–192
Bulimia nervosa, 249
Burns, David, 63–64
Butler, Timothy, 283–284

C

Campbell, Joseph, 284
Campus Life, 312–313
Career, developing skills for, 9
Career exploration, 289–29
Career services, 313
Catastrophic thinking, 146
Cheating, 6, 84–86
Chlamydia, 251
Chunking of information, for memory,
    101
Class attendance, 78
Classism, 225
Classmates, getting to know, 79
Classroom survival tactics, 78–79
Cognitive restructuring, 146
Cognitive symptoms, 144–145
College guide for career success, 294–295
College Money Handbook, 193
Communication, 210
    evaluating responses, 212
    Gazda approach to, 211
Competence, development of, 14
Computer-assisted career programs, 290
Concentration, 84
    excessive, 80
    improving, 85
    lack of, 80
Continuous personal growth, developing
    skills for, 9
Conventional personality trait, 287
Cornell method of note-taking, 81
Creative visualizations, 147
Credit cards, 189–190
Credit problems, 193
Critical thinking, 155–181
    arguments, 164–166
        defined, 164
        fallacious, 164

insufficient premises, 166
invalid, 165
irrelevant premises, 165–166
unacceptable premises, 165
unsound, 164
Bloom's taxonomy of thinking,
    157–159
critical thinking, 159–162
declarative knowledge, 156
developmental process, thinking as,
    156–159
divergent thinking, 163
metacognition, 156
models, 156, 159–164
problem solving, 162–164
procedural knowledge, 156
relativism, 157
Cultural opportunities, 313
Culture, 225

D

Date rape, 208–210
Debt stress, 193
Decision-making skills, 10
Decision to attend college, 37
Declarative knowledge, 156
Dejection, with loneliness, 205
Demographic changes, 223
Depletion, with loneliness, 205
Depression, 206
Developmental areas, 14
Developmental process, thinking as,
    156–159
Dictionary of Occupational Titles, 290
Direct deposit of income, 188
Disarming techniques, 64
    to deal with procrastination, 64
Discrimination, 225
Divergent thinking, 163
Diversity, 221–240
    ageism, 225
    anti-Semitism, 225
    classism, 225
    culture, 225
    demographic changes, 223
    discrimination, 225
    embracing, 7
    ethnocentrism, 225
    heterosexism, 229
    homophobia, 225

multicultural competencies, 225–226
multicultural view, development of, 230–231
multiculturalism, 222
pluralistic society, 224
prejudice, 225
  power of, 229
  sources of, 228–229
privilege, 225
race relations, 235–236
racism, 225
sexism, 225
DOT. *See Dictionary of Occupational Titles*
Dwinell, Patricia, 205
Dysfunctional thoughts, record of, 64
  to deal with procrastination, 64

E

Earn and Learn: Your Guide to In-School Educational Employment Programs, 193
Eastern philosophical approach, 254–255
Emmett, Rita, 62–64
Emotions, management of, 14
Employment projections, 293
  fastest-growing occupations, 293
  occupations with largest employment growth, 293
Energy level, 75
Enterprising personality trait, 287
Environment for study, 84
Ethnocentrism, 225
Excessive concentration, 80
Exercise, 249–250
Exhaustion stage, of prolonged stress, 267
External regulation, 33–35, 51
Extrinsic motivation, 33

F

Factors enhancing motivation, 40
Faking attention, 80
Fallacious, 164
Fastest-growing occupations, 293
Fight or flight response, 267
Fill-in-the-blank questions, 139
Financial aid, 192–193
  private programs, 192
  special programs providing, 192
Financial Aid Guide, 193
Financial management, 181–200
  banks, 188–189
  budgeting, 191–192
  College Money Handbook, 193
  credit cards, 189–190
  credit problems, 193
  debt stress, 193

direct deposit of income, 188
grants, 192
investing, 199–200
loans, 192
meanings of money, 182–184
military personnel, aid for, 192
overdraft privileges, 188
service fees, 188
shopping, 190
student employment, 192–193
truth in lending legislation, 190
university work program, 192
First-generation students, 90–91
Food guide, 247
Food labels, reading, 248
Frankl, Viktor, 264
Fuller, Thomas, 191

G

Gazda, George, 211
  approach to effective communication, 211
  global rating scale, 212
Genital herpes, 251
Genital warts, 251
Gerstein, Larry, 205
Ginter, Earl, 205
GOE. *See The New Guide for Occupational Exploration*
Gonorrhea, 251
Grading system, 86–87
Grants, 192
Guiding philosophy, 8

H

Hands-on approach to learning, 122. *See also* Haptic learning
Haptic learning, 122
Harassment, sexual, 208
Health maintenance skills, 11
Herpes, 251
Heterosexism, 229
HIV, 252, 252–253
Holistic health, 237–238
  AIDS, 252
  anorexia nervosa, 249
  bulimia nervosa, 249
  eastern philosophical approach, 254–255
  exercise, 249–250
  food guide, 247
  food labels, reading, 248
  HIV, 252
  nutrition, 246–247
  physical benefits, 245
  psychological benefits, 245
  sex, 250–253

sexually transmitted diseases, 250–252
  AIDS, 252–253
  chlamydia, 251
  genital herpes, 251
  gonorrhea, 251
  HIV, 252–253
  human papillomavirus, 251
  spiritual growth, 245–246
  spiritual life, 254–255
  stress, 250
  western philosophical approach, 254
Holland, John, 287
Homophobia, 225
Honesty, academic, 84–86
HPV. *See* Human papillomavirus
Human papillomavirus, 251
Human relations skills, 10, 210

I

Identified regulation, 33–35, 51
Identity
  establishing, 14
  purpose-in-life skills, 11
Income sources of students, 7
Inhibition of listening, 80
Instrumental behavior, 33
Insufficient premises, 166
Integrated regulation, 51
Integrity, development of, 14
Interactive learning, 121
Interdependence, development of, 14
Interests, 287
Interpersonal communication/human relations skills, 10
Interpersonal intelligence, 119
Interpersonal relationships, development of, 14
Interview, job, 292–293
Intrapersonal intelligence, 119
Intrinsic motivation, 33, 51
Introjected regulation, 33–35, 51
Introversion-extroversion, 123
Intuition-sensation, 123–124
Invalid arguments, 165
Inventory of life-skills development, 23–26
Investigative personality trait, 287
Investing, 199–200
Irrelevant premises, 165–166
Isolation, with loneliness, 205

J

Jefferson, Thomas, 191
Job, career, distinguished, 283
Job interview, 292–293
Jung, Carl, 123

K

Kinesthetic learning, 122
Kurfiss, J.K., 165

L

Lack of concentration, 80
Lack of motivation, 39–40
Ladder of motivation, 31
Laws governing procrastination, 63–64
Learned helplessness, 266
Learning disabilities, 7
Learning skills, 97–112
  autonomous learners, 98–99
  chunking, for memory, 101
  factors optimizing, 102–106
  imaging, 105–106
  left side of brain, functions of, 105
  long-term memory, 101–102
  memories, creation of, 100–102
  memory, learning, connection
    between, 99–100
  mental clutter, clearing, 103
  mental hooks, use of, 106–107
  prevention response, 104
  processing of information, 105–106
  remediation response, 104
  reorganizing of information, 102–103
  right side of brain, functions of, 105
  short-term memory, 101
  stress, 104
  time mangement, for study, 103
Learning styles, 113–134
  body-kinesthetic intelligence, 119
  brain fitness, 127–128
  interpersonal intelligence, 119
  intrapersonal intelligence, 119
  left brain, 115–116
  linguistic intelligence, 119
  logical-mathematical intelligence, 120
  multiple intelligences, 119–120
  musical intelligence, 119
  Myers-Briggs Type Indicator, 123
  perceptual learning modalities,
    121–122
    auditory learning, 122
    haptic learning, 122
    kinesthetic learning, 122
    olfactory learning, 122
  perceptual learning style inventory,
    129–130
  personal learning style, 125–126,
    133–134
  personality, 122–125
    introversion-extroversion, 123
    intuition-sensation, 123–124
    perceiving-judging, 124–125
    thinking-feeling, 124

  personality types, 131–132
  right brain, 115–116
  spatial intelligence, 119
  whole brain learning, 114–116,
    125–126
    brain exercises, 114–116
Left brain, 115–116
  functions of, 105
  thinking characteristics, 115
Levine, Arthur, 308
Levoy, Gregg, 284, 308
Life-skills, development of, 3–28
Linguistic intelligence, 119
Listening
  factors inhibiting, 80
  inhibition of, 80
  skills, 79–80
Loans, 192
Loci, as memory tool, 106–107
Logical-mathematical intelligence, 120
Loneliness, 204–210
  dimensions of, 205
  effects of, 205–206
Long-term memory, 100–102

M

Man in Search of Meaning, 264
Manner of learning, 113–134
Marable, Manning, 222
Marking text, 84
Maslow, Abraham, 30–32
Matching questions, 139
Math tests, 136, 139
Mature interpersonal relationships,
  development of, 14
MBTI. *See* Myers-Briggs Type Indicator
Mead, Margaret, 222
Meanings of money, 182–184
Memory, 100–102
  improving, 85
  learning, connection between, 99–100
Mental clutter, clearing, 103
Mental hooks, use of, 106–107
Metacognition, 156
Military personnel, aid for, 192
Minority population, 88–89
Model for development, application of
  life skills, 11
Model of time management, 56–61
Models of critical thinking/problem
  solving, 159–164
Models of knowledge, 156
Money management, 181–200. *See also*
  Financial management
Moral learning, 315–316
Motivation, 29–52
  academic motivational orientation
    assessment, 49–52
  amotivation, 34, 51

  boosting, 42
  decision to attend college, 37
  development of, 40–42
  external regulation, 33–35, 51
  extrinsic, 33
  factors enhancing, 40
  identified regulation, 33–35, 51
  instrumental behavior, 33
  integrated regulation, 51
  intrinsic, 33, 51
  introjected regulation, 33–35, 51
  maintaining, 40–42
  motivation ladder, 31
  persistence, 34–35
  perspective toward world, 40–42
  physiological requirements, 31
  recognition, 31
  relationship to academic success,
    38–39
  security, 31
  self-actualization, 31
  self-determined behavior, 33
  self-esteem, 31
  social science perspective, 33–42
  student perspective, 36–40
  students with, without, contrasted,
    39–40
  types of, 35
Multicultural competencies, 225–226
Multicultural view, development of,
  230–231
Multiculturalism, 222. *See also* Diversity
  demographic changes, 223
  development of multicultural view,
    230–231
  multicultural competencies, 225–226
  pluralistic society, 224
  prejudice
    power of, 229
    sources of, 228–229
Multiple-choice questions, 138–139
Multiple intelligences, 119–120
Musical intelligence, 119
Myers-Briggs Type Indicator, 123
Myers, Isabel, 123

N

Nickerson, Raymond, 165
Nontraditional students, 89–90
Nonverbal communication, 213–214
Note-taking, 79–83
  Cornell method, 81, 95
  factors inhibiting listening, 80
  listening skills, 79–80
  separate notebooks, 79
  system for, 80
  tips for, 83
Nutrition, 246–247

O

Objective exam analysis worksheet, 151
Objective tests, 138–139
  fill-in-the-blank questions, 139
  matching questions, 139
  math tests, 139
  multiple-choice questions, 138–139
  short-answer questions, 139
Occupational exploration, 290–291
Occupational Outlook Handbook, 290
Occupations, fastest-growing, 293
Occupations with largest employment
  growth, 293
Olfactory learning, 122
Online personality assessment. *See*
  TypeFocus
OOH. *See Occupational Outlook Handbook*
Organization of time, 55–76, 84, 136
  achieving values-congruence, 56
  model of, 56–61
  for study, 103
Organization skills, for time
  management, 57–58
  carry-through, 60–61
  to-do list, 58–59
    examples of, 59
Overdraft privileges, 188

P

Parental consultation, 8
Participation in class, 79
Patterns of meaning, 85
Perceiving-judging, 124–125
Perceptual learning modalities, 121–122
  auditory learning, 122
  haptic learning, 122
  kinesthetic learning, 122
  olfactory learning, 122
Perceptual learning style inventory,
  129–130
Performance anxiety, 143
  recognizing, 143
Perry, William, 157
Persistence, 34–35
Personal learning style, 125–126,
  133–134
Personality, 122–125, 285–286
  differences in, 264–266
  introversion-extroversion, 123
  intuition-sensation, 123–124
  perceiving-judging, 124–125
  thinking-feeling, 124
Personality clusters, 287
  artistic personality trait, 287
  conventional personality trait, 287
  enterprising personality trait, 287
  investigative personality trait, 287
  realistic personality trait, 287
  social personality trait, 287

Personality types, 131–132
Physical fitness/health maintenance skills,
  11
Physiological requirements, 31
Pluralistic society, 224
Politics, student participation in, 8
Post-orientation needs, 13
Pre-orientation needs, 12–13
Prejudgment, 80
Prejudice, 225
  power of, 229
  sources of, 228–229
Preparation before test, 136–137
  cramming, 137
  preparation tips, 136
Print learning modality, 121
Privilege, 225
Problem solving, 10, 162–164
Procedural knowledge, 156
Processing of information, 105–106
Procrastination, 73–74
  dealing with, 64
  laws governing, 63–64
  scale, 61–62
Professors, getting acquainted with, 79
Prolonged stress, 267
  alarm stage, 267
  exhaustion stage, 267
  resistance stage, 267
Promptness for class, 78
Psychological hardiness, 264–266
Purpose, development of, 14
Purpose-in-life skills, 11

R

Race relations, 235–236
Racism, 225
Rape, 208–210
Realistic personality trait, 287
Recognition, 31
Record of dysfunctional thoughts, 64
Reducing stress, 268–273
Relationships, 203–220
  acquaintance rape, 208–210
  agitation, with loneliness, 205
  alcohol use, 209
  assertiveness, 214–215
  communication, 210
  date rape, 208–210
  dejection, with loneliness, 205
  depletion, with loneliness, 205
  depression, 206
  evaluating communication responses,
    212
  Gazda approach to effective
    communication, 211
  human relations skills, 210
  isolation, with loneliness, 205

  loneliness, 204–210
    dimensions of, 205
    effects of, 205–206
  nonverbal communication, 213–214
  rape, 208–210
  sexual harassment, 208
  sexual relationships, 208
  suicide, 206
    myths about, 206
    truth about, 206
Relativism, 157
Remediation response, 104
Reorganizing of information, 102–103
Repeating information, 85
Repertoire of skills, importance of, 5–6
Resistance stage, of prolonged stress, 267
Responsible member of world,
  developing skills to become, 9
Resume, 291–292
Review sessions, 136
Rhodes Scholars from UGA, 4
Right brain, 115–116
  functions of, 105

S

Sacks, Oliver, 114
Scalise, Joseph, 205
Schedule
  to deal with procrastination, 64
  making, 64
Schick, Jr., Theodore, 155
Schmitt, David E., 40–41
Scoring, 263
Seating in class, 78
Self-actualization, 31
Self-determined behavior, 33
Self-esteem, 31, 64
  to deal with procrastination, 64
Self-exploration, 15–16, 284–285
Self identity, 321–324
Self-worth, performance, distinguishing,
  146
Selye, Hans, 259
Service fees, 188
Sex, 250–253
Sexism, 225
Sexual harassment, 208
Sexual relationships, 208
Sexually transmitted diseases, 250–252
  AIDS, 252–253
  chlamydia, 251
  genital herpes, 251
  genital warts, 251
  gonorrhea, 251
  HIV, 252–253
  human papillomavirus, 251
Shopping, 190
Short-answer questions, 139
Short-term memory, 101

Sinetar, Marsha, 284
Skill development, 3–28
   key areas of, 9–11
   life-skills wheel, 27–28
Skills, 288–289
Skills assumptions, 14–15
Skills repertoire, importance of, 5–6
Social personality trait, 287
Social readjustment scale, 261–263
Social science perspective, motivation, 33–34
Spatial intelligence, 119
Sperry, Roger, 114
Spiritual life, 254
State anxiety, 265
STDs. *See* Sexually transmitted diseases
Stereotyping, 225–226, 237–238
Stress, 104, 250, 259–279
   learned helplessness, 266
   personality differences, 264–266
   prolonged stress, 267
      alarm stage, 267
      exhaustion stage, 267
      resistance stage, 267
   psychological hardiness, 264–266
   reducing stress, 268–273
   scoring, 263
   social readjustment scale, 261–263
   state anxiety, 265
   stressful activities, 260–263
   trait anxiety, 265
   type A personality, 265–266
Stressful activities, 260–263
Student affairs, 312–313
Student employment, 192–193
Study, time management, 103
Study environment, 84
Study groups, 136
Study guides, construction of, 136
Study habits, 83
Styles of learning. *See* Learning styles
Subject matter, selectivity regarding, 85
Success visualization, to deal with procrastination, 64
Suicide, 206
   myths about, 206
   truth about, 206
Sullivan, Harry Stack, 203–204
Syllabus for class, 78
System for note-taking, 80

T

Test anxiety, 143–145, 153–154
   managing, 145–147
   physical reactions to, 147
Test-taking skills, 135–154
   abdominal breathing, for stress, 147
   catastrophic thinking, 146
   cognitive restructuring, for stress, 146
   evaluation of test, 141–143
   objective exam analysis worksheet, 151
   objective tests, 138–139
      fill-in-the-blank questions, 139
      matching questions, 139
      math tests, 139
      multiple-choice questions, 138–139
      short-answer questions, 139
      true/false questions, 139
   performance anxiety, 143
      recognizing, 143
   preparation before test, 136–137
      cramming, 137
      general preparation tips, 136
      seek information about test, 137
   test anxiety, 143–145, 153–154
      managing, 145–147
      physical reactions to, 147
Textbook, marking, 84
Thinking-feeling, 124
Thoughts, dysfunctional, record of, 64
Time management, 55–76, 84, 136
   achieving values-congruence, 56
   disarming techniques, 64
   energy level, 75
   for study, 103
   mindset, 63–64
   model of, 56–61
   organization skills, 57–58
      carry-through, 60–61
      to-do list, 58–59
   procrastination, 73–74
      dealing with, 64
      laws governing, 63–64
   procrastination scale, 61–62
   record of dysfunctional thoughts, 64
   schedule, 64
   self-esteem, 64
   time management, 67–68
   to-do list, 69

   values-congruence, 56
   visualization of success, 64
To-do list, 69
Traditional hiring practices, moving away from, 6
Trait anxiety, 265
True/false questions, 139
Truth in lending legislation, 190
Type A personality, 265–266
TypeFocus, 290
Types of motivation, 35

U

Unacceptable premises, 165
University work program, 192
Unsound arguments, 164

V

Value system, 285
Values
   clarification of, 279
   importance to students, 8
Values-congruence, 56
Vaughn, Lewis, 155
Visual learning, 121
Visualization, creative, 147
Visualization of success, 64
   to deal with procrastination, 64
Vocabulary development, 84

W

Waldroop, James, 283–284
Warts, genital, 251
Weber, Alan, 283
Weekly planning, 71–72
Western philosophical approach, 254
Whitman, Walt, 205
Whole brain learning, 114–116, 125–126
   brain exercises, 114–116
Work values, 299–300

Z

Zen, 284

CPSIA information can be obtained
at www.ICGtesting.com
Printed in the USA
LVOW02s0529190516

488763LV00002BA/2/P

9 780757 597505